CISTERCIAN STUDIES SERIES NUMBER TWO HUNDRED FIFTY-EIGHT

Gregory the Great

Moral Reflections on the Book of Job

Volume 3

Books 11–16

CISTERCIAN STUDIES SERIES NUMBER TWO HUNDRED FIFTY-EIGHT

Moral Reflections on the Book of Job

Volume 3

Books 11–16

Gregory the Great

Translated by

Brian Kerns, OCSO

Introduction by

Mark DelCogliano

Cistercian Publications
www.cistercianpublications.org

LITURGICAL PRESS
Collegeville, Minnesota
www.litpress.org

A Cistercian Publications title published by Liturgical Press

Cistercian Publications

Editorial Offices
161 Grosvenor Street
Athens, Ohio 54701
www.cistercianpublications.org

A translation of the critical edition by Marcus Adriaen, *Moralia in Iob*, in Corpus Christianorum, Series Latina 143, 143A, 143B.

Biblical quotations are translated by Brian Kerns, OCSO.

ISBN 978-0-87907-358-9 (Volume 3)

1	2	3	4	5	6	7	8	9

Library of Congress Cataloging-in-Publication Data

Gregory I, Pope, approximately 540–604.
    [Moralia in Job. Selections. English]
    Gregory the Great : moral reflections on the Book of Job, vol. 1,
preface and books 1-5 / translated by Brian Kerns, OCSO ;
introduction by Mark DelCogliano.
        pages cm. — (Cistercian studies series ; number two hundred forty-nine)
    Includes index.
    ISBN 978-0-87907-149-3 (hardcover)
    1. Bible. Job I-V, 2—Commentaries—Early works to 1800.   I. Kerns, Brian, translator.   II. DelCogliano, Mark, writer of introduction.   III. Title.

BS1415.53.G7413   2014
223'.107—dc23   2014015314

Contents

Abbreviations

General

Publications: Books and Series

CCSL Corpus Christianorum, Series Latina. Turnhout: Brepols Publishers, 1954–.

CS Cistercian Studies series. Kalamazoo, MI, and Collegeville, MN: Cistercian Publications.

LXX Septuagint

PL Patrologiae cursus completus, series Latinae. Ed. J.-P. Migne. 221 vols. Paris.

Praef Praefatio

SCh Sources Chrétiennes. Paris: Les Éditions du Cerf, 1942–.

Introduction

Mark DelCogliano

T he third of the six parts of Gregory the Great's *Moralia in Job* is unique. In part 1 (books 1–5) Gregory covered Job 1:5–5:2 (84 verses), commenting at a very leisurely pace as he mostly stuck to his original plan of interpreting each verse three times: first the historical or literal interpretation, then the typical interpretation (geared toward what Christians believe or need to believe), and finally the moral interpretation (what Christians need to do).[1] In the other parts he abandoned this plan, for the most part jettisoning the historical interpretation and focusing chiefly on the typical or moral interpretation (and sometimes both). This new approach enabled him to pick up his pace, as it were, resulting in a greater coverage of verses in each part: in part 2 (books 6–10), Job 5:3–12:5 (179 verses); in part 4 (books 17–22), Job 24:20–31:40 (173 verses); in part 5 (books 23–27), Job 32:1–37:24 (165 verses); and in part 6 (books 28–35), Job 38:1–42:16 (145 verses).

In part 3 (books 11–16), however, Gregory covered Job 12:6–24:20 (324 verses)—the greatest number of verses in any of the six parts. Why? The *Moralia* had its origins in oral discourses that Gregory delivered to a circle of monks and clerics in Constantinople while he was serving as papal ambassador there in the first half of the 580s.[2] These oral discourses were taken down by notaries, and upon his return to Rome in 585 or 586, Gregory revised them for wider

---

[1] On Gregory's exegetical practice, see Gregory the Great, *Moral Reflections on the Book of Job*, trans. Brian Kerns, CS 249 (Collegeville, MN: Liturgical Press), 17–26.

[2] See CS 249:8–11.

circulation, adding much to them and also improving the literary style of his originally spoken comments. But as he himself tells us, he never had the chance to revise the third part. Accordingly, it is not only the most compressed part of Gregory's exposition of Job, since it covers the most biblical verses, but it alone among the six parts affords the best access to Gregory's original discourses in their oral form. As such, it is in a sense Gregory's earliest surviving literary work, since the five other parts of the *Moralia* that he was able to revise were finalized only after his return to Rome in the mid-580s, and his other extant works were written during his papacy.[3]

It appears that Gregory's editing of the third part was mostly limited to the organization of the transcripts of his oral discourses into the six books of this part. This formatting of the material prompted him to add brief remarks at the beginning of each book, providing readers with information that would facilitate their understanding of his commentary, such as a review of the figurative referents of the characters in Job (book 11), summaries of the moral qualities of Job as a saint who also represents the church (books 12–14), and brief transitional notes (books 15–16). Gregory also added brief comments at the beginning and end of part 3 (11.I.1 and 16.LXIX.83): while the latter are perfunctory, the former are a kind of apology for the third part's unique character.

In the *Letter to Leander*, the dedicatory epistle that functions as the preface to the *Moralia*, Gregory explains that he was forced to leave the third part "almost as it was, that is, as I spoke it," because his audience in their eagerness to have him advance his commentary on Job "refused to allow me to correct the earlier draft further."[4] In the opening section of the third part, he says much the same thing: "I have left in this part much that was written down while I was speaking" (11.I.1). But here Gregory attempts to make a virtue out of necessity. First, he claims that he should not be reproached for

---

[3] See CS 249:11–13.
[4] *Letter to Leander* 2, CS 249:50.

employing stylistic variety in such a long work, for just as variation in culinary fare pleases the palate of those accustomed to the same food, so too should diversity in style please the reader. The second reason is pragmatic: he had so much to say in this part that it would not have fit into a single codex unless it had been said with "extreme brevity." Gregory opines that for those who are not free to read and study all the time, "the brevity of this part may well be congenial, where we do not so much say what we think as indicate what should be said." And so in this third part he intends to offer his readers a kind of outline or sketch—an indication of what should be said—of what would have been a much longer treatment had he had the opportunity to express himself fully (saying what he thought).

In terms of literary style and diction, however, the third part does not seem much different from the other parts, though perhaps Gregory is less given to prolixity. The chief difference lies in the rapidity with which he interprets the biblical verses, sometimes in two or three senses, moving from one verse to the next in quick succession. Absent are the long digressions, excursuses, and minitreatises that one finds in the other parts. The hallmark of the third part is focus. For example, in commenting on Job 14:4 (11.LII.70), which speaks of purity and impurity, Gregory provides in short compass a moral and christological (typical) interpretation of the verse: humans are conceived impurely but try to become pure; accordingly, they struggle with temptation. But those who are victorious over their temptations should never attribute their purity to themselves but to the one who is pure of himself, namely, the Redeemer. This reference to the Redeemer gives Gregory the chance to make a few christological comments: unlike ours, Christ's conception was not impure, not from the union of a man and woman, but instead he proceeded from the Holy Spirit and the Virgin Mary. He says all this in about a page or so; surely he could have said more and could have added further nuance and elucidation. But he makes the main points clearly, succinctly, and without ambiguity.

The present volume is the third of a projected six volumes containing a new translation of the *Moralia* by Br. Brian Kerns, OCSO, published by Cistercian Publications under the editorial care of Dr. Marsha Dutton. Congratulations to both on reaching the halfway point of this monumental venture, and Godspeed on bringing it to completion.

> Mark DelCogliano
> Minneapolis, Minnesota
> March 12, 2016
> The 1412th Anniversary of the Death of
> Saint Gregory the Great

BOOK I I

I. 1. Although no one should blame me for changing my style in an extended work like this one, lest anyone should reproach me for varying my style of speech, I explained the reasons in the letter prefixed to the work, why I completed the third part of this work without emendations to conform to the pattern of the first two parts. Having completed these two parts, we continue the work from Job 12:6, where it is said, *The tents of robbers spread out,* and the exposition of this third part begins and is carried through until Job 24:20, where we read *the sweetness of their worm.* There are so many words in this part that they cannot fit in one volume, unless they are spoken with extreme brevity. The one who is free from other occupations can read the other multiplied words. For the person who is not free to read and study, however, the brevity of this part may well be congenial, where we do not so much say what we think as indicate what should be said.

Accordingly, since I have left in this part much that was written down while I was speaking, accept this variation of style on my part, kind reader, with an impartial disposition, since diversity in cooking methods often pleases those who eat the same food. As often as you take up the individual parts to read, always be eager to commit to memory that original cause that I have proposed, namely, that blessed Job is called a sufferer, and therein is the passion of the Lord and the sufferings of his Body the church portrayed. His friends play the role of heretics, who, as I have said often enough, when they try to defend God end up displeasing him. When they falsely counsel the saints, they deeply discourage them. Not everything heretics say, however, is foolish or strays from the knowledge of truth; rather they mix prudence with stupidity and falsehood with truth. When they ask a question out of concern for truth, they easily get falsehood out of it.

The same holds true for blessed Job's friends: sometimes their speech is contemptible, sometimes admirable. The holy man accordingly sometimes reproves and condemns what they say, but at other times he agrees with and approves it; he even applies to the profit of rectitude those things that they say correctly but ill-advisedly. So he has only contempt for those who ridicule his poverty, and while his body sits on the dung heap, he shows them the great height of virtue on which he sits before them, while he declares that the riches of the present life amount to nothing, since he also tells them that reprobate sinners have abundant riches.

II. 2. *The tents of robbers spread out; they insolently provoke God, even though it was he who gave them everything they have.** It is easy for people to despise riches when they have them. It is hard, on the other hand, to consider riches worthless when they do not have them. From this obvious fact it clearly appears how much contempt blessed Job had in his mind for worldly possessions, when at the very time that he had lost everything, he said that the abundance possessed by reprobate sinners was nothing. He said, *The tents of robbers spread out; they insolently provoke God.* Evil people, you see, wax more proud against God precisely because their riches come from God's bounty and contrary to their own deserving, and those who ought to be incited to better behavior by the good things they receive are made worse by those gifts.

3. But we must learn how it is that they are called robbers, when it is immediately added, *even though it*

*Job 12:6

was he who gave them everything they have. If they are robbers, you see, it means they took something away by force, and God is certainly no helper for the violent. How then does God give that which robbers wickedly take? We must realize, however, that it is one thing when almighty God mercifully grants something, but it is another thing entirely when he angrily allows a thing to be possessed. Whatever the crooked thieves do, that most impartial steward only allows to happen out of his sense of justice, so that those who are allowed to steal might increase their guilt with their mental blinders on, and that those who suffer the theft might in the loss presently sustained be penalized for a fault previously committed.

Suppose somebody waits in a mountain gorge to ambush wayfarers, while the traveler has perhaps done some evil thing sometime in the past; almighty God decides to avenge the evil he has done in the present life, so he delivers the traveler into the hands of the one who set the ambush, either to be robbed of possessions or even to be killed. So that which the robber unjustly desires, that most impartial Judge justly allowed to happen, so that the former might receive recompense for his unjust act and the latter might someday be punished more severely, because it was through his thoroughly wicked will that almighty God justly punished the guilt of the first one. The one wronged is purified. The wrongdoer's guilt is increased, so that he might someday either return to repentance from his deep wantonness or, because he did not return, be thrown down as deeply in eternal damnation as he was long put up with in his wickedness.

So God dealt mercifully with the former that he might stop sinning, but with the latter in strict justice, so that his guilt might increase unless he returned to repentance. In the former the evil is purified when he is treated with violence; in the latter the evil is multiplied by what he does. It is just, therefore, that almighty God allows that to happen that he forbade anyone to do, so that where he now waits for those who do not convert and long puts up with them, he may someday strike them more severely. So it is well said, *The tents of robbers spread out; they insolently provoke God, even though it was he who gave them everything they have.* That which wicked people take, God himself gives them, he who could have opposed their robbery if he had wished to show mercy.

4. The above description can also be understood spiritually. Some people, you see, often receive the gift of teaching, but they grow proud concerning these gifts, and they want to seem important in the eyes of others. So when they wax proud in front of their neighbors concerning God's gifts, they provoke God. Nor is it without merit to call them robbers, because they do not practice what they say, and they steal the words of the just and use them in their speeches. Because, however, it is grace that has given them these very heavenly words, grace that, on the other hand, has left their lives with bad habits, they are robbers in themselves, although whatever good they have, they have received from God. The next verse:

III. 5. *Question the beasts, and they will certainly tell you. Ask the birds of the air, and they will show you. Speak to the earth, and it will answer you. Even the fish of the sea will teach you.*[*] What should we understand by beasts if not those of slow perception? What by birds of the air if not wise people who think high and heavenly thoughts? Concerning beasts, furthermore, that is, those of slow perception, it is written, *Your animals will dwell there.*[*] That the wise think lofty thoughts and fly among the words of our Redeemer, it is also written,

*Job 12:7-8

*Ps 67:11

*So that the birds of heaven may come and dwell in its branches.** What should we understand by earth, but those with earthly thoughts?* That is why the first man who deserted heaven was told, *You are dust, and to dust you shall return.** What should we take the fish of the sea to mean, if not the curious ones in this world? Of them the psalmist speaks: *The fish of the sea that travel the ocean paths.** They busy themselves in important investigations about the world, as though sniffing around hidden waves. What all this information teaches us he adds, saying,

IV. 6. *Who is unaware of the fact that God's hand has created all this?** It is as if he said, "Either among those of slow perception, or among those whose wisdom searches the heights, or among those given over to worldly actions, or among those occupied with earthly affairs direct the inquiry of your search; they will all admit that God is the Creator of all this, and they unanimously recognize his power, even if they do not all unanimously live accordingly." That which each one of the just says and even lives, you see, that same message the unjust are often forced to admit concerning God, even if it be only with their voice. It happens that evil people do homage to the Creator of the world by their words of confirmation, even if their acts oppose that same Creator. Their brazen behavior assails him, but they cannot deny that he is Creator of all.

The text, however, can also be understood profitably according to the bare literal sense, because each creature considered in itself lends its own voice of witness, as it were, which is the very form that it has. We question beasts, birds, earth, or fish when we look at them, and they unanimously answer us that God created everything. When we take in their forms with our eyes, they testify that they did not make themselves. By the very

*Matt 13:32
*see Phil 3:19

*Gen 3:19

*Ps 8:9

*Job 12:9

fact that they were created, by the form that they present, they, as it were, give forth a voice of confession to their Creator. He, because he created everything, arranges the way in which they ought to be governed. The text continues,

*Job 12:10

V. 7. *In his hand is the soul of every living creature and the spirit of all human flesh.** The word *hand* denotes power. Accordingly, the soul of every living thing and the spirit of all human flesh are in his power who made them, that he might himself dispose of their actions, who guaranteed that to be that did not exist before. The words *soul*, however, and *of every living creature*, may represent the lives of beasts. Almighty God gives life to the souls of beasts all the way to the formation of the senses of the body, but to the spirits of humans all the way to spiritual understanding. In his hand, therefore, is the soul of every living creature and the spirit of all human flesh, since he grants the former the ability of the soul to give life to the flesh, and in the latter he enlivens the soul, that it might reach the understanding of eternity.

We must remember, nonetheless, that the spirit of humankind in the Bible is usually presented in two ways. Sometimes, you see, spirit equals soul, and sometimes it renders spiritual agency. Spirit equals soul, then, when it is written about our very own Head, *Bowing his*

*John 19:20

*head, he gave up his spirit.** If, you see, the evangelist meant to say that spirit was something else than soul, when the spirit left him, the soul would surely have remained. Spirit also renders spiritual agency, as when it is said, *He makes his angels spirits, and his ministers*

*Ps 103:4

*burning fire.** Actually, preachers are sometimes called angels in the Bible, and angels are equivalent to messengers. The prophet says, *The lips of the priest hold knowledge; men should seek the law from his mouth.*

He is the angel of the Lord of Hosts.* Accordingly, al-   *Mal 2:7
mighty God makes his angels spirits, because he makes
his preachers spiritual. In this passage, if the soul of
every living thing represents the very life of the body,
by the spirit of all human flesh is meant the spiritual
agency of intelligence.

VI. 8. *Does not the ear judge words, and the eater's
jaw the taste?** Virtually no one is unaware that our   *Job 12:11
body's five senses, namely, sight, hearing, taste, smell,
and touch, sense and discern everything, and they draw
the power of sense and discernment from the brain. The
brain senses internally, and it is the only judge presiding
over perception. Through its own procedures it distin-
guishes the five senses, while God performs the miracle
that consists in the fact that the eye does not hear, nor
does the ear see, nor does the mouth smell, nor do the
nostrils taste, nor do the hands smell. Since our sense
perception in the brain governs all the senses, not one
of these senses can do anything else except the task it
has received from the Creator's disposition.

From these exterior bodily organs, therefore, the interior spiritual faculties must be derived, so that through
what concerns our external relations we might connect
with what is hidden in us and escapes our perception.
We must unquestionably notice that, although wisdom
is one, she dwells less in one, more in another. One
person excels in this way, another in that. Wisdom, like
the brain, uses us as if we were bodily senses; although
she is herself never unlike herself, through us she does
works that are always diverse and unlike one another.
This is true to the extent that one person receives the gift
of knowledge, another the gift of wisdom; one person
might have diverse tongues, another the gift of healing.

9. In the words that blessed Job uses when he says,
Does not the ear judge words and the eater's jaw the

taste? he seems to include as well something about the elect and the reprobate sinners. The words of wisdom, you see, that the reprobate sinners hear, the elect not only hear but also taste, that their hearts may taste that which is not heard by the reprobates' minds but only by their ears. What we only hear with our ears is something different from that which we taste as well. We call that which we taste *food*. The elect accordingly hear the food of wisdom in such a way as to taste it. They savor through love that which they hear and savor it to the very marrow. The knowledge of the reprobates, on the other hand, does indeed reach as far as the knowing mind insofar as its sound is conceived, so that they hear of virtues, but their heart is cold, and they know not how those virtues taste.

By the words quoted, blessed Job reproved his friends' naiveté, as well as the arrogance of those who boast of wise teaching. It is one thing to know something about God and another thing entirely to taste intellectually what one knows. So he is right to say, *Does not the ear judge words, and the eater's jaw the taste?* It is as if he openly told the arrogant ones, "The words of doctrine that reach your ears also touch my intelligent jaws through their interior taste." Nevertheless, those of tender age, even if their understanding is correct, should not carelessly leap into the preaching office, so he adds,

VII. 10. *There is wisdom in age, and in many years there is prudence.*[*] Those words that are rooted in wisdom and are strengthened by life experience and activity, you see, are set firm. Yet long life is granted to many whom the grace of wisdom does not adorn, so it is rightly shown next on whose judgment these gifts depend:

VIII. 11. *With him is wisdom and fortitude, and he has counsel and understanding.*[*] It is not improper that we take these words to refer to the only-begotten Son of

*Job 12:12

*Job 12:13

the eternal Father, that we might understand him to be the wisdom and fortitude of God. Paul testifies the same reality to our understanding when he says, *Christ is the power of God and the wisdom of God.** He is always with him, because *In the beginning was the Word. The Word was with God, and the Word was God.** God has counsel and intelligence, counsel in that he distributes what is his own, intelligence in that he knows what is ours.

*1 Cor 1:24

*John 1:1

The word *counsel* may also refer to that very delay of hidden judgment, namely, that he sometime later strikes sinners, not because he does not see their sin, but so that their sentence of condemnation is deferred for the sake of their doing penance, and his counsel seems to hand it down late. Accordingly, that which an open sentence sometimes indicates externally lay hidden before time in the counsel of almighty God.

IX. 12. *If he should destroy, there is no one who would build; if he should shut a man in, there is none who would open.** Almighty God destroys the human heart when he abandons it, but he builds it up when he fills it. Nor does he destroy a human mind by attacking it, but by leaving it alone, since it is enough for its ruin that it be dismissed. It often happens therefore that, if the hearers' hearts are not filled with almighty God's grace, because their guilt requires that absence, it is in vain that a preacher warns them externally. Every mouth that speaks is mute, unless God cries out within the heart, since it is he who inspires the words that are heard. That is why the prophet says, *If the Lord does not build the house, they labor in vain who build it.** That is also why Solomon says, *Consider the works of God, that no man can set him right, whom God has rejected.**

*Job 12:14

*Ps 126:1

*Eccl 7:14
Vulg

It is no wonder that a preacher is not heard in the heart of a sinner, when the Lord himself is sometimes opposed by the misbehavior of his foes when he speaks. That is

why Cain could be warned by God's voice and still could
not change.* Because of his malicious guilt God had already deserted his heart internally, when he was talking to him externally to prove his guilt. So Job was right to continue, *If he should shut a man in, there is none who would open.* All people who do wrong, what else do they do but build a prison for themselves in their conscience, so that guilt might corner their soul, even if no one should accuse them externally? It is God's judgment that people should be left alone in their blindness and malice; they are then closed up inside themselves, so that they may not find a way to escape, since they by no means merit escape.

*see
Gen 4:6-7

It often happens, you see, that some people desire to have their evil actions behind them, but they are burdened with the weight of these same acts, and they are locked up in a prison of evil habits and cannot get away from themselves. Others desire to punish their own sins, and what they think they are doing right gets them into worse trouble, so it happens in a lamentable fashion that what they think is an escape they find to be a blockade. So it was with the renegade Judas when he caused his own death in reaction to his sin and received the penalty of eternal death, so that his sorrow for sin was worse than the sin itself.*

*see
Matt 27:5;
Acts 1:19

13. Let him say it then: *If he should shut a man in, there is none who would open.* Just as no one resists the free call of God, so no one questions the justice of God when he abandons. For God to shut in, accordingly, means that he does not open the door for those who are already shut in. That is why he tells Moses about Pharaoh, *I will harden his heart.* When he says *harden*, he is of course talking about his own justice, since he does not soften the unrepentant heart through grace. He shuts a man in, consequently, when he abandons him in the darkness of his own actions.

*Exod 4:21

It is as though Isaac wanted to open the shut door for his firstborn son when he tried to prefer him to his brother by blessing him. The Lord, however, found that son unacceptable whom the father preferred, and the one the Lord preferred the father albeit unwillingly blessed; this happened in order that he who had already sold his birthright to his brother for a meal might not receive the blessing that belongs to the firstborn son, which he had forfeited out of the belly's longing for food. He who keeps following the earth, pursuing the wind, and desiring to inherit a blessing is unacceptable. He found no path of repentance, even though he sought it with tears,* because, you see, lamentation bears no fruit; it eagerly desires perishable things with groans. Accordingly, Isaac could not open for his son, whom almighty God, judging justly, locked up in the prison of his own evil intent. The next verse:

^{*see}
Heb 12:17

X. 14. *If he holds back the waters, all the land will dry up; if he releases them, the land will be overturned.** If water is taken to mean the knowledge of preaching, it is as it is written: *Words out of a man's mouth are deep water, and the fountain of wisdom is like an overflowing waterfall.** When the water is withheld, everything dries up, because when the knowledge of preaching is taken away, the hearts of those who could have flourished in eternal hope straightway wither, so that they might remain barren and without hope, since they love what keeps moving away and know not how to hope for that which will last. If, on the other hand, the word *water* is taken to mean the grace of the Holy Spirit, then, as Truth tells us in the gospel, *As for him who believes in me, as Scripture says, "Rivers of living water will flow out of his belly."**

*Job 12:15

*Prov 18:4

*John 7:38

The evangelist forthwith adds, *He said this about the Spirit which those who believed in him were to*

*John 7:39
*receive.** The plain perception in these words spoken by Job, to wit, *If he holds back the waters, all the land will dry up*, is appropriate, because if the grace of the Holy Spirit is taken away from the hearer's mind, the intellect immediately dries up, which seemed already to grow vigorous through hope in the hearer. The fact that he specified waters, not water, indicates by the use of the plural the sevenfold grace of the gifts of the Holy Spirit; it is as if, you see, each one were doused with as many waters as he was filled with the different gifts. In this regard, he properly adds: *If he releases them the land will be overturned.*

15. What else but the sinner is meant by earth? To him the sentence is pronounced, *You are dust, and to*
*Gen 3:19
*dust you shall return.** Accordingly, the sinner remains unchangeably earth when he disdains obedience to the Lord's commands. He stiffens his neck by pride, and he closes the eyes of his mind to the light of truth. We
*Hab 3:5-6
LXX
find it written, *His feet stood still, and the earth moved.** That is, when truth is embedded in the heart, the mind's constancy is shaken, and if the grace of the Holy Spirit is by God's favor poured out with the preacher's voice, the earth is immediately overturned; that is, the obdurate sinful mind is shaken out of its determined obstinacy, that henceforth it might submit itself tearfully to the Lord's commands in the same degree as it formerly stiffened the neck of its heart by pride against the Lord.

As you may see, then, when the waters bestowed by God flood the earth of the human heart, it accepts injuries freely. We on the other hand are used to inflicting violent injuries on others; we who bestow possessions on others are the same ones who formerly took away the possessions of others by force. We now discipline the flesh by abstinence, but we formerly stooped to overindulgence of the flesh by the fatal pleasures of disgraceful living; if we now love our persecutors, we previously refused to love even those who loved us. When, therefore, the human mind is inundated by the gift of God, we begin to act against our former habits; so the earth is overturned, because we who were formerly preeminent are forced down to the ground, and the face that was formerly pressed down to the lower regions is now raised up on high.

16. We may, as an example of this truth, call one witness out of many: Paul. He took letters he had received against Christ to Damascus, but on the road there he was filled with the grace of the Holy Spirit, and he was forthwith converted from his cruel purpose.* He later received the lashes for Christ's sake that he had himself gone to inflict on the Christians.* Whereas he had formerly lived according to the flesh and tried to put God's saints to death, he was glad later on to give up the life of his own flesh for the lives of the saints. Those cold thoughts of his cruelty were turned into warm and affectionate thoughts, and he who was previously a blasphemer and persecutor became in time a humble and dedicated preacher.* He who formerly saw his highest gain in the killing of Christ in his disciples now esteemed Christ as his very life and death as a gain.* The earth therefore was overturned when the water was poured out, because as soon as Paul's mind received the grace of the Holy Spirit, it changed the condition of his inflexible cruelty.

Concerning that condition, the Lord intones this lament against Ephraim through the prophet: *Ephraim has become a loaf under the ashes, which is not turned.* A loaf under the ashes naturally has ashes on top of it, while its cleaner half is against the ground; the upper half is as much dirtier as it holds ashes on top of it. Accordingly, what else does the mind that thinks worldly

*see Acts 9:1-3

*see 2 Cor 11:23-25

*see 1 Tim 1:13

*see Phil 1:21

*Hos 7:8

thoughts cover itself with but a pile of ashes? But if we wanted to turn around, we could present the clean face we had pressed to the ground and shake off the ashes from our head.

If, then, we rid our mind of the ashes of earthly thoughts, we as it were turn the loaf that is under the ashes, so that our very intention should now be put aside, which the ashes of base thought formerly pressed upon us. Our clean face can then be turned up so that our good intention may no longer be pressed to the earth by the pile of worldly desires. We can in no way bring this about, unless we are inundated by the grace of the Holy Spirit, because if almighty God sends out the waters, they certainly overturn the earth. The next verse:

*Job 12:16

*Job 12:13

XI. 17. *With him are fortitude and wisdom.** He had said a little earlier, *With him are wisdom and fortitude.** Yet now he says, *With him are fortitude and wisdom.* Remember, almighty God became man by the mystery of his fatherly love, so he first revealed the doctrine of meekness, and he later showed the greatness of his fortitude in judgment. So Job is right to mention wisdom before fortitude, since it is said of the only-begotten Son of the Father, *With him is wisdom and fortitude.* On the other hand, he is coming as Judge, and he will appear in his dreadful power; when the unrepentant sinners have been banished, he will show his chosen ones in the eternal Kingdom that he is the Wisdom of the Father. So it is rightly said in the later sentence that fortitude is with him first and then wisdom. Consequently, in the words that he spoke formerly, *With him are wisdom and fortitude*, he clearly indicates that having taught us in his meek character how to believe, he shows subsequently the dreadful power of Judgment. The later words, *With him are fortitude and wisdom*, demonstrate more lucidly that he first overthrows the reprobate sinners in

Judgment by his power and then shines out in the minds of his chosen ones with the perfect light of the eternal Kingdom. Before that day of Final Judgment, however, he does not stop judging the acts of mortals every day with secret arrangements. So he now turns to events of the present time and continues,

XII. 18. *He knows both the deceiver and him who is deceived; the counselor he brings to a fool's end, and the judges to folly.** If everyone who tries to deceive his neighbor is an evil person, and the Truth tells evil people, *I never knew you. Out of my sight, you evildoers,** how is it that we are told in this passage that the Lord knows the deceiver? God's knowing, however, is sometimes called *intelligence* and sometimes called *approbation*. He knows the wicked in the sense that he judges them by insight— for he would not have judged any wicked people, if he had not seen through them—yet on the other hand he does not know the wicked, because he does not approve of their doings. Accordingly, he both knows the wicked, because he is wise to them, and does not know, because he does not find them in their own brand of wisdom.

**Job 12:16-17

**Matt 7:23

In the same way we say that honest people know no falsehood, not because they do not know how to censure lies they hear told by others, but because they both know that very deception by scrutiny and do not know it by affection. In other words, they do not do that themselves that they reprove when others do it. It often happens that people hide in ambush and set traps in their depravity against the lives of strangers, and when somebody unwittingly falls into these traps, others wonder if God sees these things happen and why he allows them to happen, but *He knows both the deceiver and him who is deceived.*

He knows the deceiver, because he often secs the evil he has already done, and he allows him to fall into other sins by his just judgment. He knows the deceiver, because he lets him fall into the hands of his own acts and abandons him, that he may rush on to worse crimes, as it is written, *Let the evildoer still do evil and the filthy still be filthy.** He also knows the one who is deceived, because people often do evil things that they know about, so God allows them to be deceived, precisely in order that they may also fall into evils that they do not know. This consequence tends to become for some deceived ones the beginning of purification and for others of punishment.

*Rev 22:11

19. *The counselor he brings to a fool's end.** When they even do anything good without a good intention but act for the sake of reward by way of worldly benefit, that half verse is shown true. If the only-begotten Son of the Father on high, through his becoming man himself, announced eternal life, he is called the Angel of great counsel; we correctly take the counselors to mean the preachers, then, because they offer their listeners the counsel of life. On the other hand, if any preacher preaches eternal life in order that he may reap temporal benefits, he is certainly brought to a fool's end, because his labor tends to that end that his integrity of mind ought to avoid.

*Job 12:17

20. So he rightly adds, *And the judges to folly.** All those who preside over the examination of other people's behavior are rightly called judges. But if those who preside do not inquire about the life of their subjects with care and do not know whom they should correct or how, the judges are led to folly, because they who should judge evil acts have not learned what should be judged. The next verse:

*Job 12:17

XIII. 21. *He loosens the belts of kings and girds their loins with rope.** Those who know how to control the motion of their own limbs are rightly called kings. When, however, the mind is touched by pride at this

*Job 12:18

self-control, almighty God often deserts such proud ones and allows them to fall into impure acts. Accordingly he loosens the belts of kings when he undoes the restraint of chastity because of the sin of pride in those who seemed to have control over their own members. What do we take rope to mean if not sin? Solomon says, *His evil deeds take hold of the wicked man, and he is tied up with the rope of his sins.** The pleasure of the flesh rules in the loins, you see, so the strict judge of consciences, who loosens the belts of kings, ties up their loins with rope insofar as the girdle of chastity has been untied, in other words insofar as the pleasure of sin is dominant in their members, in order that those whom pride secretly defiles he might also publicly expose in all their offensiveness. The next verse: *Prov 5:22

XIV. 22. *He brings forth undistinguished priests and deposes aristocratic ones.** The uprightness of subjects is a high source of pride for priests. That is why an illustrious preacher rightly asks his disciples, *What is our hope, our joy, and our crown of glory in the Lord's sight if not you?** When priests neglect the lives of disciples, however, and bring forth no fruit in God's sight from their advancement, what else do we call them but undistinguished? They earn absolutely no distinction hereafter before the inflexible Judge, because they never took pride in the present behavior of their disciples by insistent preaching. On the other hand, he is right to say, *and deposes aristocratic ones.* If, you see, in his just judgment he abandons the minds of rulers, those minds will not seek the reward of internal recompense, and they will be deposed, because deceived, and instead of eternal glory they will exult over temporary rule. So the aristocrats are deposed, because when they neglect the true reward of the heavenly kingdom, they fall into their own pleasures here below.   *Job 12:19

*1 Thess 2:19

XV. 23. *He stops the lips of truthful men and takes*
*Job 12:20 *away the old man's knowledge.** When the priest does
not do the good that he talks about, the gift of speech is
also taken from him, in order that he may not presume to
speak that which he does not practice. That is what the
prophet says: *God tells the sinner, "Why do you proclaim*
*Ps 49:16 *my justice and adopt my covenant with your mouth?"** So
the psalmist himself prays as follows: *Never take away*
*Ps 118:43 *the word of truth from my mouth.** Accordingly he is considering the fact that almighty God confers the word of
Truth upon those who do the truth and that he takes it
away from those who do not do it. Those therefore who
have petitioned God not to take away this word from their
mouths, what are they after but the grace of good works?
It is as though they said openly, "Do not let me go astray
from good works, lest while I lose the way of living well,
I lose as well the gift of speaking the righteous word."

It often happens, you see, that teachers who brazenly
teach what they neglect to do end up desisting from
speaking about the good they disdain to do, and they
start teaching their pupils the evil that they really do.
So by the just judgment of almighty God, those who
refuse to live a good life no longer involve their tongue
in goodness. Inasmuch as their minds have been gripped
by the love of earthly things, they always speak about
those same worldly pursuits. That is why Truth says in
the gospel, *Out of the abundant heart the mouth speaks.
The good man brings forth good things out of his good
treasure, and the evil man out of his evil treasure brings*
*Matt
12:34-35 *forth what is evil.** John says for his part, *They belong to*
*1 John 4:5 *the world, so their speech belongs to the world.**

So Job was right to say, *He stops the lips of truthful men and takes away the old man's knowledge.* At
first, you see, they truthfully preached about heaven,
but then worldly objects attracted them, and they sank

to lower pursuits; in this way the lips of truthful men were stopped and the old men's knowledge taken away, because when they were attracted by worldly objects, they no longer followed the precepts of their forebears, so that they might hold the chair of authority merely for the enjoyment of pleasure, as it were, not for the purpose of industriousness.

24. It makes more sense to understand these lips in relation to the Jews, who spoke the truth before the Lord's incarnation, since they believed and proclaimed that he was coming. Yet after he appeared in human flesh, they denied that he was the one. Accordingly, the lips of truthful men were stopped, because the one who they had said was coming they denied when he was here. The knowledge of the old men was taken away, because . they by no means followed what they remembered that their fathers foretold by believing it. Thus they promised that Elijah at his coming would turn back the hearts of sons to their fathers, so that the knowledge of old men, which is now taken away from the hearts of the Jews, might by the Lord's mercy return at the time when the sons should begin to understand what the fathers proclaimed in relation to the Lord.

If, on the other hand, we take the old men to mean those same Jews who, persuaded by unbelief, tried to contradict the word of Truth, the knowledge of the old men was taken away later, when the Gentile church, which was then very young, took it. The psalmist spoke of this: *I understand better than the elders.** Because the church held that knowledge by practicing it, the psalmist demonstrates that she understood more than the elders when he forthwith adds, *Because I sought out your commands.* Because she zealously put into practice what she learned, she received the understanding of what she should teach. So he again rightly adds,

*Ps 118:100

XVI. 25. *He pours contempt upon princes and lifts up the oppressed.** As long as the Jewish people remained obedient to the law and none of the Gentiles knew God's commandments, the former seemed to be the masters of faith, and the latter lay oppressed in the depths through unbelief. When, however, the Jews denied the mystery of the Lord's incarnation, the Gentiles

believed it, and the princes* fell into contempt. Then those who had been oppressed with the guilt of unbelief were raised up in the liberty of true faith. Jeremiah saw this fall of the Israelites long before and said, *The Lord became like an enemy; Israel fell headlong; all*

his palaces collapsed; his ramparts were thrown down.*

Palaces in cities are for ornaments, ramparts for defense. The gifts that defend us are one thing, and those that adorn us are something else. Of course prophecy, teaching, different kinds of tongues, and the power to heal are all, as it were, like palaces to the mind. Even if not everyone has these palaces, nevertheless all are able to stand defended by faith and justice, even if they do not seem at all ornamented with high virtues. As for us, faith, hope,

and charity* are not our palaces but our ramparts, and if we neglect them, we lie open to the ambush of the enemy. As for Judea, because God hid prophecy and teaching, as well as signs and miracles, Judea's palaces collapsed. On the other hand, since God allowed faith, hope, and charity to be taken away because of Judea's hardness of heart, he was intent on doing away with her ramparts. Jeremiah followed the correct order, then, in speaking first of her palaces and later of her ruined ramparts.

When, you see, the sinful soul is abandoned, first the gifts of the virtues, bestowed for the sake of manifestation of the spirit, are pulled down, and later the foundation of faith, hope, and charity is destroyed. The Lord bestowed on the Gentiles all these gifts taken away from the faithless people, and to adorn the minds of the faithful, he used what he hid from the unfaithful. That is why it is written, *The beautiful homes divide the spoil.** He hid the spoil of the virtues from the Jews, you see, but the homes of the Gentiles' hearts are those that he deigned to dwell in, and he gave them the beauty of the gifts. This happened when the Jewish people received the word of God only according to the letter that kills, and the converted Gentiles penetrated it through the spirit that gives life.* So Job soon adds,

*Ps 67:13 LXX

*2 Cor 3:6

XVII. 26. *He unveils the deep darkness, and he brings out into the light the shadow of death.** Whenever, you see, the believers understand mysterious elements in the dark sayings of the prophets, what else does that indicate than an unveiling of deep darkness? That is why Truth himself spoke to his disciples in parables and said, *What I tell you in darkness speak out in daylight.** When we clear up mysterious enigmas concerning allegories by explaining them, we say in daylight what we hear in darkness. As for the shadow of death, that was the harshness of the law, which restored the balance by punishing all sinners with bodily death.

*Job 12:22

*Matt 10:27

Our Redeemer, however, softened the harshness of the legal penalty through his gentle disposition, and after that he determined that bodily death should no longer be required as a penalty for sin; rather he made known how dreadful a thing spiritual death is, and in so doing, without any doubt, he brought out into the light the shadow of death. Indeed this death in which the body is separated from the soul is a shadow of that death in which the soul is separated from God. Into the light accordingly the shadow of death is brought forth when spiritual death is understood, and bodily death is consequently no longer feared.

The matter, however, can be understood in yet another way. They in truth are not wrongly called princes who are always the masters of their own thoughts with great discernment and consideration, and who suppress all foolish emotions by the power of wisdom. Yet it often happens that the soul is secretly lifted up in the exaltation of pride on account of its very own wisdom and falls under the spell of those vices that it boasted of having overcome. So he is right to say, *He pours contempt upon princes.* Then again, those who seem to wallow in vices sometimes have recourse to the tears of repentance and rise up against the sins in which they previously lay. So he again rightly adds, *and lifts up the oppressed.* Some of them, you see, are enlightened by God's bounty, and they see the base shame of the sins in which they lie; they wash the stains of their deeds with tears and suppress their bodily emotions beneath them, those emotions under which they were previously themselves oppressed.

27. This turn of events is naturally brought about by a superb arrangement of almighty God, in order that all the events of this life might be regarded as uncertain, and so that none might wax proud on account of his chaste way of life, because *he pours contempt upon princes.* Nor should any despair because of the oppression of their own vices, since *he lifts up the oppressed.* When these things happen on account of God's secret counsels, the obvious sentence is passed upon each person, so he is again right to add, *He unveils the deep darkness.*

28. The Lord does unveil the deep darkness when he indicates the obvious sentence passed by his own secret counsels, in order that he might show forth what he thinks of each person. Because, you see, the Creator now sees everything while remaining unseen himself in his counsels, the psalmist rightly says of him, *He has made darkness his covering.** But it is as if light shone forth from this darkness when he shows what he thinks about any of these acts that he sees. Since anyone who is

*Ps 17:12

oppressed by the burden of his own sins and is brought forth to the status of righteousness sees death itself for the first time, in which he had been accustomed to sink but which he had been unable to look at, he rightly adds, *He brings out into the light the shadow of death.*

The shadow of death is the doing of evil by imitating the ancient enemy, as if it were outlined with the very form of the body. Of such action it is said, in order to signify a certain person, *His name is death.** The evil thought of such action often escapes the notice of people's minds, and because of the fact that it is unknown, it prevails further. Accordingly, the shadow of death is brought out into the light when the doing of evil by the ancient enemy is exposed to the minds of the saints, so that it might be stopped. The next verse:

*Rev 6:8

XVIII. 29. *He multiplies the nations and destroys them, and once they are overthrown, he again completely restores them.** Perhaps this verse could be understood in the sense that the Lord multiplies the nations and destroys them in this way: people are daily born only to die; once they are overthrown, the Lord again completely restores them, in the sense that they who were dead will rise again. But we take a better sense from the words if we think of the nations as regards what happens in their souls. He multiplies the nations and destroys them, then, when he increases their progeny with fertility yet abandons them in their faithlessness. Once they are overthrown, he again completely restores them, because those he had abandoned in the misfortune of unfaithfulness he sometimes leads back to the state of faith. When, however, these are reinstated in spiritual wholeness, that ancient people who seemed to be faithful to God became reprobate in heart and were cast off. They were deceived by their own faithlessness and rose up against him whom they previously foretold. The next verse:

*Job 12:23

XIX. 30. *He transforms the hearts of the princes of the people of the land and deceives them, letting them travel aimlessly through a pathless wasteland. They will grope about as in the darkness, not in the light, and he* *Job 12:24-25 will make them stagger like drunken men.** The hearts of the princes of the land were transformed when the chief priests and leaders of the people in Judea by their own counsel set themselves to block the path of him whose coming they had formerly announced. When they tried to blot out his name by persecution, they were deceived by their own malice, and they endeavored to make their way aimlessly through pathless deserts, because no way could be open to them in their hard-heartedness against the Creator of the universe. They saw miracles, they feared his power, but they refused belief. Still they demanded signs, saying, *What sign do you work, that we* *John 6:30 may see and believe you? What do you do?** So Job is right to say, *They will grope about as in the darkness, not in the light.*

Anybody, you see, who hesitates among so many clear miracles is like someone who gropes about in darkness, because he does not see what he feels. But anyone who wanders is led now here and now there. Yet it was shown that they were once believers who *John 9:33 said, If he were not from God, he could do nothing.** Now, however, they denied that he was from God and contemptuously said, *Isn't he the carpenter's son? Isn't his mother named Mary? Aren't his brothers James, Joseph, Simon, and Jude? Aren't all his sisters here with* *Matt   us?** So Job rightly adds, *He will make them stagger like* 13:55-56 *drunken men.* Surely they saw him raise the dead, and they knew he was mortal. Who then would not believe him to be God, when they saw him raise the dead? Still, because they saw that he was a mortal man, they felt it to be beneath them to believe him to be the immortal God.

Accordingly, for the very reason that almighty God displayed himself before them in such a guise, he who could both display divine acts and suffer human nature, he made them stagger like drunken men in such a manner that their pride, which preferred contempt of the mystery of his incarnation to discipleship thereof, might both vaunt itself against his humanity and internally wonder at the luminous power of his divinity. All of this was made present to the eyes of blessed Job through the spirit of prophecy, so he rightly adds,

XX. 31. *This is all.** In God, you see, he beheld all that was to follow as present, him to whom neither the future comes nor the past leaves, but before his eyes everything is present at once. Furthermore he saw these very future events enacted in one way and spoken in another. So he adds, *My eye sees them, and my ear hears them.** Words are useless, however, if they lack meaning. So he again adds, *I understood them all.** Whenever something is seen or heard, if no understanding is had, it is certainly no prophecy. For example, Pharaoh saw in a dream what was going to happen to Egypt,* but he could not understand what he saw. So he was obviously no prophet. King Belshazzar saw the fingers of a hand, writing on the wall, but he was no prophet either, since he had no understanding of what he had seen.* So in order that blessed Job may declare himself as someone having the spirit of prophecy, he asserts that he has not only seen and heard but also understood everything. Moreover, his next words bear him witness that he is not arrogant concerning what he has understood:

XXI. 32. *If you have knowledge, so do I. I am in no way inferior to you.** Note well that by these words Job revealed the depth of his humility in that he denied that he was the inferior of those whose lives his own holy way of living far surpassed. As far as their knowledge

*Job 13:1

*Job 13:1
*Job 13:1

*see Gen 41:1-8

*see Dan 5:5

*Job 13:2

was concerned, he affirmed his own their equal; by his knowledge of heaven he far surpassed their thoughts of earth, and he had the spirit of prophecy as well.

XXII. 33. *Nevertheless I will speak to the almighty*
*Job 13:3   *One; I want to argue with God.** We speak to the almighty One when we implore his mercy, but we argue with him when we appeal to his justice and discuss our actions with careful inquiry. Well, at least Job argues with God, he who obeyed his commands here below and as a judge comes with him later to judge the peoples, just as the Lord told those preachers who left all things, *You who have followed me, in the new world, when the Son of Man sits on his majestic throne, will also sit on*
*Matt 19:28   *twelve thrones and judge the twelve tribes of Israel.** The Lord also spoke through Isaiah: *Help the man who is oppressed. Give judgment for the orphan. Defend the*
*Isa 1:17-18   *widow. Then come and argue with me.**

It is surely right that they should argue with God about their wards in judgment, those who abandon the present world completely for the word of God. Accordingly, speaking belongs to prayer, arguing to judgment. Job then speaks to almighty God now, so that he may later argue with almighty God, because he later comes with God as judge, he who associated with God here and now in familiar prayer. Holy Church, however, whose role blessed Job plays, as we have already frequently said, not only judges evildoers later, when the day of Final Judgment arrives, but also even now unceasingly judges all those who act wickedly and who think foolish thoughts. The next verse:

XXIII. 34. *I will first show you up as liars and fol-*
*Job 13:4   *lowers of crooked teaching.** By these words we are obviously shown directly that Job's friends oppose the holy man's judgment, in similarity to the heretics. Obviously, you see, they cannot be representing catholics

when they are called followers of crooked teaching. In such a statement of the case the fact that they are called those who make up lies must also be included. Just as a building is made up of stones, you see, so lies are made up of words. Where there is guileless speech and a sense of truth, it is as if a fortified construction rose, not out of anything that is made up, but out of nature. The next verse:

XXIV. 35. *If only you would be silent, that you might be considered wise.* Just as behind a closed door we do not know what is hidden inside a house, so also when a fool remains silent, it is often unknown whether he is wise or foolish, provided, of course, that nothing else that he does exposes the quality of his mind, even if he is silent. So the holy man, seeing his friends wishing to look like something they were not, warned them to be silent lest they should look like that which they really were. That is why Solomon says, *If the fool should be silent, he would be considered wise.* Of course when the fool does speak, because he blurts out his own words, he is unable to weigh wise words; after Job has imposed silence, he rightly adds,

XXV. 36. *Hear now my reproof, and pay attention to the judgment of my lips.* He is right to tender his reproof first and mention judgment afterward, for unless the fool's swelling pride is first lanced by a reproof, the fool will never understand the just man's judgment. The next verse:

XXVI. 37. *Does God stand in need of your lie, that you should utter deception for his sake?* God does not need a lie, because truth requires no support from the medium of falsehood. The heretics, however, because they understand God in a twisted way, find no security in truth. It would be as if they needed a false shadow to confirm a ray of light. So they speak deceptively on his

*Job 13:5

*Prov 17:28

*Job 13:6

*Job 13:7

behalf and beguile weak minds on how to think about God by foolish seduction. The next verse:

XXVII. 38. *Are you taking his place, and are you* *trying to judge for God's sake?* * When fools see what prudent people do, all such deeds seem to them blameworthy. They forget their own inexperience and weakness, and the more rigorously they judge them, the more completely they forget their own weakness. Righteous people, on the other hand, when they find fault with the actions of the wayward, are always aware of their own shortcomings, so even if they scold them verbally, yet they do so with a compassionate attitude, because it is for the one alone who because of his almighty nature cannot sin to deal without compassion with the sins of men and women. Accordingly, since blessed Job's friends had reproved his actions in such a way that it was as if they had done nothing reprehensible themselves, Job rightly says now, *Are you taking his place, and are you trying to judge for God's sake?* To take his place is surely to assume his authority in judgment, and those who blame all the weaknesses of the other person while having no weakness of compassion inside themselves attempt to judge for God's sake, as it were. The next verse:

XXVIII. 39. *Will it please him from whom nothing can be hidden, or will he be fooled like a man by* *your deceit?* * The heretics display their deceit before God, because they keep saying things that never please him for whose sake they speak; rather, they offend him even as they pretend to defend him, and they fall to the ground while opposing him whom they seemed to serve by their preaching. That is why the psalmist says, *That you might destroy the enemy and the defender.* * All the heretics are certainly almighty God's enemies and defenders, because whenever they pretend to

*Job 13:8

*Job 13:9

*Ps 8:3

defend him, they then oppose his truth. Since however nothing can escape God, he judges their interior attitude, not their apparent external service. Accordingly, since God is not fooled like a person by their deceit, Job is right to add,

XXIX. 40. *He will accuse you, because you surreptitiously assume his place. As soon as he stirs forth, he will frighten you, and his dread will fall upon you.** *Job 13:10-11 This matter, namely, that he says God's place is surreptitiously assumed, can be understood in two ways. There are some people, you see, who really understand truth in their hearts and who nevertheless speak falsely about God externally. They do not want their double-dealing to be exposed, in that they both know the truth internally and oppose it externally. So it is well said at this point, *He will accuse you, because you surreptitiously assume his place.* It is as though he said plainly, "You are as guilty in his sight of falsehood as you see within yourselves what is true."

There are indeed some people who, when they return to their own mind's eye, contemplate God's justice and righteousness and are shaken with prayers and tears; yet when the time for contemplation is over, they boldly return to their evildoing ways so that they might seem to be unseen by the light of justice, as though their evildoing took place behind God's back. These people, accordingly, themselves surreptitiously assume the place of God while he, as it were, sees them, because while they are in his presence, they flatter him with tears, and when they seem to leave his presence, their behavior becomes base. The more worthy they are of blows because of their evil acts, the more they think of God's just judgment in the secret place of their thought. So he adds,

41. *As soon as he stirs forth, he will frighten you, and his dread will fall upon you.* The nature of almighty

God is unshakable, so he cannot be moved to anger in judgment. Nevertheless, the very severity of his jurisdiction is referred to in human words as God's being moved, since by it human depravity is struck with blows. Righteous people fear God before his wrath can be moved against them, and they fear a serene God, lest they should encounter him moved. Base people, on the other hand, only fear blows when they are already receiving them; dread of him awakens them from the slumber of sluggishness only then when vengeance throws them into confusion. That is why the prophet says, *Nothing but harsh treatment will make them hear and understand.** When, you see, they start to feel the flogging for their contempt and scorn of God's commandments through his vengeance, then they will understand what they have heard. The psalmist says for his part, *When he slew them, then they sought him.** So it is well said here, *As soon as he stirs forth, he will frighten you, and his dread will fall upon you.* In the hearts of reprobate sinners, fear does not give birth to rest, but the penalty brings forth fear.

*Isa 28:19

*Ps 77:34

XXX. 42. *Your memory is compared to ashes.** All those who are conformed to this world by thinking thoughts of earth try to leave their memory in this world through all their actions. Some by war inscriptions, others by the high walls of their houses, others by eloquent teachings in books urgently strive to build themselves monuments for their names to be remembered. But when their life is itself hastening toward a speedy end, what is there that will remain fixed in it, when it is swiftly moving and has indeed passed? The wind in fact picks up the ashes, just as it is written: *Not so are the wicked, not so; they are like dust driven by the wind from the face of the earth.** Rightly therefore is the memory of fools compared to ashes, because it is

*Job 13:12

*Ps 1:4

placed there where the wind takes it. However much, then, each person strives for the fabricated glory of his name, he makes his memorial like ashes, because the wind of mortality picks it up without delay. Of the just man contrariwise it is written, *The just man's memory is eternal.** By the very fact, you see, that he prints his acts in God's sight alone, he fixes the memorial of his name in eternity.

*Ps 111:7

XXXI. 43. *Your necks are brought down to the ground.** Just as the eye often means the sense of sight, so the neck customarily signifies pride. The neck accordingly is brought down to the ground when each proud person is humbled by death, and proud flesh decays and rots. Let us consider the different carcasses of the rich that lie buried in tombs and what form of death might lie in dead flesh, as well as the decay of corruption. They were certainly the ones who were distinguished by special honors, grew proud concerning their possessions, despised others, and boasted as if they were the only ones that mattered. But they did not weigh carefully what they were headed for, nor did they know what in fact they were. Their neck has been brought down to the ground, because they lie scorned in rotten decay, those who grew proud in vanity. Their neck is brought down to the ground, because the decay of corruption proves how much the power of the flesh is worth.

*Job 13:12

XXXII. 44. *Be silent a little while, that I may speak whatever my mind suggests to me.** He indicates to those who have spoken in the carnal sense, on whom on that account he imposes silence, that he may speak those words that the mind suggests to him. It is as if he said frankly, "I do not speak according to the flesh, but according to the spirit, because I hear through the spiritual sense what I declare through the exercise of my bodily

*Job 13:13

faculties." So he immediately ascends to the heights and lifts himself up mystically. Then he transforms the verbal attack he had launched into words of mystery and says,

XXXIII. 45. *Why do I tear my own flesh with my teeth and carry my soul in my hands?*[*] In Holy Scripture teeth are sometimes taken to mean holy preachers, and at other times internal senses. For example, the bride is told concerning the holy preachers, *Your teeth are like flocks of shorn sheep coming up out of the water.*[*] Hence one of them was told, after the Gentiles had been figuratively portrayed, *Slaughter and eat.*[*] In other words, obliterate their past and change them into the church, into your own members.

On the other hand, the prophet Jeremiah bears witness that *teeth* may be taken as internal senses; he says, *He has broken my teeth one by one.*[*] The teeth break up food so that it may be swallowed. So we are not wrong in taking teeth to mean internal senses, since they take each single thought and, as it were, chew it and break it into small pieces, after which they transmit it to the stomach of the memory. The prophet says they are broken one by one, because according to the size of any sin a blindness of the intelligence is generated in the senses, and, according to what people have done externally, their ability to understand internally and invisibly is blunted.

So the prophet rightly says elsewhere, *Any man who eats sour grapes will have his teeth blunted.*[*] What else is a sour grape but sin? A sour grape is certainly one that is unripe. Whoever desires the satisfaction of the pleasures of the present life, as it were, hastily eats unripe fruit. Accordingly, those who eat a sour grape have their teeth blunted, because those who are fed by the pleasures of the present life have their internal senses bound

*Job 13:14

*Song 4:2

*Acts 10:13

*Lam 3:16

*Jer 31:30

so that they cannot chew, that is, understand spiritual realities anymore, because insofar as they take pleasure in external things, they are blunted as far as internal reality is concerned. As long as the soul feeds on sin, it cannot eat the bread of justice, because its teeth are bound because of a habit of sin, so they cannot eat the justice that is relished internally.

So since we have said that the *teeth* in this passage mean the internal senses, it is very much incumbent upon us to consider what the just people are wont to do. If they find any carnal thoughts in themselves, however small, they often disown them in their internal senses, and they attack them violently in themselves; they turn against and afflict themselves, and they accuse themselves of even the slightest misdeed, torturing themselves grievously, and they punish themselves by repentance. They act in this way in order that they may themselves be found irreprehensible in the sight of the eternal Judge as far as possible, and so that those who see them judge themselves in this way may be incited to amend their own more serious faults.

That is indeed what blessed Job had done in front of his friends, who were clutching at worldly fame and boasting of transient wealth. Nevertheless, he was unable to induce them to apply their minds to understand the usefulness of his own trials, so that they could really distinguish the fact that almighty God not only grants prosperity but sometimes graciously inflicts adversity as well. That is why he says in this passage, *Why do I tear my own flesh with my teeth?* He could have said openly, "Why do I shatter with my internal senses whatever carnal thoughts may be in me, if I cannot influence those who watch me?" So he is right to add, *I carry my soul in my hands.*

46. To carry one's soul in one's hands means to display the intention of the heart in one's actions. It is a characteristic of righteous people, you see, that in all their words and all their actions they have in view not only their own intent but also their neighbor's edification. Sometimes, in fact, they are their own judges, so that they might, on occasion, lead back halfhearted listeners to consider their own case. Sometimes they display good works, so that those who witness them might be embarrassed for not imitating the goodness they see. It is written, *Let them see your good works* *and glorify your Father who is in heaven.** Accordingly, those who realize their intentions in action carry their souls in their hands.

*Matt 5:16

On the other hand, when righteous people fail to render aid to their neighbors, either by judging themselves or by displaying good works in whatever they do, they fall back on words of pain. So Job now says rightly, *Why do I tear my own flesh with my teeth and carry my soul in my hands?* In other words, "Why do I either judge myself harshly in front of others or display my intention in my actions, if I do not forward the advantage of my neighbors by punishing evil or by displaying what is good?" Even so, righteous people never cease, even while speaking in this way, to offer a good example to their neighbors. Accordingly blessed Job is still offering and displaying to his friends the virtue of patience, as he says,

XXXIV. 47. *Even if he should kill me, I will still* *hope in him.** You will never find the virtue of hope in prosperity. He is really a patient man who although worn out by adversity is not turned away from the object of his hope. As for the attitude of the reprobate sinner, we find it written, *He will praise you as long as it profits* *him.** This is how the righteous mind differs from the

*Job 13:15

*Ps 48:19

unrighteous, namely, that it proclaims the praise of almighty God even in the midst of adversity, that it is not discouraged by the loss of possessions or crestfallen by the loss of external fame. Rather such men and women show what kind of people they were when they owned property precisely in this circumstance: that even without possessions they are still steadfast. The next verse:

XXXV. 48. *Nevertheless I will declare my ways before him, and he will be my Helper.** The apostle Paul says, *If we judged ourselves, we would surely not be judged.** Accordingly the Lord is then found to be our helper when we now in the fear of God confess our sin. That is why the elect can never go easy on their own faults, so that they might find the Judge lenient toward them. They certainly hope to find him their helper afterward, him whom they now fear as a strict Judge. Those who take their sin lightly now, you see, will not be spared the penalty afterward. Let Job say then, *Nevertheless I will declare my ways before him.* Let him then add the purpose of this declaration: *He will be my Helper.* The next verse:

XXXVI. 49. *No hypocrite will appear in his presence.** Since it is decreed that when the Judge comes he will put the sheep at his right hand and the goats on his left, why is it said here that no hypocrite will appear in his sight?* If there is a hypocrite among the goats, will he not appear at the Judge's left hand? We must realize, however, that there are two ways in which we come into the Lord's presence. By one of them we carefully scrutinize our sins here below, place ourselves in God's presence, and tearfully judge ourselves. Every time, you see, that we bring our Creator's power to mind, we stand in his presence. So Elijah, the man of God, correctly said, *As the Lord, the God of Israel, lives, in whose presence I stand.**

*Job 13:15-16

*1 Cor 13:31

*Job 13:16

*see
Matt 25:33

*1 Kgs 17:1

The other way we enter God's presence is at the Last Judgment, when we stand before his tribunal. Hypocrites accordingly will enter the Judge's presence at the Last Judgment. For the time being, however, they neglect the consideration and lamentation of their sins and refuse to enter the Lord's presence. While righteous people contemplate the intransigence of the Judge who is coming, they bring their sins to mind and weep over the things they have done; they judge themselves lest they be judged.

The hypocrites, on the other hand, insofar as they please people externally, neglect the internal examination of themselves and are wholly guided by the word of their neighbors; they esteem themselves saints, because that is what they think others hold them to be. When they scatter the seed of self-praise in their minds, they never bring themselves to knowledge of their guilt, and they never consider how they have offended the internal Judge. They never fear his intransigence, because they trust human praise and think they have pleased God. If they were to bring his dread before their minds, the very fact that their motive is impure while they please people would make them fear him more. So Job is right to say, *No hypocrite will appear in his presence.* They do not place God's intransigence before their eyes as long as they want to appear attractive in the eyes of humans. On the other hand, if they change their attitude and put themselves in God's presence, they will assuredly no longer be hypocrites. The next verse:

XXXVII. 50. *Listen to my words, and let your ears take in the riddle.** Since he uses the word *riddle*, he lets us know that he is using figurative language. So he fittingly follows up on the role of the faithful people:

XXXVIII. 51. *If I should be judged, I know that I will be found innocent.** These words are not inconsis-

*Job 13:17

*Job 15:18

tent with what we know about blessed Job, since he is himself speaking publicly about himself what Truth had said secretly to his enemy about him, namely, *Have you noticed my servant Job? There is none on earth like him.** Certainly what this man says of himself is less important than what God says about him. It is one thing, you see, for him to be just, and something else for there not to be anyone like him. Accordingly he thinks humbly about himself, he who, while being incomparably just, only says that he can be found just in some way, not that he is more just than others.

Nevertheless there is a question it seems we might ask about his words. He said earlier, *I will declare my ways before him,** and later he will say, *You will have me swamped by the sins of my youth.** Furthermore, when he is considering his sins carefully, he adds still later, *You have sealed my sins as if in a bag.** But here he says, *If I should be judged, I know that I will be found innocent.* Sinfulness and innocence cannot be found together, but the holy man attributes a guilty state to himself and his purification to almighty God; he knows himself for a sinner, nor does he forget his justification by God's favor. But while he was performing good works, he deserved the abundant grace of undergoing trials. At this moment he is glad to be found innocent by the Judge, he who was buffeted by trials before Judgment. That is why, when he will say long afterward, *You have sealed my sins as if in a bag,* he will immediately add, *but you have healed my guilt.** So he who says he is found innocent in Judgment certainly does not deny that he is justly buffeted, even if the Lord's object in buffeting him was not to wipe away his sins but rather to increase his merit. The next verse:

XXXIX. 52. *Where is the one who will enter into judgment with me? Let him come forward.** The saints

*Job 1:8

*Job 13:15
*Job 13:26

*Job 14:17

*Job 14:17

*Job 13:19

conduct themselves in their works in such a way with God as their guide that absolutely nothing can be found externally by which they may be accused. In their thoughts, they are so circumspect and apply such extreme caution that if possible they always stand without blame in the internal Judge's sight. But however much they may succeed in their external behavior in avoiding base actions, they are by no means able to do equally well internally so as never to fall short in their thoughts. Human consciousness, you see, to the extent that it fails internally, is always in motion. That is why even the saints often fail in their hearts. So let blessed Job, as much with his own voice as with that of all the chosen ones, speak out and say, *Where is the one who will enter into judgment with me? Let him come forward.* He has no external actions, you see, for which he can be blamed, so he boldly looks around for an accuser. But since even the hearts of righteous people sometimes reprove themselves for foolish thinking, for that very reason perhaps he adds,

*Job 13:19

XL. 53. *Why am I consumed in my silence?** He is consumed in his silence, he who reproaches himself for foolish thinking and is stung internally by the pang of conscience. It is as if he said frankly, "Just as I have lived in such a way that I may fear no external accuser, would that I had lived in such a way that I might have within myself no conscience to accuse me." He who finds within himself something to make him burn is consumed in his silence. The next verse:

*Job 13:20

54. *There are two things I do not want done to me; then I will not hide from your face.** In this passage how should we take the word *face* of God, unless it be his censure, whereby he sees our sins and punishes them? No one hides from his face, not even a just person, if the two things he asks about are not withdrawn. Concerning these, Job goes on to say,

XLI. 55. *Let your hand be far from me, and may dread of you not frighten me.** What else but the time of grace and redemption is petitioned through the voice of prophecy by these two things? The law, you see, held the people bound under the threat of punishment, so that whoever should sin under the law would be punished by death. Nor did the people of Israel serve the Lord out of love, but out of fear. Justice, however, can never be fulfilled through fear, because, as John says, *Perfect love casts out fear.** Paul, on the other hand, encourages the adopted sons, saying, *You have not received a spirit of servitude, that you should still live in fear, but you have received a spirit of adoption as sons, whereby we cry, "Abba, Father."** *Rom 8:15

Blessed Job accordingly speaks with the voice of the human race, desiring to get beyond the harsh penalties of the law and wishing to leave fear behind and reach love; so he prevails upon almighty God and tells him what two things he would have him remove far away from him. He says, *Let your hand be far from me, and may dread of you not frighten me.* That is, "Take away the harsh penalty, relieve the weight of fear, but infuse in me a spirit of safety by means of the radiant grace of love. For if I do not get away from the penalty and from fear, I know I will not escape your intransigent judgment, because no one can be found just in your sight who serves you not by love, but by fear." In this way he seeks the very presence of his Creator, as it were familiarly and bodily, in order that he may hear what he does not know, and by what he knows he may be heard in that presence. So he forthwith adds,

56. *Call me, and I will answer you. Or at least I would speak, and you answer me.** When God appeared to human eyes through the flesh he had assumed, he showed men and women the sins they had committed without knowing it. So he adds,

*Job 13:21

*1 John 4:18

*Job 13:22

XLII. 57. *How many crimes and sins I have commit-*
*Job 13:23 *ted! Show me my wickedness and my misdeeds.** Nevertheless we can understand the verbs *call* and *answer*
in another way. For God to call means that he cares for
us by loving us and choosing us. As for us, to answer
means to obey his love by good works. So he appropriately adds, *Or at least I would speak, and you answer
me.* We speak by seeking his face through desire. God,
on the other hand, answers those who speak when he
appears to us who love him. But those who eagerly desire eternity carefully reprove themselves and scrutinize
their own actions; they try to make sure that there is
nothing in themselves that might offend their Creator's
intimate presence. So he adds, *How many crimes and
sins I have committed! Show me my wickedness and
my misdeeds.*

What the righteous people have to do in this life is
find themselves, and once they have found themselves,
they must start living a better way of life by weeping
over themselves and correcting themselves. Although
there is no difference between crime and sin according
*1 John 3:4 to the apostle John, who said, *Wrongdoing is sin,** in ev-
eryday usage crime seems worse than sin; most people
will freely admit they are sinners, but to call oneself a
criminal is sometimes embarrassing. There is, however,
a difference between crime and fault, in that a crime
surpasses the penalty for sin, whereas a fault does not
surpass that penalty. We are ordered, you see, by the law
to offer a sacrifice, and this injunction certainly includes
sin as well as fault.

Furthermore crime is sometimes an act, whereas
fault is often only a thought. That is why the psalmist
*Ps 18:13 says, *Who knows his faults?** Sins of act, of course,
we know all the more easily to the extent that they are
external to us. As for sins of thought, however, they are

hard to know, because they are committed in the invisible realm. Accordingly, whoever is driven by desire for eternity eagerly wants to appear pure in the sight of the coming Judge; such people examine themselves in the present time all the more carefully and consider diligently how they may stand openly hereafter before the Judge's dreadful appearance; they implore him that he would show them how they have displeased him, so that they may punish themselves for it by repentance and render themselves unjudgable here by judging themselves.

58. In this matter, however, it is necessary to realize how devastated we are by the penalty of our exile, since we have become so blinded that we no longer know ourselves. We commit evil acts, but we do not realize that they are evil until after they are committed. Of course the mind driven away from the light of truth finds nothing in itself but darkness, and it often steps into the pit of sin without knowing it. This fact is certainly clear about the blindness of exile alone, since the mind is excluded from the enlightenment of the Lord, and it has lost sight of itself because it did not love its Maker's face. So he adds,

XLIII. 59. *Why do you hide your face and consider me your enemy?* * The human race had contemplation of intimate light in Paradise, but by pleasing itself it abandoned itself and lost the Creator's light and face. Humans fled to the trees of Paradise because after sin they dreaded the sight of the Creator, whom they were accustomed to love. But see how after sin they receive the penalty, and after the penalty they return to love, because they discover the consequence of sin. They dreaded God's face in their sin, but upon being awakened to sin they seek that face in the penalty, that they might now flee the darkness in which they were blinded

*Job 13:24

and might shudder bitterly at the very fact that they could not see their Maker. The holy man is now struck by such a desire that he cries out, *Why do you hide your face and consider me your enemy?* because, "If only you saw me as a friend, you would not deprive me of the light of your vision." He then adds the changeability of the human heart:

*Job 13:25

XLIV. 60. *Why do you show your power against a leaf blown by the wind and pursue dry straw?* * What indeed are humans but a leaf that, as you can see, fell from a tree in Paradise? What are they but a leaf blown away by the wind of temptation and lifted up by gusts of desires? The human mind surely suffers as many temptations as the gusts of wind move through the air. Anger often disturbs the mind, and when anger cools, silly, inept joy takes its place. The mind is driven by pinpricks of lust, and the fever of avarice causes it to move far and wide to encompass the things that belong to the earth. Sometimes pride lifts up the mind; sometimes, on the other hand, irrational fear causes it to fall to the ground.

Since therefore the mind is lifted up and carried by so many gusts of temptations, people are rightly compared to leaves. So Isaiah is right when he says, *We have all fallen away like leaves, and our evil deeds have carried us away like the wind.* * Our evil deeds have unquestionably carried us off like the wind, us who are stabilized by no weight of virtue; yes, our evil deeds have given rise to empty pride. After leaves, humans are again called straw, and rightly. At their creation they were a tree; in temptation they became leaves of themselves; after that they looked like straw in exile. Because they fell from a high place, they are leaves; because they were near the earth through their flesh, even if they seemed to stand, they are called straw. But

*Isa 64:6

it was because they lost the green freshness of interior love that they are now dry straw.

Let the holy man then reflect on the low meanness of humankind and the supreme inflexibility of God and say, *Why do you show your power against a leaf blown by the wind and pursue dry straw?* It is as if he bitterly wept over himself and said, "Why do you with such impeccable righteousness attack the one whom you know very well to be a weakling in temptation?" The next verse:

XLV. 61. *You are writing bitterness against me.*   *Job 13:26

Everything we speak passes away, but our written words remain, so he says not that God speaks but that he writes bitterness when his trials keep buffeting us for a long time. Humankind the sinner was once told, *You are dust, and to dust you shall return.* Angels often appeared to   *Gen 3:19
men and women to give them precepts. Moses was the lawgiver who strictly restrained sin. The only-begotten Son of the heavenly Father himself came to redeem us and by dying destroyed death.* He announced to us   *Heb 2:14
that eternal life that he demonstrated in himself. That sentence of death that was handed down in Paradise concerning our flesh, however, was not changed from the very beginning of the human race until the end of the world: *Who is the man who lives and will not see death?* This point the psalmist supports with insight: *Ps 88:49
You are dreadful; who can resist you? Your wrath is from of old. It is he, you see, whose anger was once   *Ps 75:8 Vulg
roused against humans who sinned in Paradise and who passed sentence on us concerning mortal flesh, which neither now nor ever until the end can be lifted. Let him therefore say, *You are writing bitterness against me.* So he again adds,

XLVI. 62. *You will my destruction for the sins of my youth.* Here is a righteous man who has not discovered   *Job 13:26

that he sinned in his youth but is afraid of his youthful actions. But what we must realize is this: just as age increases in the body, so also in the mind. The first stage of people's life is certainly infancy, when even if their life is innocence, they do not know how to say that they live in innocence.[1] To that stage succeeds the next, that of childhood, in which they can now say what they want. Then comes adolescence, which is obviously the first stage when they are free to act. After that, young adulthood follows, which, as you know, is connected with physical strength; after that comes old age, which, thanks to the passing of time, corresponds with maturity.

Accordingly, since we have said that adolescence is the first stage fit to perform good works, it is of righteous people that we speak: when they enter the stage of high mental maturity, they sometimes bring to mind the memory of their first actions, and they engage in self-reproach concerning their first stages of life to the extent that they have grown wise in mental gravity. They find that they have been indiscreet, because they have later reached the pinnacle of discretion. So Holy Job now rightly dreads the sins of adolescence. If, however, we are to take these words in the literal sense, we must consequently ask ourselves how much greater are the sins of old age than those of youth, since the righteous so intensely dread those sins that they committed at a more immature stage. The next verse:

XLVII. 63. *You have put my feet in irons; you have kept watch over all my paths; you have kept guard over my footsteps.** God has placed our feet in irons, because he has bound our sinfulness by the unrelenting sentence

*Job 13:27

---

[1] This is a pun on the Latin *infancia*, which the English *infancy* transliterates. It alludes to the obvious fact that the newborn child cannot speak, so he or she cannot say that he or she is innocent.

of his strict justice. He watches all our paths, because he carefully judges everything whatsoever about us. Paths, you see, are normally narrower than roads. If we are not wrong in taking roads to mean actions, then we are surely right in taking paths to mean the very thoughts of actions. God accordingly keeps watch over all our paths, because he even weighs the thoughts in each and every one of our acts. Furthermore, he keeps guard over our footsteps, because he scrutinizes the intentions behind our actions to see how correctly they are made, lest any good work should be undertaken without a correct desire.

Footsteps could also signify evil acts. The foot in the body is the step on the road, and when we do something bad, we often give a bad example to those who see it; in so doing, as it were, we leave a distorted print for those who follow us by turning our foot off the road, since we incite the hearts of other people to scandal through our actions. It is exceedingly difficult, however, to keep watch over ourselves, not boldly to perform evil acts, not to falter in our intention to do good works, and to keep our evil thoughts from mocking us in the midst of righteous acts. Almighty God, however, takes good care to sift all these circumstances, and he weighs everything in judgment. But when are people who are confined by the weakness of their flesh able to rise up with assurance against all that hinders them and maintain righteousness with their thoughts unimpaired? So he shrewdly adds,

XLVIII. 64. *I am wasting away like a rotten thing; I am like clothes eaten by moths.** Just as the moth that emerges from a garment eats it up, so humans have rottenness in themselves, and they are consumed by it. That is the thing by which they are consumed to the point that they no longer are. It can be understood in another way, however, if it should be said in the voice of

*Job 13:28

the one who is tempted, *I am wasting away like a rotten thing; I am like clothes eaten by moths.* We waste away like a rotten thing, because our corruptible flesh wears us out. Since an impure temptation arises from nowhere else but us ourselves, that temptation consumes our flesh like a moth, as though we were a garment from which it emerged. In ourselves we assuredly have that by which we can be tempted. It is just like the moth consuming the garment, the very garment from which it emerged.

We should know, moreover, that the moth bores its way through the garment without a sound. And a thought often pierces the mind in such a way that the mind is itself unaware of it until afterward, when it feels the sting. It is well said therefore that we are eaten up like a garment by a moth, because we sometimes do not know that we are wounded by our temptations, unless they should afterward stab us in the mind. This weakness of ours the holy man now obviously considers when he again shrewdly adds,

XLIX. 65. *Man, born of woman, living but a short time, is full of abundant misery.** In Holy Scripture the word *woman* is used either to indicate her sex or her weakness. It is certainly used for the sex in the words, *God sent his Son, born of a woman, born under the law.** It is used to indicate weakness as in these words by a certain wise man: *A man's wicked deeds are better than a woman's kind services.** A man, whoever he may be, is called strong and discreet, but a woman is taken to mean a weak or indiscreet mind. Furthermore, it often happens that even a discreet man quickly falls into sin, and another who is indiscreet and weak displays good works. He who is indiscreet and weak, however, is sometimes given grounds for pride by the fact that he did well, and he then falls into a graver sin. Every discreet person, however, when he realizes that he has

*Job 14:1

*Gal 4:4

*Sir 42:14

done something bad, forces himself back to a more exact following of a strict rule of conduct, and in this way he grows stronger in justice, on the same path from which he seemed to have temporarily fallen away from justice. Concerning this matter it is well said, *A man's wicked deeds are better than a woman's kind services.** Even the sin of a strong man sometimes becomes an occasion of virtue, and the virtue of the weak an occasion of sin. In this passage of Job, therefore, what does the word *woman* signify but weakness, where it is said, *Man, born of woman?* He might as well say plainly, "What physical strength will he have who was born of weakness?"

*Sir 42:14

66. *Living but a short time, he is full of abundant misery.* See how Holy Job's words briefly describe the penalty of humankind, how our life is restricted and our misery multiplied. If, you see, we carefully consider all that is done here on earth, it is penalty and misery. When we have to minister to the corruption of the flesh for the necessary and granted continuation of life, it is misery: clothing to combat the cold, food to combat hunger, and coolness against the heat are needed. Health of the body is preserved only with a great deal of caution; even when preserved it is lost; once lost it is only restored with much labor, and even when it is restored, it is always in doubt.

What is all this but miserable mortal life? We love our friends, fearful lest they might be offended; we fear enemies, and we are insecure concerning them, especially the ones we fear. We often speak with confidence to our enemies as though they were friends; sometimes we take the harmless words of our neighbors, who perhaps love us very much, as though they were hostile words; we who never wish to be deceived or to deceive err seriously by caution. What indeed is all this but miserable human life? That having lost the heavenly fatherland we enjoy our exile and are loaded with cares, and yet we pretend not to notice their weight with our many thoughts, that we are deprived of the inner light and yet desire to endure our blindness for a long life— what else is all this but our innate penalty of misery? But even if we wish to remain in this life for a long time, the very course of mortal life presses forward to make us leave it. So the holy man rightly adds,

L. 67. *Man is like a flower which falls and withers; he flits like a shadow; he never remains in the same state.** Like a flower we fall, because our flesh is conspicuous, but then it withers and returns to decay. What are we who are born in the world but flowers of the field? Let us cast the eyes of our heart over this vast present world and see how it is as full of flowers as of people. The life of the flesh is accordingly like the flower in the grass. So the psalmist says well, *As for man, his days are like grass, and he grows like the flower of the field.** Isaiah for his part says, *All flesh is grass, and its boasting is like the flower of the field.** Like the flower, therefore, we emerge from concealment, suddenly appear in public, and just as quickly leave the public, only to return to concealment in death. The greenness of flesh displays us, but the aridity of dust carries us away from view. Like a flower we appeared where we were not before; like a flower we withered after appearing but a short time.

68. Each day and moment by moment we are impelled further toward death, so Job rightly adds, *He flits like a shadow; he never remains in the same state.* But since the sun also never stops pursuing its course, nor fixes itself in one place, why is the course of a person's life compared to a shadow instead of to the sun, unless it is because we have lost the Creator's love and equally

*Job 14:2

*Ps 102:15
*Isa 40:6

the warmth of his heart, and we are therefore left with our cold wickedness alone? In the words of Truth, *Wickedness will spread, and the love of many will grow cold.**   *Matt 14:12
Those then who do not have their heart warmed by the love of God or keep the life that they love certainly flit like a shadow. In that case it is also correctly written about them, *He followed a shadow.**   *Sir 34:2

So it is well said, *He never remains in the same state.* Infancy, you see, passes into childhood, childhood into adolescence, adolescence into young adulthood, young adulthood into old age, and old age into death. So the course of the present life, by means of its very phases, is impelled forward to the loss of itself. In fact, it always sustains a loss precisely there where it thinks it is making progress in its walk of life. Accordingly we cannot have a fixed state here below where we have come in order to pass through, and our life here itself means to pass out of life every day. Such movement the first humans obviously could not have before sinning, because time passed while they stood still.

After they sinned, however, they placed themselves in a kind of slippery state of temporary being. When they ate the forbidden fruit, they forthwith discovered a defect in their status, and that changeability we suffer, not only externally but also internally, whenever we attempt to rise up to better actions. The mind, you see, by the weight of its changeability, is forever impelled to be something other than what it is, and unless it is held fast in its present position by the stringent discipline of self-control, it forever lapses into worse behavior. That mind that abandoned the one who always remains lost the status that it could have kept. So now when it tries to be better, it has, as it were, to strive against the current of a stream. But when its intention of ascending is deflected, it is led to the lowest point without struggle.

Since ascent requires struggle and descent allows rest, the Lord warns those who are to enter the narrow gate, *Strive to enter the narrow gate.** When he was about to speak of the entrance of the narrow gate, he prefaced it with the verb *strive*, because unless the striving of the mind is engaged, it does not overcome the world's water, by which the soul is always borne down to the lowest point. Accordingly, since the soul falls and withers like a flower, and since it flits like a shadow and never remains in its own state, let us listen to what follows that consideration:

*Luke 13:24

LI. 69. *Do you judge it worth your while to open your eyes on a being of this sort and to enter into judgment with him?** Job undoubtedly considered both the power of almighty God and his own weakness before he set both God and himself before his eyes. He considered who would enter into judgment with whom. He saw humankind in this corner and the Creator in the other, that is, dust and God, and he rightly said, *Do you judge it worth your while to open your eyes on a being of this sort?* For almighty God to open his eyes means to exercise justice, and to see him whom he would strike. It is as though he closes his eyes when he does not wish to see him whom he does not wish to strike. So Job straightway adds concerning Judgment itself, *To enter into judgment with him.* Since, however, he has contemplated God's coming for Judgment, he again considers his own weakness. He sees that he could not be pure of his own accord, he who came out of impurity in order to exist, so he adds,

*Job 14:3

LII. 70. *Who can make pure him who is conceived of impure seed? Is it not you alone who are?** He who alone is pure of himself is able to purify the impure. Humans, you see, live in corruptible flesh, and they have the impure seeds of temptation implanted in themselves, be-

*Job 14:4

cause they have certainly brought them along from their origin. Even their conception is undoubtedly impure because of the pleasure of the flesh. That is why the psalmist says, *Behold, I have been conceived in iniquity, and my mother brought me forth in sin.** That is why we are often tempted, even against our will. That is why we suffer from the impurity in our own mind, even if we fight against it by the use of reason, because although we were conceived impure, we tend toward purity, and we try to overcome that which we are.

*Ps 50:7

Any who win the victory over the impulse of hidden temptation and impure thoughts, however, should never attribute their purity to themselves, because no one can make pure the one who is conceived of impure seed except him who alone is pure of himself. Therefore, those who finally arrive at the goal of purity of soul should look back at the road they have traveled from their conception, and they should gather from that road the knowledge that they do not have purity of life by their own virtue, they whose impurity brought about the beginning of their life.

This passage, however, may be understood in the sense that blessed Job had an insight into the incarnation of the Redeemer and saw him as the only man in the world who was not conceived of impure seed; rather, he entered the world through the Virgin in such a way that he should have no impure conception. He did not come forth from the union of a man and a woman, but he proceeded from the Holy Spirit and the Virgin Mary. He alone accordingly was really pure in his flesh, he who could not be touched by pleasure of the flesh, for he also did not come here through pleasure of the flesh.

BOOK 12

Honest people customarily think how transitory this life is just as seriously and devoutly as they consider the eternal happiness of their heavenly homeland. They inwardly look upon those things that remain and wisely await the external disappearance of fading things. In this way blessed Job, after he had passed sentence on the loss of human time, saying, *Man, born of woman, lives but a short time*, and again, *He flits like a shadow and never remains in the same state,** adds more words about the shortness of his life:

I. 1. *The days of man are short, and the number of his months is before you.** He considers that to be as nothing before us which passes away so swiftly. Since, however, even those things that fade still stand before almighty God, he asserts that the number of our months is before him. Or at least *days* mean a short time, whereas *months* express, as it were, an increased extension of days. Our days are accordingly short, but since our life extends to the hereafter, the number of our months is said to be before God. That is why Solomon says, *Length of days is at his right hand.** The next verse:

II. 2. *You have determined his limits, and they will not be passed.** Nothing that happens to people in this world is done without the hidden counsel of God. He foresees everything that will follow, and he decided before the world was made how the ages would develop. He decreed even then both how much prosperity in this world would follow people's steps and how much adversity would strike them, lest unlimited prosperity should exalt God's chosen ones or too much adversity depress them. God also decreed the length of people's lives in this mortal life. Although almighty God added fifteen

*Job 14:1-2

*Job 14:5

*Prov 3:16

*Job 14:5

years to King Hezekiah's life, the day when he let him die was also the one on which God foreknew that he was going to die.* Concerning this matter we ask how the prophet can tell Hezekiah, *Put your house in order, since you are going to die; you shall not live.** When the sentence of death was passed on him, his life was forthwith extended because of his tears.

*see
2 Kgs 20:6

*2 Kgs 20:1

But the Lord told him through the prophet the time at which he should die, although he deferred that time of death for him through his generous mercy, that time that he foreknew before the ages. Neither was the prophet wrong, accordingly, when he warned Hezekiah of the time of his death, the time when that man should die, nor was the Lord's decree overturned, because it was also preordained before the ages that the years of Hezekiah's life should increase by God's generosity. Furthermore the length of his life, which was unexpectedly increased externally, was internally decreed without adding foreknowledge. So Job was right to say, *You have determined his limits, and they will not be passed.*

3. The matter can, however, be understood spiritually, because we sometimes try to grow in virtues, and we receive certain gifts while we are disappointed as regards others, and we are then depressed and dejected. We never reach the level of virtue we want to reach, you see, because almighty God knows our inner potential, and he imposes a limit on our spiritual advancement. He does so in order that when we try to attain some virtue and are unable to do so, we might not become proud concerning that which we are able to reach. For example, that famous preacher who had been pulled up to the third heaven and even attained the knowledge of the secrets of Paradise* was unable after that revelation to be quiet and untempted. Almighty God, however, has imposed limits on humans that none will be able to cross;

*2 Cor 12:2-4

so he raised them up to contemplate the highest reality
and led them back again to put up with their weakness,
so that they might realize their own capacity and limits.
When they try to grasp security and cannot, lest they
exceed themselves by pride, they are always forced by
humility to keep to their own limits. The next verse:

III. 4. *Back away from him a little, that he may rest
until the day comes that he longs for like a hired ser-*

*Job 14:6

vant. In this passage the word for *back away* means to
remove the force of the whip. Who, you see, is able to
rest when God backs away? He alone is repose, and as
long as anyone is away from him for any period of time,
that person is restless. Therefore *back away from him*
presupposes *your striking arm.* Job is smart to add, *Until
the day comes that he longs for like a hired servant.* As
long as the hired servant has not reached the end of his
task, he is that far from receiving his salary. In the same
way any of the saints who are still living the present life
and realize how far they are from leaving it sigh because
they are also far from eternal joy. Accordingly what does
it mean to say, *Back away from him a little, that he may
rest*, except "Take away the whip of the present life now
and show him the happiness of eternal rest"?

That is why he adds concerning this rest, *Until the
day comes that he longs for like a hired servant.* The day
that we long for like a hired servant comes to us precisely
when we are given eternal rest as a recompense for our
labor. As long as he beholds the form of the present life,
blessed Job presses his point, namely, that the human
race is still full of misery and despicable. He also declares to what extent those creatures that are without
physical senses seem to surpass humans when he says,

IV. 5. *There is hope for a tree. If it should be cut
down, it might sprout again and put forth new limbs.
If its root should rot in the ground, and its trunk die in*

the dust, it will blossom anew at the touch of water and put forth leaves, just as when it was first planted. When a man dies, however, he is stripped and decomposed. Where is he then, may I ask? Since the literal meaning of these words is clear, we must render the internal sense and search out how they should be understood spiritually. In Holy Scripture the word for tree sometimes indicates the cross, sometimes the just person (or even the unjust), and sometimes the incarnate wisdom of God. The cross is symbolized by the wood, for example, in the words, *Let us put wood in his bread.* Putting wood in bread certainly means to lay the cross on the Lord's body.

Job 14:7-10

Jer 11:19

Second, the word for wood signifies the just person (or even the unjust), as the Lord says through the prophet, *I the Lord have brought down the lofty tree, and the lowly tree I have raised up.* The voice of the selfsame Truth tells us, *All those who exalt themselves will be humbled, and the one who humbles himself will be exalted.* Solomon says for his part, *In whatever direction a tree falls, whether to the north or to the south, there it will stay.* On the day of death, you see, the just one falls to the south, but the sinner to the north, because the just are led to joy through spiritual warmth, whereas sinners, with the apostate angel who said, *I will take my seat on the mount of the covenant, at the edge of the north,* are condemned in the coldness of their hearts.

Ezek 17:27

Luke 14:11; 18:14

Eccl 11:3

Isa 14:13

In the third place the incarnate wisdom of God is prefigured by the tree, since it is written about him, *Wisdom is the tree of life for those who take hold of it.* He says himself, *If in the green wood they do these things, what will be done in the dry?* So in this passage of Job under discussion where a tree fares better than a person, what do we take that *person* to mean except anyone who is self-indulgent? What does the word *tree* represent but

Prov 3:18

Luke 23:31

the life of any just person? So *there is hope for a tree. If it should be cut down, it might sprout again.* When the just are done to death by suffering for the sake of truth, they recover the freshness of eternal life. The one who sprouts here anew through faith sprouts there in open vision. *It might put forth new limbs,* because the faithful often grow in love for the heavenly country because of a just person's suffering, they receive the freshness of spiritual life, and they give thanks for his having striven manfully here for God's sake. The next verse:

V. 6. *If its root should rot in the ground, and its trunk die in the dust, it will blossom anew at the touch of water and put forth leaves, just as when it was first planted.* What is the just person's root if not holy preaching? That is his source of life, and it is what he lives on. What do we take the words for earth or dust to mean but sinners? The voice of the Creator tells them, *You are earth, and to earth you shall go,* or rather, as our trans-

*Gen 3:19

lation puts it, *You are dust, and to dust you shall return.** The root of the just accordingly rots in the ground, and their trunk dies in the dust, because their preaching is held in contempt by the hearts of depraved sinners and deprived of all power. Their trunk moreover dies in the dust, because their body is killed at the hands of persecutors. The voice of wisdom has it thus: *In the eyes of fools they seemed to die, and their departure was

*Wis 3:2

esteemed as affliction.**

Those, however, whose root rotted in the ground and whose trunk died in the dust will sprout at the touch of water, because they created the seed of virtue in the hearts of the chosen ones by the example of their own work through the inspiration of the Holy Spirit. The word for water, you see, sometimes indicates the dew of the Holy Spirit, as when it is said, *If anyone is thirsty, let him come to me and drink. The one who drinks the water*

I give will never be thirsty again.* *It will put forth leaves,* just as when it was first planted.* Putting forth leaves after the trunk has been cut down means that after the bodily death of the just, they lift up the hearts of many by the very example of their suffering and show the freshness of truth by their correct faith. It is well said, *Just as when it was first planted.* All that the just do here on earth is a second planting, because the first planting is obviously not the works of the just but the foreknowledge of the Creator. Just as all that the chosen ones do is first internally foreseen and planned, so it is later perfected externally. So it is well said, *It will put forth leaves, just as when it was first planted.* In other words, it will show forth its freshness in completed actions, the freshness it had at first in the Creator's foreknowledge.

7. The root of the just person can also be understood as human nature itself, by which the just person exists. This root obviously rots in the earth, when the nature of flesh weakens and is reduced to dust. Its trunk dies in the dust, because the dead body loses its form. But it sprouts at the touch of water, because it rises at the coming of the Holy Spirit. *It will put forth leaves, just as when it was first planted.* It returns to that form, you see, that it was created to receive if it had refused sin when it was given a place in Paradise.

8. The passage could perhaps even be understood of the Lord himself, him who is the head of all goodness, following that lead that we have already mentioned, namely, his own words: *If they do these things in the green wood, what will be done in the dry?** He called himself green wood, and us he called dry, because he had in himself the power of divinity, whereas we who are only humans are called dry wood. The tree accordingly has hope if it should be cut down, because it recovers its greenness; so, even if he could be cut down

*John 7:37;
4:13

*Luke 23:31

through the passion, he returns to fresh life through the glory of the resurrection. Its branches spread out, because the faithful are multiplied after his resurrection, and they grow in number far and wide.

Its root rotted in the earth, as it were, because the faithless Jews held his preaching in contempt. Its trunk died in the dust, because the persecutors' hearts swelled with pride from the wind of their unbelief, and they held him in contempt and disdain for being able to die in the flesh. At the touch of water it blossomed anew, because by the power of God his dead flesh returned to life according to that which was written: *God raised him* *Acts 3:15   from the dead.** Since God is Trinity, the Holy Trinity, that is, the Father, the Son, and the Holy Spirit, raised up the dead flesh of the same Son, the only-begotten One. It put forth leaves, just as when it was first planted. After the apostles, being fainthearted at his death, gave in to dread and denial, their root withered. But then they received back the freshness of faith through the glory of his resurrection. Compared with this tree what is any one person but dust?

VI. 9. *When a person dies, however, he is stripped* *Job 14:10   and decomposed. Where is he then, may I ask?** No one is without sin, except that one who did not come into this world from sin. We are all bound by guilt, so we all die because of the very loss of justice. We are stripped of the garment of innocence granted us first in Paradise, and by subsequent death we are decomposed. The sinner accordingly dies in guilt, is stripped of justice, and decomposes in the penalty. This nakedness of his sinful son the father was pleased to cover when he returned, *Luke 15:22   and he said, *Quick, get the best robe.** The best robe is surely the garment of innocence, which humans in the fullness of creation received but sadly lost, deceived by the serpent. Opposing this nakedness, another writer says, *Happy are those who are on their guard, keeping watch over their garments, lest they go around naked.* We unquestionably keep watch over our garments when we observe the precepts of innocence in our minds, so that when guilt makes us naked in front of the Judge, repentance may cover us, as we recover our lost innocence. He is right to say, *Where is he then, may I ask?* Sinful humans, you see, refused to stay there where they were created, and here where they fell they are forbidden to stay long. They willingly lost the fatherland, and unwillingly they are expelled from this place of exile that they love. Where, then, are they, may I ask, who are not in his love, where true being is? The next verse:

VII. 10. *Just like water that leaves the sea, and the river bed that empties and dries up, so when a man sleeps, he will not rise again.*[1] The sea is the mind of man, and just like waves of the sea are the thoughts of the mind, which sometimes swell with anger and then calm down with kind dispositions; hate troubles the water of the mind with bitterness. When a person dies, the waters of the sea recede, because, as the psalmist says, *On that day all their thoughts will perish.* Somewhere else it is written about the dying person, *Love and hate will perish together.* The riverbed accordingly empties and dries up, because when the soul is led away, the body remains empty. Just like a streambed, the dead body is

*Rev 16:15

*Job 14:11-12

*Ps 145:4

*Eccl 9:6

---

[1] As the following paragraph shows, Saint Gregory interprets *dormierit* as the sleep of death. So although literally the line reads, "So when man sleeps, he does not get up again," it might actually be more correct to translate, "When a man dies, he will not rise." Early church writers often speak of death as sleep following Saint Paul, whom, in fact, Gregory quotes later in paragraph 11. By contrast, the early Wisdom literature, including Job, had no belief in a resurrection after death.

empty. In this matter it is to be carefully observed that the present life, as long as the soul remains in the body, at any rate, is compared to sea and river. Seawater of course is salty; that of a stream is sweet. So we who live here are sometimes affected by a certain amount of peevishness, but sometimes we are found to be serene, mild, and charming; accordingly, the course of the present life is characterized by comparing it to the stream and to the sea.

11. What follows, however, seems too harsh: *When a man dies, he will not rise.* Why in that case do we labor, if we do not expect the reward of resurrection? Why does he say here, *He will not rise*, when it is written, *We shall all certainly rise, but we shall not all be changed?** Elsewhere he says, *If we have hoped in Christ for this life alone, we are of all men the most to be pitied.** Truth himself says, *All those who are in the tombs will hear his voice, and those who have done good will come out for the resurrection of life.** The next line, however, shows the discernment of the previous one. Here is how he goes on:

VIII. 12. *Until heaven is destroyed, he will not awake, or arise from his sleep.** Clearly he will not rise, but *until heaven is destroyed*, because unless the end of this present world arrives, the human race will not awake from the sleep of death to life. Therefore, he does not mean that humankind does not rise in any sense at all, but that the human race positively does not rise before the skies fall. It is to be noticed also that previously he said humankind was dead, and then later he described humankind not as dead but as sleeping; so now he tells us that we are absolutely not going to rise from sleep until heaven is destroyed. What is the purpose of speaking in this way, unless he clearly makes us understand that he is talking about sinful humankind, whose death

*1 Cor 15:51

*1 Cor 15:14

*John 5:28-29

*Job 14:12

is compared to a tree sprouting anew, whose death is death to the life of justice?

When, however, he is talking about bodily death, he prefers to call it not death but sleep, doubtless wishing to insert the hope of resurrection, because just as quickly as a person rises from sleep, so at the Creator's nod does one rise from bodily death. The word *death*, you see, is a subject of sheer terror to untrained minds, but the word *sleep* has no fear in it. That is why Paul counsels his disciples with the words, *I do not want you brothers to be unaware of those who have fallen asleep, lest you should be saddened like those who have no hope. If we believe that Jesus died and rose again, so God will also bring with him those who have fallen asleep in Jesus.*[*]

*[*1 Thess 4:13-14]*

But how is it that the famous preacher calls the Lord's death *death*, but the death of the Lord's servants not *death* but *sleep*? Is it not because he understands the untrained hearts of his listeners and prepares the remedy of his preaching artfully, unhesitatingly admitting the death of the one who they knew had already risen? On the other hand did he not call them sleepers rather than dead, those who had not yet risen, so that he might give his hearers hope in the resurrection? He had no fear of calling him dead who the listeners knew had already risen, but he was afraid to call them dead whom they had trouble believing able to rise. Accordingly blessed Job does not doubt that those who have suffered bodily death will rise again to life; so he prefers to say they are sleeping rather than dead. The next verse:

IX. 13. *Who will grant me the favor of your protection in hell?*[*] Before the coming of the Mediator between God and humankind, every person, however pure and acceptable his life may have been, went down to the dungeons of hell; so there is no doubt that the human beings who fell by their own volition could not by their

*[*Job 14:13]*

own volition return to the repose of Paradise until the one came who by the mystery of his incarnation opened the road to Paradise for us. That is why after the sin of Adam, we are told that a flaming sword was placed at the entrance of Paradise, a sword that was also described *see Gen 3:24 as turning,* because whenever the time should arrive, it might then be turned away. We have said that the souls of the just went down to hell but not that they were held in the place of punishment. Rather we are to believe that there are higher places as well as lower places in hell and that the just rest in the higher places, while the unjust are tortured in the lower places. That is why the psalmist, because of the advance grace of God, said, *You* *Ps 85:13 *delivered my soul from the lower depths of hell.** Blessed Job, accordingly, knowing he was going down to hell before the Mediator's arrival, pleads for his Creator's protection there so that he might remain a stranger to the place of punishment and, while he is given his rest, might be hidden from retribution. So he adds,

*Job 14:13   X. 14. *May you hide me until your anger is spent.** Every day the wrath of almighty God exerts the force of its severity to the end; he especially strikes down with suitable penalties those who live unsuitable lives. His wrath strikes indeed here, but the blow passes in the end; temporarily it is felt, but at the end of the world it is over. This very anger, insofar as it concerns the souls of the elect, has already passed at the Redeemer's coming, because the Mediator between God and humans led them back from the dungeons of hell to the glory of Paradise, when he loyally went down to hell. We must, however, keep in mind on this subject that the word *wrath* does not fit the divine nature, because no disturbance falls upon the simple Godhead. That is why we are told, *You, however, are supreme in power, and you judge in serenity, governing us with great con-*

*sideration.** Since, then, the souls of the just were to be   *Wis 12:18
freed at the Mediator's coming from the parts of hell
that were not places of punishment, this fact was also
foreseen by the just man. He adds a petition:
XI. 15. *Will you please set me a time when you will
remember me?** But when the fullness of time came,*   *Job 14:13
*God sent his Son born of a woman, born under the
law, that he might redeem those who were under the
law.** It is this redemption, accordingly, that the man of   *Gal 4:4-5
God foresees, the redemption that would liberate many
even of the Gentiles, as Job said earlier, *Even if you
hide the knowledge in your heart, nevertheless I know
that you remember all things.** So he makes his petition   *Job 10:13
before almighty God, that he would set him a time for
his remembrance of him. That is why the Lord said in
the gospel, *If I should be lifted up from the earth, I will
draw all men to myself.** He means, of course, all the   *John 12:32
elect. When the Lord returned from hell, you see, he
did not bring the reprobate sinners along with the just,
but from there he freed all those who, as he well knew,
had believed in him.

That is why he also said through the prophet Hosea,
*O death, I will be your death. I will be your bite,
Gehenna.** When we kill, we see to it that the victim is   *Hos 13:14
no more. When we bite, however, we take away a part
and we leave a part. The Lord absolutely killed death
in his chosen ones, so the death of death is assured.
Since, however, he took away part of hell and left a
part, he did not kill hell absolutely, but took a bite out
of it. So he says, *I will be your death, O death.* That is,
"I absolutely am killing you in my chosen ones." *I will
be your bite, Gehenna,* because, "Having taken away
my chosen ones, I partly stab you." Blessed Job knew
about this coming to hell of our Redeemer, so let him
make his petition for what he foresaw was going to

happen, and let him say, *Please set me a time when you will remember me.* The next verse:

*Job 14:14

XII. 16. *Do you think a dead man will live again?** It is the practice of just people, because they hold sure and firm knowledge themselves, to say things as though they had some doubt concerning them, in order that they might transfer the words of weak people to themselves. Then by a decisive answer they directly contradict that weakness and doubt. Inasmuch as they are perceived as giving utterance to a doubt, they condescend to the weak to a certain extent. On the other hand, inasmuch as the decision they render is firm, they lead the doubting minds of the weak to a more assured position.

When they act in this way, they certainly follow the example of our Head. When the Lord was drawing near to his passion, he actually used the words of weaklings himself and said, *My Father, if it is possible, let this cup pass away from me.** He took up their fear so that he might rid them of it. Then through obedience he showed them the strength of fortitude and said, *Yet not my will but yours be done.** This was in order that when something we do not wish threatens us, we might pray through weakness for it not to happen, so that we might be prepared through fortitude for our Creator's will to be done, even against our own will. By this example, accordingly, the words of the weak should sometimes be used by the courageous; in this way the hearts of the weak might be inspired to make robust declarations and thereby be gratefully strengthened. So blessed Job, once he had, as it were, taken up the words of doubters, saying, *Do you think a dead man will live again?* forthwith added his firm opinion and said,

*Matt 26:39

*Matt 26:39

XIII. 17. *All the days that I do battle now, I am waiting for my change to come.** He is waiting with extreme longing for his change to come, and he surely

*Job 14:14

implies how sure he is of the resurrection, giving notice how much he despises the course of his present life that he calls warfare. A soldier's life certainly always tends toward an end, and the time of that end is daily awaited. So he despises the course of this life, and he demands a fixed position. Just because he fights in changing situations, he is in a hurry to reach an unchanging condition. For the just, indeed, the load of their state of corruption in this life is burdensome. Because insomnia tires them out, they long for sleep, that the fatigue and worry of sleeplessness might be mitigated. On the other hand, sleep itself sometimes kills a person.

Hunger exhausts the body, and in order that its urgency might be driven off, food is earnestly sought. Yet even food is often a burden, which we need in order to banish our sluggishness and exhaustion. Accordingly the burden of corruption is heavy, and if it were not so, Paul would never have said, *The creature is unwillingly a subject of futility, because of him who made it a subject in hope; yet the creature will be freed from its slavery to corruption; its freedom will be the glory of the children of God. We know in fact that the whole creation groans in turmoil until now.** So let the holy man desire   *Rom 8:20-22
the state of incorruption and say, *All the days that I do battle now, I am waiting for my change to come.* What he will do when that change comes he adds now:

XIV. 18. *You will call me, and I will answer you.**   *Job 14:15
We are said to answer a person when we perform actions in return that correspond with that person's deeds. In that change, therefore, the Lord calls, and humankind responds, because in front of the glory of incorruption humans stand forth incorruptible, after corruption is over. For now, you see, as long as we are subject to corruption, we by no means answer to our Creator, because while corruption is still a long way off from

incorruption, there is no similarity that comes close to our answer. Concerning that change we find it written, *When he appears, we will be like him, because we will*

*1 John 3:2   *see him as he is.* At that time, accordingly, we will truly answer to God who calls, when we shall rise incorruptible at the command of supreme incorruption. Because no mere creatures can bring this about by themselves, but only by the free gift of almighty God does the change into such blinding glory of incorruption happen, he is right to add,

XV. 19. *You will stretch out your right hand to the*
*Job 14:15   *works of your hands.* It is as if he clearly said, "For that reason corruptible creatures can keep on going toward incorruption, namely, that they are held up by your powerful hand and by the favor of your countenance, that they may stand." Human creatures, you see, by the very fact of being creatures, must of their own volition slip below themselves, but humans have received from the Creator both the gift of being rapt in contemplation above themselves and of being held in themselves by incorruption. Creatures, then, lest they slip below themselves, so that they may continue incorruptible, are held up by the right hand of their Creator in the state of unchangeability.

The word for his right hand can also mean the Son,
*John 1:3   because *Everything was made by him.* Accordingly, almighty God stretched out his own right hand to the work of his hands when, in order that he might lift up the lowly human race, lying prostrate in the meanest depths, to the very heights, he sent his only-begotten Son to become incarnate for that very purpose. This incarnation bestowed on us the grace that we who have fallen into corruption by our own volition may one day answer to God's call and reach the glory of incorruption. Who could estimate the extent of God's generous mercy

in this regard, that he leads us on to such a height of glory, after we have sinned? God weighs with care the evil we have done, and he still mercifully lightens it through the grace of his kindness. So he adds,

XVI. 20. *You have certainly counted my footsteps, but you forgive my sins.* God counts our footsteps when he keeps track of every single action of ours for the sake of retribution. For what do footsteps mean here, if not our every action? Consequently almighty God both counts our footsteps and forgives our sins, because he both considers our actions carefully and yet mercifully lightens them when we do penance. He sees the callousness of sinners; nevertheless, he softens them with his prevenient grace for the sake of repentance. He counts our faults, therefore, when he changes our hearts to weep for all the sins we have committed. He mercifully lightens our faults, because we punish them ourselves, and he by no means judges us at the Last Judgment, as Paul testifies, *If we judged ourselves, we would certainly not be judged.* Whereupon Job adds,

XVII. 21. *You have sealed up my sins as if in a bag, but you have healed my wickedness.* Our sins are sealed up as in a bag, because the things we do externally, unless we do away with them by the intervention of repentance, are kept hidden in a certain secret place for the judgment of God, in order that they might be brought out from hiding some time or other for public judgment. That is why Moses also says, *Are they not collected before me and sealed up in my storehouse? On judgment day I will requite them.* When, however, we are subdued by the whip of punishment for the evil we have done, and when we weep for it through repentance, God seals and heals our wickedness, because he neither abandons unpunished sins here below nor reserves them for punishment at the Judgment. Accordingly he seals the sins,

*Job 14:16

*1 Cor 11:31

*Job 14:17

*Deut 32:34-35

because he carefully keeps a record of them here below for punishment, but he heals them, because he fully lightens them through blows of the whip. For example, he both seals and heals the wickedness of his illustrious persecutor, whom he had thrown to the ground, as he told Ananias about him, saying, *He is a vessel whom I have chosen, that he may carry my name to the gentiles, to their kings, and to the children of Israel. I will show* *Acts 9:15-16   him how much he must suffer for my name.**

God threatens with future sufferings for past actions Paul, whose sins are sealed in his breast. Yet God also heals his sins by sealing them, and he calls Paul a vessel of his choice. At least our sins are sealed up in a bag when we always weigh carefully in our heart the evil we have done. What then is our heart but God's bag? When we frankly look into our hearts to see how many our transgressions are, we carry our sins as though sealed up in God's bag. Did not David hold his sin sealed up in a bag when he said, *I know my wickedness, and my sin* *Ps 50:5 LXX   is always before me?** Since, however, our kind Creator lightens the sins for us, which we recognize by insight and repentance, after saying he kept our sins sealed in a bag, Job rightly adds, *You have healed my wickedness.* It is as though he openly said, "What you have once sealed so that I might penitently see it, you are sure to arrange that it is not seen in retribution." The next verse:

XVIII. 22. *The mountain totters and falls, and the rock is moved from its place. Water hollows out the stone face, and the earth erodes little by little from the action* *Job 14:18-19   of water. In like manner do men perish before you.**
What is described here in rapid succession is falling cliffs, the moving of rocks out of their place, the hollowing out of stone faces by water, and the slow erosion and loss of soil by the action of water. It is incumbent upon us, however, to study with careful attention what

follows: *In like manner do men perish before you*. How is it that human ruin is compared to the falling of mountains, the moving of rocks, the hollowing out of stone faces, and the loss of soil by erosion due to the action of water, unless it be that we are given to understand clearly that there are two kinds of temptations? In the first it happens even to the mind of the just through some unforeseen event that they are tempted so suddenly that the temptation strikes them and lays them low in an unexpected result, in such a way that they do not even perceive how they have fallen until later.

The second kind, however, enters the mind little by little and infects the resisting soul with light notions; it wears out all sense of righteousness in the soul, not by its excess but by its constancy. Accordingly, to signify the one kind of temptation that often lays the just low by an unexpected invasion, let it be said, *The mountain totters and falls, and the rock is moved from its place*. That is, the holy mind, whose place was justice, is moved by a sudden shove to sin. On the other hand, since there is another kind of temptation, which injects itself slightly into a person's heart and corrupts and exhausts all its resistance and fortitude, let it be said, *Water hollows out the stone face*. The constant gentle caresses of lust obviously wear away the mind's resistance, and the slow, shrewd advance of vice tires the robust fortitude of the mind's resolution.

So he adds, *The earth erodes little by little from the action of water*. Just as the soil suffers erosion gradually as water flows into it, so a vice creeping up noiselessly overcomes even the stoutest mind. So he rightly adds, *In like manner do men perish before you*. That is, because in your just judgment you allow the one who seems to stand high to be spiritually defeated by a sudden temptation, you cause the mountain to totter and fall. Since the will is converted to vice, the rock is moved to a new place. You let a slight but clever temptation (but also constant) prevail in the minds of those who are considered steadfast; this fact resembles the water that hollows out the stone face and the running water that causes slow erosion of the soil, in that the mind's constancy is weakened by some slight motion that enters it.

23. Let us consider David, how much like a high mountain he was, when he was able to contemplate such exalted mysteries of God in the spirit of prophecy. Now let us look at him when he suddenly stumbled and fell. While he was walking on his roof deck, he conceived a desire for another man's wife and took her; then he had that man killed with loss to his own army.* The mountain fell in a sudden crash when that mind that was accustomed to heavenly secrets was overcome by an unexpected temptation and was driven to such a monstrous disgrace. The rock was moved from its place when the soul of the prophet was shut out from the secrets of prophecy and lowered him to disgraceful thoughts.

*2 Sam 11

Let us see also how the water hollows out the stone face and how the earth erodes little by little from the action of water. Solomon was led to the extremity of forging idols for the temple by excessive and repeated intercourse with women. He who first built the temple of God enjoyed continual intercourse with women and was so prostrated by infidelity that he was not afraid to adorn the temple with idols. So it happened that continual wantonness of the flesh ended up in faithlessness in the mind.* What else is this accordingly but water hollowing out the stone face and the slow erosion of the earth by the action of water? By the gradual creeping up of sin, the soil of his heart runs away to ruin.

*1 Kgs 11:4-8

Let blessed Job then consider both kinds of temptation, the sudden strong one as well as the weak and long-lasting; let him consider the fall of humankind, and from those things that happen externally let him grasp internal contemplation and say, *The mountain totters and falls, and the rock is moved from its place. Water hollows out the stone face, and the earth erodes little by little from the action of water. In like manner do men perish before you.* That is, just as these beings devoid of sense sometimes crumble quickly and sometimes wear away gradually at the slow running of water, so also the one whom you have created endowed with reason you either prostrate with a sudden temptation or allow to be worn away by a long and slow-acting one. Job forthwith explains this same rational creature with the following words:

XIX. 24. *You have strengthened him a little, in order that he might cross over into eternity.** Humans have been strengthened a little, because they were empowered to live here a short time in order that they might cross over into eternity, where no end would terminate their life. But in this brief span of time where they are strengthened, they gather that by which they might find in eternity either everlasting joy or unavoidable punishment. So, since men and women are strengthened a little, in order that they might cross over into eternity, Job forthwith adds reasonably,

XX. 25. *You change his countenance, and you send him forth.** Human countenances change when their species is decimated by death, but they are sent forth, because they are forced to leave what they willingly possessed in order to cross over unwillingly to eternity. While they are led on to eternity, however, they have no idea what is to happen to those things they acquired and possessed so long, those things that they leave behind. So he adds,

XXI. 26. *He knows not whether his sons will be honorable or dishonorable.** Just as those who are still alive

*Job 14:20

*Job 14:20

*Job 14:21

do not know where the souls of the dead are, so the dead have no idea how the life of those who live in the body is lived after they have gone, because the life of the spirit is far from the life of the flesh. Just as embodied creatures are different from disembodied creatures, so also their thoughts are different. We must not think in that way of the souls of the saints, however, because they see the glory of God internally, and we must certainly not believe that there is anything externally that they do not know. Concerning sensual people, on the other hand, because they love their own children best, blessed Job asserts that they do not know them in the hereafter, since they loved them too much here, for he says that they know not whether they are honorable or dishonorable, those whose constant care preoccupied them here.

Then again, if we prefer to understand the verse spiritually, there is nothing against taking the word for *sons* to mean works. Remember, Paul said about women, *She will be saved by the bearing of children.*[*] It is not that the woman who prefers to live in continence will not be saved, since she bears no children, but when he speaks of salvation through the birth of children, it is taken to mean that she shares in eternal salvation through the merit of good works. Honorable sons therefore are good works, dishonorable ones evil works. People often attempt to do good in their intention, but because many thoughts interpose themselves in the meantime, it is always uncertain how their works fare in the sight of almighty God. Whether their sons be honorable or dishonorable, accordingly, they do not know, because when those sons are subjected to close scrutiny, whether their works be approved or rejected, they do not know. Here below, then, humans are subjected to harsh trouble, and they are led hereafter in fear

*1 Tim 2:13

and uncertainty. So he again adds something about this trouble we find in the present life:

XXII. 27. *But yet while he lives his flesh will have pain, and his soul will mourn over itself.** Concerning married people, Paul says, *Such people will suffer tribulation of the flesh.** As for tribulation of the flesh, even those who live a spiritual life here can suffer that. Why then does he speak particularly of married people having tribulation of the flesh, when it is no stranger to those who live a spiritual life? Is it not because those who take pleasure in delight of the flesh usually suffer even greater tribulation from that same flesh? It is well said, therefore, that *His soul will mourn over itself.* Those, you see, who want to take pleasure in themselves are by that very fact already a cause of mourning for leaving the source of true joy. The true joy of the soul is undoubtedly its Creator. Accordingly, it is fitting that we should always find in ourselves a cause for sorrow, when we have forsaken the Creator and sought happiness in ourselves. The next verse:

*Job 14:22

*1 Cor 7:28

XXIII. 28. *Eliphaz the Temanite answered and said, "Will a wise man answer as though talking to the wind and fill his stomach with heat?"* * We have already said often enough that blessed Job is a type of Holy Church universal and that his friends play the role of heretics who, as though defending God, seize an opportunity for inept speeches and spout insulting words against good people. To them all that the faithful people say is wind, and they find it distasteful. That is why Eliphaz now says, *Will a wise man answer as though talking to the wind?* They take the words of good people not as reasonable speech but as provocations of madmen. That is why he adds, *and fill his stomach with heat?* Even when they know their words are insulting, they always

*Job 15:1-2

try, as we have said, to disguise themselves as though
they were defending God. So he adds,

XXIV. 29. *You accuse him with words, who is not
your equal, and you say things which are not expedient
for you.*[*] They suppose that nobody has any fear of God
except the one whom they have been able to lead to the
stupid action of joining their own confession. So he
adds, *As far as you could, you have rid yourself of fear,
and you have done away with prayer in God's presence.*[*]
The words *done away with* mean stolen. It is as though
he said, "You arrogate justice to yourself, and you disdain the petitioning of your Creator for grace." When
the heretics, you see, find nothing really wrong against
good people, they make up accusations against them, in
order that they may appear righteous themselves, and it
often happens that they go on to openly insulting words.
So he forthwith adds,

XXV. 30. *Wickedness has taught your mouth, and
you imitate the tongues of blasphemers.*[*] Wickedness
teaches the mouth when the worst speeches are conceived from an evil life. Since blessed Job was as free
in his words as he was righteous in his actions, he is
reproved by his friends both for an evil life and for a
bold tongue. They play the role of heretics to whom
he says, *Wickedness has taught your mouth.* It is as
though he said outright, "You have learned your crooked
speech from your life, which is even more crooked." As
for the heretics, they often pretend reverence for God
while they contradict his mysteries, and they consider
it humility when they deny the truth. Some of them
even think that they do wrong if they confess that God
assumed real flesh, or if they believe that he could really
have suffered death for us in the flesh. So when they
try to pay greater honor to God, as it were, they are
forced to deny him true praise for his kindness. What

*Job 15:3

*Job 15:4

*Job 15:5

is greater praise of his goodness than that he should make us worthy of his receiving us when we seemed to be unworthy of him? Holy Church confesses his real flesh and real death, and while she is speaking thus, the heretics think she is insulting God. That is why Eliphaz now says, *You imitate the tongues of blasphemers.* So if any adversity comes upon the church in this world, they say it happened because of this very insult of her confession. So he again adds,

XXVI. 31. *Your own mouth will condemn you, not I.*
Your own life will answer you. Since the heretics suppose   *Job 15:6
that it was the error of the church's confession that brought the misfortune of adversity upon her, they assert that her own lips answer her that sinful eloquence was the cause of her trial. Sometimes, however, they prefer to put her down reasonably, as it were. So Eliphaz tries to reprove blessed Job as though by the use of reason and says,

XXVIII. 32. *Were you the first man to be born, or were you formed before the hills? Have you listened to God's counsel, or is his wisdom inferior to you?* He   *Job 15:7-8
might as well say, in other words, "You who speak of the eternal God should remember that you belong to time, and when you argue about his wisdom, you should remember that you know nothing about his counsel." Since, however, the heretics' words take up God's defense precisely for the purpose that they might seem learned themselves, and even as they seem to defend God's glory they parade their own knowledge before people, these words of Eliphaz testify to that fact. In fact, he begins to talk about God's wisdom. Yet he soon falls back on his own pride. Here is what he says: *What do you know that we do not know? What do you understand that we are ignorant of?* These words prove clearly and un-   *Job 15:9
equivocally the extent of the mental pride that produces whatever sounds like a defense of God. The next verse:

XXVIII. 33. *Both our old men and our ancients are*
*Job 15:10   *much more aged than your fathers.** John testifies that
all the heretics left our holy universal church where he
*1 John 2:19   says, *They went away from us, but they were not of us.**
But they wanted to commend their assertions as tradi-
tional in the minds of foolish people, so they testify that
their own ancient fathers say that even the doctors of
the church were the teachers of their own confession.
When they disdain the contemporary preachers, they
boast of the teaching of the more ancient fathers, and
this is false presumption; they do it in order to profess
that the early fathers also held what they say themselves.
Inasmuch as they cannot rightfully make any additions,
they would find support in the fathers' authority. But
since it is written, *Him whom God loves he chastises,*
*Heb 12:6   *and he beats every son he receives,** Holy Church often
struggles in this life against many adversities, while
reprobate sinners, in the same degree that their life is
free of struggle, are kept free of reward. Yet the heretics
see the sufferings of Holy Church and despise her, supposing that she who is buffeted by so many misfortunes
is guilty of sinful faith. So he adds,

XXIX. 34. *Is not God's consolation a great thing*
*Job 15:11   *to you? Yet your speech denies it you.** It is as if he said
plainly, "If you would correct your profession of faith,
you would have had comfort from your trials long ago."
The next verse:

XXX. 35. *Why is your heart lifted up, and why are*
*Job 15:12   *you thinking elevated thoughts, with your eyes staring?**
The minds of righteous people are often so fascinated
by contemplation of higher realities that their faces appear dumbstruck to others. But since the heretics do
not know how to exercise the power of contemplation
secretly, they suppose that the just and those with correct understanding do this hypocritically rather than

honestly, because they have no idea how that which they cannot themselves have could really exist in others. The next verse:

XXXI. 36. *Why is your spirit so puffed up against God, that you spout such bold speeches from your mouth?* * Discouraged by certain urgent requirements, the just are often forced to admit what they have done, as blessed Job has been, he whom hard knocks have depressed after a just life. But when unrighteous people hear their words, they suppose that they were spoken in pride rather than truthfully. They evaluate these words of righteous people, you see, from their own hearts, and they do not believe that genuine good deeds could be spoken of in a humble fashion. Just as it is a grievous fault for people to arrogate to themselves what does not belong to them, so there is often no fault if they humbly speak out the good that is in them. So it often happens that righteous and unrighteous people speak similar words, but their hearts are always far different. The Lord is offended by the words unrighteous people speak, yet the righteous speak the same words, and God is pleased.

    The Pharisee entered the temple and said, *I fast twice a week, and I give tithes from all my possessions.* * But the publican went away justified, rather than the Pharisee. King Hezekiah also, when he was suffering from a bodily ailment and had arrived at the end of his life, was heartbroken and prayed thus: *I earnestly beseech you, O Lord, remember how I have lived honestly before you with a perfect heart.* * The Lord, on his part, neither despised nor denied this avowal of perfection but forthwith answered his prayer. See how the Pharisee justified himself in his works, and Hezekiah even claimed that he was just in his thoughts. The one offended God, while the other pleased him. Why is this, unless almighty God evaluates the words of each one by his thoughts, and

*Job 15:13

*Luke 18:12

*Isa 38:3

those words do not sound proud to his ears that were spoken with a humble heart? Accordingly blessed Job was by no means inflated with pride against God when he declared his works, because he spoke humbly about what he honestly did.

But the heretics customarily mix up some things that are true with their erroneous words, and although blessed Job's friends are positively wrong in reprehending him, they might say some things that are true, which they learned from his constancy. If all their speeches had to be refuted, the apostle Paul would never have alluded to Eliphaz's opinion in these words: *I will catch the wise in their craftiness.** Since, therefore, even when they spoke the truth against blessed Job, they did not speak it correctly, let us clear away the blemish of indiscretion in their words, so that we may behold the light of their truth. The next verse:

*1 Cor 3:19

XXXII. 37. *What is man, that he should be spotless?** By the very fact that he is called *man*† he is understood to be of earth* and weak, since man† is derived from earth.§ How, then, could those be spotless who willingly fell into weakness, once they were made out of earth? So he adds, *Who is there born of woman who could appear just?** The woman proposed the first act of injustice to the man in Paradise. How, then, will he appear just when he is born of her who was the one who proposed the act of injustice? The next verse:

*Job 15:14
†Lat homo
*humo
†homo
§humo

*Job 15:14

XXXIII. 38. *Behold, none of his holy ones is immovable, and even heaven is unclean in his sight.** He says the same thing with the word *heaven* as he said before with the words *holy ones.* Of these same *holy ones* we find it written, *The heavens declare the glory of God.** By their nature all things are changeable in themselves, but as long as they eagerly desire always to cling to unchangeable truth, by clinging they bring it

*Job 15:15

*Ps 18:2

about that they may be unchangeable. When they stick to unchangeable truth with all their hearts, they sometimes receive the gift of being led above themselves and overcoming that in themselves that was changeable. What, then, is changeability, if not some kind of death? Whereas death changes a thing to something else, it, as it were, kills one thing so that something else that did not exist might begin to be.

Of the Creator of all things it is written, *He alone has unchangeability.** He obviously is unchangeable in himself. James says for his part, *With him there is no change, no shadow of alteration.** The shadow is changeability itself, which would cover the light, as it were, if it changed it by some alteration. In God, however, no change enters, nor does any shadow of alteration cut off his light. So he is right to say, *Heaven is unclean in his sight.* Not even those who become preachers of purity can of themselves be perfectly pure before the intransigent Judgment of God, since John testifies in these words: *If we say we have no sin, we deceive ourselves.** Accordingly, if none of his holy ones is unchangeable, and heaven is unclean in his sight, who could presume on his works of justice in his sight? So he adds,

XXXIV. 39. *How much more detestable and worthless, then, is that man who drinks up evil like water?** First he denied that humans would be pure and just of themselves; now he says that they are both detestable and worthless. He calls them detestable, obviously because of impurity and stain, but worthless because of injustice and a deficient life. *Detestable* and *worthless*, however, could also be understood differently. Sometimes bad people seem to do some things right, but their evil works ruin their good works. Because evil displeases God very much, even that which looks good does not please him.

*1 Tim 6:16

*Jas 1:17

*1 John 1:8

*Job 15:16

Those whom God finds detestable in the evil they do are also worthless in their good works, because while their evil deeds make them abominable before God, not even that which appears righteous in them pleases God. So he is right to say, *He drinks up evil like water.* The food we eat, you see, is swallowed more slowly, because it is first chewed up so we can swallow it. Our drink, however, is swallowed without delay, because it has no need for chewing. Guilt, then, is incurred by a stupid person without regret, so its evil is drunk up like water. The one who commits unlawful acts fearlessly swallows the drink of injustice, as it were, without hindrance. The next verse:

XXXV. 40. *I will teach you. Listen to me. I will tell you what I have seen.** All haughty people have this special characteristic, that when they perceive something that is right, be it ever so small, they twist it for the purpose of pride: thus where they might be raised higher than themselves by intelligence, there they rather fall into the pit of pride through self-aggrandizement. In this way they suppose themselves more learned than the scholars, they demand reverence from their betters, and they pretend to teach those higher than themselves, as though they had authority. That is why we are now told, *I will teach you. Listen to me.* Since he who reports what he hears has less authority than he who is an eyewitness, Eliphaz says, in order that he might arrogate greater authority for himself, *I will tell you what I have seen.* Since, however, heretics are sometimes abashed by the condemnation of their forefathers, whose doctrines they nevertheless publicly proclaim as though authoritatively, whose silliness rightly rebuffs them, this very boldness of the heretics is correctly implied by Eliphaz when he says,

XXXVI. 41. *Wise men acknowledge themselves and do not hide their forefathers.** They exult in their praise

*Job 15:17

*Job 15:18

of them, and they boast that they were virtually the only ones to have governed the church. So he again adds, *The earth was granted to them alone, and no stranger got past them.* They suppose that the earth was bestowed on their ancestors alone, because they think that only the teachers of their own errors truly governed the church. Who is the stranger if not the apostate angel? That is why the psalmist says about all the evil spirits together, *Strangers rose up against me, and those in power sought my life.* Accordingly the heretics suppose that the hearts of their teachers were not subject to the apostate angel, so they deny that the stranger got past them.

    For that stranger to get past people obviously means to plant evil thoughts in their hearts. That is why the prophet says about evil spirits attacking the constant soul, *They said to my soul, "Bow down that we may get past."* Now Eliphaz the Temanite wants Job to listen to the words he is about to say, and he knows very well what he wants to say, but he does not know that such words should not be said to blessed Job. So let us listen to the statements he makes against blessed Job. We should not think about the person they are spoken to but merely what is actually said. The next verse:

    XXXVII. 42. *The wicked man is proud all his life.* The elect are usually proud as well in some of their thoughts and acts. Since they are elect, however, they cannot be proud all their lives, because before they end their lives their hearts change and measure up to the standard of humility, leaving pride behind. Evil people, on the other hand, are proud all their lives, because they end their lives in such a way that they by no means abandon pride. They are well aware of their temporal prosperity, yet they neglect to reflect where they are being led in eternity. They put their trust in the life of the flesh, and they suppose that what they have in the

*Job 15:19

*Ps 53:5

*Isa 51:23

*Job 15:20

present will remain theirs forever. Pride hardens in the soul; all their kin become objects of contempt; they do not even suspect how suddenly death can surprise them or imagine how unstable their happiness is. If they did see the instability of this fleeting life, they would never hold what is unstable for stable. Therefore he rightly adds,

XXXVIII. 43. *The number of years of his tyranny is uncertain.** Such people ought never to have become proud, even if they could have been certain about the number of their years, for knowing how long they would live, they would also have foreknowledge of when they should retreat from pride. Yet once we know that the present life is always uncertain, sudden death ought always to be feared, to the extent that it can never be foreseen. He is right, therefore, to call the pride of the wicked a tyranny. He is rightly called a tyrant who illegally rules over a common republic.

But it is necessary to know that all proud people in a way run their own tyranny. For what one person does sometimes as head of a republic, having received the honor of power, another of a province, another of a city, another of his own household, another by his own secret wickedness exercises power over himself in his own thoughts. Nor does the Lord look at the quantity of evil a person *can* do but how much such a one *wants to* do. When we have no external power, we are our own tyrant, when wickedness governs internally. Even if we do not hurt our neighbors externally, we desire the power to hurt internally.

Since almighty God weighs the heart, the wicked in God's eyes have already done the evil they thought of. It is for this reason that our Creator willed that our end should be hidden from us, that since we do not know when we will die, we ought always to be found prepared

*Job 15:20

for our death. So after he said, *The wicked man is proud all his life*, he rightly adds, *The number of years of his tyranny is uncertain.* He might as well say, "Why is he proud of his certainty, when his life is led under the penalty of incertitude?" Almighty God, however, not only reserves future punishment for those who act wickedly but also complicates their lives even now by punishing their sins, so that by their very sinful acts they may strike themselves, and that they may always anxiously look around themselves and fear that evil from some that they remember to have done against others. Again Eliphaz adds concerning such an evil person,

XXXIX. 44. *The dreadful sound is always in his ears; in time of peace he suspects an ambush.* Nothing is more auspicious than a simple heart, because when people relate to others in a simple manner, they have nothing to fear from them. If they have innocence, they are like a strong tower. They have no suspicion that they will suffer anything that they do not remember having done themselves. That is why Solomon wisely says, *In the fear of the Lord there is confidence and courage.* He also says, *The fearless mind is like a continuous banquet.* Fearless tranquility is itself like an unending meal.

    Job 15:21

    Prov 14:26

    Prov 15:15

The evil mind, on the other hand, is always in trouble, because it is either planning the evil it would do to someone else or worried that it might be done to itself. Whatever evil it is devising against its neighbor, it is dreading that its neighbors are devising the same against itself. All around it there is suspicion and fear. Anyone it remembers, it believes to be an adversary. Accordingly, whoever lacks fearless tranquility, in his ears, beyond any doubt, is always heard the dreadful sound.

It often happens to such people, whoever they may be, that when their neighbor speaks simply, without hostility, they suspect an ambush in time of peace. Those who always act craftily do not suppose that anyone would act toward them in a straightforward manner. It is written, *When the evil man reaches the deepest sin,* *Prov 18:3* *he reaches contempt.** He is caught up in the darkness of his own wickedness, so that he finally despairs of light. So he adds,

XL. 45. *He does not believe he can retreat from the* *Job 15:22* *darkness, but he sees the sword all about him.** As long as he thinks he is being attacked from ambush on every side, he despairs of salvation, and his wickedness keeps increasing. Sometimes, however, such criminals also expect judgment from on high, and they are afraid that it is coming upon them. Yet when they seek the recompense of the present life, senseless avarice wins them over, and the judgment they started to fear they now regard with contempt. In fact, they imagine the possibility of dying in sin, yet they do not stop sinning. So he adds,

XLI. 46. *While he is exerting himself to find bread,* *Job 15:23* *he knows the day of darkness is ready in his hand.** We take *bread* to mean the recompense of the present life, but we take *the day of darkness* to mean the time of punishment. Sometimes the sinners consider that the wrath of the heavenly Judge is present in their own action, but they do not turn away from evil so that the wrath may also turn away from damning them. Their consciences accuse them, and they are afraid of the stroke, yet they keep on doing more and more actions that deserve the stroke. They ridicule the idea of conversion, have no hope of forgiveness, and grow proud in sin, but they have an internal witness of their evildoing, and that witness is fear. Even if they seem externally to commit crimes boldly, they are forced internally to tremble at these crimes. That is why it is written, *When evildoing* *Wis 17:10* *is fainthearted, it is testimony for condemnation.** When *LXX* people do something unlawful, you see, what they have done frightens them, and that fear of evil is itself the loudest witness of condemnation, because they fear both the act and the evil, and they do not rid themselves of the evil. Concerning that evil he continues, XLII. 47. *Trouble will frighten him and distress hem him in, like a king getting ready for battle.** All the actions of criminals are hemmed in by trouble and distress, and evildoers are disturbed by anguish and distrust. One person secretly desires to snatch away what belongs to others and struggles with his thoughts to escape detection. Somebody else forsakes truth and is determined to lie and to deceive the minds of the audience; yet how laboriously and carefully such people guard themselves to keep their deception from being found out! In fact they hold in their mind's eyes the response they should make to those who know the truth, and they exercise intense concentration to plan false arguments to defeat the evidence of truth. They run about here and there to cover up and to find an answer close enough to the truth to disarm any path of discovery. But if they wanted to tell the truth, they could find it easily enough.

*Job 15:24

The road of truth is certainly broad enough, whereas the path of falsehood is rough. That is why the prophet says, *They trained their tongues to tell lies, and they wracked their brains to do evil.** So Eliphaz was right to say, *Trouble will frighten him, and distress hem him in.* Within themselves such people grow tired of the labor of fear, since they have forsaken the road of truth that is the companion of safety. They are rightly compared to a king ready for battle. The very evil that king does terrifies him; he rushes around; his conscience causes him to tremble and his desire to pant. He is afraid and proud at the same time; suspicions cause him worry, and boldness alerts his mind. We should remember also that a king ready for battle is so suspicious of enemies

*Jer 9:5

that he is even afraid of the army he is leading; he is afraid of falling and of being the target of spears with no soldiers around him.

The evildoers are accordingly hemmed in by distress like a king ready for battle. They do what is false, you see, and speak what is false, and they are afraid of losing their own soldiers, which are deceitful arguments; they would be a clear target for the lances of truth if they should be without the assistance of the weapons of deceit to defend themselves. But although their souls quake with fear, and although their consciences accuse them, nevertheless the evildoers are conquered by their own avarice. They repress their fear and take a firm grasp on boldness from sinful habits. They often go so far as to propose revenge and lift themselves up against God. They consider that they are suffering adversity sent by God whereas they did what they could to please him. So Eliphaz adds,

XLIII. 48. *He has stretched out his hand against God and armed himself against the Almighty. He rushed against him with uplifted head, and he raised his broad* *Job 15:25 *shoulders against him.** These words are clearly spoken against the head of all wickedness himself, namely, the Antichrist, who lifts up his hand against God and is said to arm himself. He is allowed to exalt himself for a short time. After he has been suffered to boast a little bit, he is punished forever all the more fearfully. The members of Antichrist are all the evildoers. Antichrist alone is going to do something extraordinary at the end of the world, but let us see how each one of the evildoers will act now in his or her own particular case. There are those, you see, who, even if they sometimes try to act against the Judgment of almighty God, are struck by the very impossibility of carrying out their plan, and they look to themselves and turn back to him whom they had intended to hold up to contempt. They could have fallen away further, if they had been able to carry out their intention, but because they were unable to complete their evil plan, they were saved. So they were brought back to themselves and realized their true condition, so that they were reduced to tears for having wanted to act against the truth.

There are others, however, who are allowed by God's just judgment to fulfill their evil purpose even more maliciously. That evil purpose instigates them and power confirms them, so that they cannot realize the error of their ways, and they are led on by the prospering of their affairs to show their external power more and more. About their purpose Eliphaz continues, *He has stretched out his hand against God and armed himself against the Almighty.* Stretching out one's hand against God means to persevere in unjust acts despite God's judgment. God's anger is greater when he allows crimes to be committed of which the very thought is shameful, so the evildoers armed themselves against the Almighty, since God allowed them prosperity in evildoing so that they both commit crimes and live on happily. About this situation, Eliphaz continues, *He rushed against him with uplifted head.**   *Job 15:26

49. Rushing against God with uplifted head means to perpetrate brazen actions that displease the Creator. He is right to say *rushed*, that is, no obstacle of adversity blocked his path of evil action. Eliphaz goes on, *He raised his broad shoulders against him.* Broad shoulders designate pride and power, in which evildoers obviously rest secure as in a well-developed body, because their affairs have prospered. Wicked people who have power, accordingly, raise their broad shoulders against God, because being proud in the possession of worldly goods, they take the lead against the precepts of truth,

as though strengthened by their very bodily weight. What is poverty if not a kind of leanness, and what is abundance of worldly goods unless a kind of fatness in the present life? The evildoers who make worldly abundance a source of pride raise their broad shoulders against God. It is a characteristic of the wicked and powerful ones that being in possession of deceitful riches, they disregard the real wealth that belongs to God. The less interest they have in the truth, the more they exalt themselves in the possession of false riches. Excessive anxiety for the possession of worldly goods blinds the soul because it occupies the mind. So Eliphaz goes on to say,

*Job 15:27   XLIV. 50. *Dullness covers his face.** The sense of sight has its seat in the face, and the most honorable organ of the body is found there. It is not incongruous for mental activity to be designated by the face, and wherever we turn the face, there we see. But dullness covers the face, because the desire for an abundance of worldly possessions weakens the mind's eyes, and that which should have been worthy of honor in them is disgraced in the sight of God because of the many anxieties that engross it. As for the evildoers who boast of their fatness, their own boasting is not enough for them, but those who are joined with them must also boast. There are those indeed who do boast about patrons they are joined to, and they even praise them to the skies for their power against helpless people. The next verse:

*Job 15:27   XLV. 51. *Fat hangs from his loins.** Fat is the heaviness of flesh, and we call those people the loins of the rich whom we recognize as their dependents, so fat hangs from these loins, because those people who join themselves to the wicked in power grow fat in turn on their own power, as though from abundance of possessions. They imitate the evil of their wicked patron, so

they do not fear God, and they oppress the poor whenever and as much as they choose; their hearts are lifted
up with temporal honors. This is the lot of the dependents of the evil one in power, so they are the fat that
clings to that one's loins. So Eliphaz again adds,
XLVI. 52. *He will dwell in deserted cities and in the
empty houses, which are no more than ruins.* A city is
called so because its citizens live together, so those cities
are deserted where compliant wicked people live, and
these latter praise the perverse ones in power by their
shouts when they sally forth to do evil actions. So it is
written, *The sinner is praised for the desire of his soul,
and he who does evil is praised.* The empty houses are
evil thoughts that these wicked people inhabit, because
all that they do aims at giving pleasure to the thoughts
of the wicked. Deserted cities and empty houses are
correctly so named, because unless almighty God, as a
result of the sins of the wicked, had left their thoughts
and manner of life to their own devices, they would
never end up committing still worse sins. He is right to
say as well, *They are no more than ruins.* Falling houses
and city buildings create ruins, because whenever any
evil people get together to perpetrate disorderly actions
and plan crimes, they display beyond any doubt their
own fall from the building of life. The next verse:
XLVII. 53. *He will not be inhabited, nor will his
wealth endure, nor will he sink his roots in the earth.*
Although we find the word *inhabited* here, I have found
be enriched in some codices. Yet even if the words are
different, the sense does not disagree. The one is rich in
virtues, you see, in whose mind almighty God dwells.
The Creator's grace, however, does not dwell in the
thoughts of the proud man and woman, so they are obviously not rich in virtues. For this reason, namely, that
they are internally empty, we are told, *He will not be*

*Job 15:28

*Ps 9:24

*Job 15:29

inhabited. Because they grow big externally, though transitorily, however, Eliphaz rightly adds, *Nor will his wealth endure*. It is as though he said plainly, "That which he seems to have externally passes, but that which could not pass away internally he does not have." So he again fittingly adds, *Nor will he sink his roots in the earth*.

If we take these words to refer to the literal earth, it is undoubtedly plain that a tree having no roots in the ground falls when swayed by the smallest wind. Proud people, then, as long as they are armed against almighty God, and as long as they run with head uplifted and raise their broad shoulders against him, do seem to stand like trees, yet their standing lacks roots, because like a small wind the hidden sentence moves against them, and their life is ended. We could, however, take *earth* in this passage to mean the reward of eternal life of which the prophet speaks: *My share is in the land of the living.** In that case, the wicked do not sink their roots in the earth, because they never plant the thoughts of their heart in the desire of eternal life. What the root means to the tree, you see, each person's inmost thought is to him, because that which is seen externally is held internally and unseen. So the prophet says, *He will take deep root and bear fruit above.** When we employ our thoughts for the relief of our needy neighbors, it is as though we sank our roots downward, so that we might bear the fruit of recompense upward. The next verse:

XLVIII. 54. *He does not escape the darkness.** If this proud man had wanted to return from sin to justice, he would escape the darkness. Since, however, he does not seek the light of justice, he does not escape darkness. Following his example, his adherents long to advance in worldly pursuits, are excited by the stimulation of avarice, and are burned up by the fires of carnal desires. So Eliphaz goes on,

*Ps 141:6

*Isa 37:31

*Job 15:30

XLIX. 55. *Flames will wither his branches.** If he   *Job 15:30
should gather any people who are seeking the eternal
fatherland, he would have some green branches. Nevertheless, those who are his adherents are also on fire with
earthly desires, and the flames of passion burn up the
souls of his followers. So his branches wither in order
that they may bear no fruit of good works, because they
yearn and long after base things through wickedness.
So Eliphaz is right to add,

L. 56. *He will be taken away by the breath of his
mouth.** The more power proud people possess in this   *Job 15:30
life, the more boldly they loosen the reins on their
tongues and speak whatever evil they wish; they fear
the words of no one, but some they sting with insults,
and others they stab with curses. They are even driven
to blaspheme the Creator at times, as the psalmist says
concerning his sort: *They have set their mouths up in the
sky, and their tongue struts upon the earth.** Remember   *Ps 72:9
how the rich man, when he is held in the flame, asks for
a drop of water on his tongue from Lazarus's fingers.*   *see
From this we may understand that where sin abounded,   Luke 16:24
the fire burned more fiercely. Accordingly, it is correctly
said in the present instance, *He will be taken away by
the breath of his mouth.* He received the sentence of
punishment, because he did not restrain the breath of
his mouth by the fear of God. The next verse:

LI. 57. *Let him not believe in vain, deceived by error,
that he can be freed by any price.** As often as we give   *Job 15:31
alms after committing a sin, it is as though we pay a
fee for some bad action. That is why the prophet says
about the person who does not act in this way, *He will
not make atonement to God, nor will he give him the fee
for the redemption of his soul.** Sometimes proud rich   *Ps 48:8-9
people oppress those in humble circumstances, and they
take what does not belong to them. Nevertheless they do

give something to others. Although they oppress many people, they sometimes aid or help certain ones; they seem in this way to pay a fee for the wicked acts they never stop committing. But the fee of alms delivers us from guilt only when we weep over what we have done and give up doing it. Those who want to keep sinning and virtually keep giving alms deliver the fee in vain, because they do not rescue their soul when they do not restrain themselves from vice. That is why Eliphaz says in this passage, *Let him not believe in vain, deceived by error, that he can be freed by any price.* The alms the proud rich give cannot free them, because they simultaneously rob the poor person, and that act does not allow their alms to rise before the eyes of God. Still, we can perhaps understand the verse in another way, if proud rich people often give alms not for the sake of their desire for eternal life but for an extension of earthly life, in which case they believe they can put off their death by means of these contributions. But *Let him not believe in vain, deceived by error, that he can be freed by any price.* Such people cannot obtain by any extravagant gift the evasion of the end that is due, because it is their own wickedness that cuts their life short. So he adds,

LII. 58. *He will perish before his days are com-*
*Job 15:32   *pleted, and his hands will wither.* The number of days for every person has been allotted by God's providence from eternity, and it can be neither increased nor decreased, unless such a contingency be also foreseen that some people live longer because of having acted righteously, or others have shortened lives because of having done wickedly. Hezekiah, for example, obtained an
see Isa 38:1-6   extension of his life by his tears. On the other hand, it is
*Prov 24:9   written about crooks, *Death is in store for the ignorant.*
LXX
     Even if a long life is not destined for the wicked in God's hidden providence, however, because they

want to live according to the flesh, they often propose to themselves a long life in their soul. So because they cannot reach the age they hope for, it is as though they perished before their days were completed. Nevertheless, we may understand the text differently. We often do in fact see people who act wickedly and do finally reach old age. How then is it said, *He will perish before his days are completed*? We often see cases where people live long, and their limbs grow weak, and yet their desires to perpetrate wicked designs do not abate.

59. There are those, you see, who, having lived a hopeless life, come to their senses; their consciences accuse them, and they leave behind the crooked paths they were following. They change their behavior, and they renounce their long familiar perversity; they run away from worldly pursuits, and they yearn after heavenly desires. Yet before they can become fixed in those same holy desires, they fall back through mental listlessness into that very behavior they had started to resolve against, and they revert to the evil practices they had managed to run away from. It often happens, you see, that even the saints conform their external actions for the common good to the ministry of civic government; feeble-minded people watch them, and their wonted pride urges them to imitate them by devoting themselves to external actions, but since they do not come to these with spiritual training, they perform them in a carnal fashion. Unless the heart first strengthens itself with persevering study and continued practice in heavenly desires, when people turn to external actions, they are torn away from any progress in good works. So we are correctly told about this wicked person, *He will perish before his days are completed*. Whatever good he may have managed to do by chance, before he is rooted in it by long practice, he falls away to external pursuits

and wickedly abandons what he seemed to have begun correctly. So Eliphaz rightly adds, *His hands will wither.* When people like that get involved in external actions prematurely, they sicken absolutely concerning all good action. So he again wisely adds,

LIII. 60. *His grapes will wither while still green on the vine, like the olive putting forth its flower. The community of the hypocrite is barren.** Note well that Eliphaz speaks in a general way about this evil man, so that the word of God might be interpreted to apply especially to his brand of wickedness. First he says, *His grapes will wither while still green on the vine, like the olive putting forth its fruit.* Then he immediately follows up with, *The community of the hypocrite is barren.* In this way he clearly shows that he is passing a sentence of condemnation on the hypocrisy of this evil person.

*Job 15:33-34

Yet now we must consider how the hypocrite withers like a grapevine in its first budding or like an olive putting forth its flower. If a severe cold temperature strikes the flowering vine because of the inconstant climate, the vine immediately withers, losing all its sap and greenness. Yes, there are those, as we have said, who after following crooked paths want to get on to the way of holiness, but before they can become rooted in good desires, some earthly prosperity takes hold in them and gets them involved in external affairs. These in turn entice their minds away from the warmth of internal love, and it is as though cold weather stopped up the heat, so that whatever flower of virtues seemed to show itself in them died. The soul grows seriously cold in worldly actions if it is not yet securely rooted in internal gifts. It is necessary, therefore, that those who know best how to decide what is profitable for human services should be the ones to accept the duties of magistrates or the performance of public works; they should also have the internal discernment to renounce external duties.

Those of weak disposition, on the other hand, who are inclined to take the place of magistrates or to perform public works, lose prestige the more public they become. When a tree's roots, you see, are not already planted deep in the soil, it is more quickly thrown down by a blast of wind when it lifts itself up on high; it falls down on the ground instantly when it grows up toward the sky without deep roots. Sometimes it is not the cold but the hot wind that withers the flourishing grapevine. When the flower drops and the severe heat touches the grape, it spoils. It often happens too that those who turn to good works without a pure intention, when they seem to be pleasing other people, are all the more intensely incited to put those works into practice, and they are eager and anxious to excel, because they know their works will please human witnesses. Yes, they are fervent, as though in a holy endeavor. What is it that happens to them, unless it is a hot wind attacking a flower, because their desire for human praise has deprived them of fruit?

So he is right to add, *Like the olive putting forth its flower.* If a dense fog covers an olive tree when it is in bloom, it is deprived of all its fruits. As for those who are beginning good works, the more their admirers start to praise them, and the more they are flattered by these praises, the more darkened their intelligence becomes, and their thoughts as well, to the point that they can no longer distinguish the purpose behind their actions. So they lose the fruit of their works as if clouded by approval. Concerning this matter we are told by Solomon, *In the morning let us go to see the grapevine, let us see if the vines have blossomed, and if the flowers have yielded fruit.** Without any doubt the grapevine   *Song 7:12

blossoms when the minds of the faithful bring forth good works. Yet they bear no fruit if from that which they have brought forth they are overtaken by errors and so weakened.

61. We should not look, accordingly, to see if the grapevine has blossomed, but rather to see if the flowers have actually brought forth fruit. It is no wonder if someone has started to do well, but it is truly wonderful if with a pure intention such a person has seen a good work through to its accomplishment. So it often happens that a pure intention is not held fast in the course of a good work, and consequently even that which we take to be a good work is lost. We often see people, in fact, who have abandoned their worldly possessions, who already seek nothing transitory, and who participate in no disputes that concern the affairs of this life. When accordingly the faithful soul displays such behavior, it brings forth a flower like an olive tree.

When, on the other hand, some of these souls again start to curry honor from the world, honor that they once spurned, and to yearn after worldly possessions, never being satisfied, possessions they once seemed to have scorned, to enjoy disputes, and to seek out occasions for wrangling with their neighbors, then it is I say that the olive tree drops the flower it had budded forth, because, you see, the soul has not persevered in the rudimentary good works it had started or brought them to perfection. But we must realize that these things always happen to those who do not seek God with a pure and simple intention. So Eliphaz rightly adds, *The community of the hypocrite is barren.* He would not lose the good he had begun to do if he were not a hypocrite. Hypocrites get together to do good works, but their togetherness is barren, because through their works they do not yearn for the fruit of eternal recompense. They seem fruitful and green in their works in the eyes of other people, but in the sight of the hidden Judge they show up as unfruitful and barren. In fact they are often motivated by avarice, and they display still greater works to human eyes, because they desire to be offered still greater rewards by humans. So he again adds,

LIV. 62. *Fire will consume their tents, because they freely take bribes.** As the body dwells in the tent, so the mind in thought. But fire consumes the tent when the heat of avarice ruins the thoughts. It often happens that the hypocrite detests the idea of taking gold or any carnal goods from men and women, but just because he does not accept them, he expects to receive more praise from them. Perhaps such hypocrites do not suppose they have received anything from other people because they refuse carnal goods. So it is to be taken for truth that sometimes a present is offered by the hand and sometimes by the mouth. The person who hands over a coin presents it with the hand, whereas the one who offers a word of praise offers a gift with the mouth. Hypocrites accordingly, even if they refuse to take an external present that might correspond to some worldly need, desire to be paid what is worth more to them, namely, undeserved praise, and such praise they crave to receive from the mouth. In that appetite of praise their hearts are warmed by an excessive desire, so it is well said, *Fire will consume their tents, because they freely take bribes.*

63. If, on the other hand, we are to take tents to mean the bodies in which hypocrites' souls abide, fire devours their tents in the sense that here the fire of avarice consumes their minds, and there their bodies also burn in the fire of hell, since the minds of hypocrites are never without a malicious thought. Whether it is some earthly object they yearn after or human praise, they

*Job 15:34

begrudge to other people what they themselves want to be offered. They try all the harder to show up others as crooked the more they want themselves to seem holy to all people. If others are scorned, the result should be that the hypocrites themselves would always appear more venerable. So it happens that the neighbor's opinion before the human tribunal causes such people's tongues to set ambushes, in order that they alone may gain esteem from those whom they yearn to please. So Eliphaz adds,

LV. 64. *He conceives sorrow and brings forth evil.*

*Job 15:35   His womb prepares deceit.** Hypocrites conceive sorrow when they think up wicked devices. They bring forth evil when they start to set afoot what they planned. By envy they conceive sorrow, and by detraction they bring forth evil. It is grave evil when crooked people start exposing others as crooked, so they can seem holy when they show that others are unholy. Remember, however, that in Holy Scripture the words *belly* and *womb* often mean "the mind." For example, Solomon says, *The spirit of man is the Lord's lamp, and it searches out all the*

*Prov 20:27   hidden places of the stomach.** The light of grace comes from heaven and brings us our spirit to give us life.

We are told that the said light investigates all the mysteries of the belly, since it gets through to the secret places in the mind, so that it may lead out to the eyes of the soul all the hidden things that it should weep over. That is why Jeremiah says, *My belly, my belly! How it*

*Jer 4:19   hurts!** In order further to explain his belly, of which he had spoken, he added, *The feelings of my heart are*

*Jer 4:19   troubled.** The womb is also rightly taken for the mind, because just as descendants are conceived in the womb, so thoughts are generated in the mind. Just as food is stored in the belly, so thoughts are held in the mind. Hypocrites' wombs also prepare deceit, because the more they want to look like the only blameless people there are, the more malice they keep conceiving in their mind against their neighbors.

Eliphaz proclaimed this discourse precisely because he assumed that blessed Job was struck down by adversity for his hypocrisy. Yet his words, even if they are by and large true, miss the mark concerning Job, about whom alone they were spoken. There was no duplicity in the actions of that holy man whom the witness of Truth praised for his simplicity of heart.

BOOK 13

I. 1. It is ordinarily the custom of unrighteous people to shift the blame for their evil practices onto righteous people with an outcry, before they can be truly accused of them themselves, and while they are afraid of being reproached for their actions, they testify against the righteous who accuse them of their wickedness, saying that they have done it themselves. The saints on their part bear these things with patience, even though they know very well that they never did the things they are accused of, and even when they realize that the very ones who are charging them for such wicked deeds are the ones really responsible for them. When they cannot correct them by preaching, they patiently put up with their behavior, and inasmuch as they cannot have the result of their conversion, they at least acquire the reward of long-suffering patience by their agency.

Therefore Holy Church says in the words of the prophet David, *Sinners have plowed my back,** obviously because while she puts up with heretics and other sinners whom she cannot correct, she holds the actions of sinners on her back. Blessed Job accordingly sees his friend Eliphaz questioning him at length out of hypocrisy, after having moved on from words of consolation to bitter invective as a pretended minister of consolation; Job typifies the church through his patience, she who also knew how to put up with such words by listening and, when her speech gains a hearing, how to dismantle an argument by reason. So blessed Job says in his turn,

II. 2. *Yes, I have often heard such arguments.** The chosen ones often hear indeed about the evil deeds of strangers, as if they were their own; they are charged

*Ps 128:3

*Job 16:2

with crimes by those who really committed them. By this answer blessed Job signifies that time to the church when she would be crushed by adversaries and supposedly vanquished by their worldly power. The next verse: *You are all burdensome comforters.** Whether it be heretics or crooks of any stripe, when they see good people struggling with adversity, they want them to take comfort in the fact that they are trying to convince them that they are guilty. Accordingly to the minds of good people, their comfort correctly seems burdensome, because they want to put the poison of error in their drink of sweet words, and while they mitigate the pain with harmless words, they quickly impose the burden of sin. Yet even when they are left without worldly honor, the chosen souls do not lose the force of internal judgment. They know, you see, how to suffer adversity externally, even while maintaining their sense of righteousness internally, unbroken and fearless. So he adds,

 III. 3. *Will windy speeches not come to an end?** Windy speeches are those that carry worldly pride instead of righteousness. Evil people often speak good words too, but they do not speak them correctly, and so the words they speak are wind. Even when their words carry sober judgment, they are inflated by pride. We have already heard it said, *You are all burdensome comforters.* What else does the blessed professor Job teach us with them, except that all should know how to weigh their words carefully, lest they speak out words of reproof in time of mourning? If there is anything people ought by rights to be reproved for, it should certainly be postponed when they are suffering affliction, lest the comforters by their reproof aggravate the pain in those whose pain they had proposed to lighten. The next verse:

 IV. 4. *Is there anything troubling you when you speak?** Evil people speak insulting words along with

**Job 16:2

**Job 16:3

**Job 16:3

their cronies, but they quickly become speechless when they hear their audience speak words just as insulting as their own against themselves. When, on the other hand, they attack good people with insulting words, no trouble for themselves arises from their insults, because they are speaking against silent people; nor are they forced to hear what they are, because the righteous people do not return insults, even when they are forced to hear what they are not. So Job says well, *Is there anything troubling you when you speak?* He might as well say it outright: "You can speak longer, because you hear nothing troublesome from me because of your act." So he adds,

*Job 16:4

*I could have spoken similar words to you.** The just man tells us what he could have done, but he does not wish to abandon justice, so he declines to do what he could have done. The next verse:

V. 5. *If only you were in my place! I would comfort you with my words, and I would bend my head over you. I would strengthen you with my mouth, and*

*Job 16:4-6

*I would move my lips as though to pity you.** Sometimes it is necessary that divine chastisement should be kindly prayed for in the case of perverse minds that cannot be corrected by any human preaching. When this is done with a great deal of love and devotion, it is obviously not the hurt but the correction of the erring one that is sought, and prayer rather than malediction is in evidence. That, we are given to understand, is what blessed Job intends with these words, in order that his friends, who were unable to show compassion for his sufferings through love, might learn by experience how they should have mercy on another person's trial. If they did so, they would be chastened by suffering, and then from their own pain they would draw the ability to afford others comfort; they would live interior lives in a more salutary fashion when they encountered any weakness externally.

It is noteworthy that he did not say, "If only I were in your place," but *If only you were in my place.* He would certainly curse himself, you see, if he chose to become similar to them himself. Rather, he wanted better things for them in wanting them to become like himself. Accordingly we comfort perverse people when they suffer trials; we announce that their internal cure is gaining ground because of the external blows they suffer. We bend our heads when we incline our minds (the principle of our being) to compassion. We strengthen them in trials when we mitigate the pain of their suffering with gentle words. There are those, you see, who do not know about the interior life and who are desperately afflicted by external misfortunes. Of them the psalmist says, *In time of misfortune they fail.** He who can always rejoice in interior hope knows well how to withstand external distress.

*Ps 139:11

6. Note, however, that he did not say "to pity you" but *as though to pity you.* I do not think that this fact should by any means be let pass heedlessly. Holy Church, you see, upholds energetic teaching with a slight admixture of gentleness; sometimes she pretends to pity but does not pity evildoers, but sometimes she pretends not to pity them while she does pity them. We will explain this better, however, if we simply relate what often takes place. Let us then place before our mind's eye two perverse individuals who are members of Holy Church; one of them is influential and bold, the other mild and subjective. If any fault should appear in the mild and subjective person, a preacher straightway censures him and reproves him in an attempt to correct him. By correcting him he frees him from guilt and restores him to the path of righteousness. What has

he done to this person except pity him by not pitying him? Because he did not delay speaking the words of correction, he freed him from guilt sooner. By frankly accusing him he did not pity him, but by correcting him he did pity him.

As for the influential bold person, when he is known to have committed a crime, time is needed so that he may be rebuked for the evil he has done. Unless preachers, you see, hold themselves in check until correction can be accepted conveniently, they will increase the evil in the one they censure. It often happens, you see, that such a person will not accept any words of reproof. What then is left for preachers to do in regard to his crime except that their sermon of admonition, which they give for the common good of their whole audience, should take as its subject such crimes of a general nature that they consider would include those the man has perpetrated, the one who is present and cannot yet be accused directly lest he become worse?

Since their invective is aimed at sin in a general way, the word of correction is conveyed to the mind without hindrance, because the influential sinner has no idea that he is the particular one being spoken to. What else is this but the fact that his preacher has not at all spared him while seeming to spare him, he spoke no words of correction to him in particular, and yet he has wounded him underneath the common admonition. So it often happens that such a person regrets the sin he has committed all the more bitterly in that he thinks his guilt is unknown, even while he feels struck.

7. The preacher's art must be plied cautiously, in order that those who grow worse when they are corrected openly may be restored to grace by a certain moderate form of correction. That is why Paul says, *Those members of the body that we consider less hon-*

orable we surround with greater honor, and to those that are less presentable we give more deference, which our more presentable parts do not require. What therefore the non-presentable parts are in the body, the influential and bold people are in Holy Church; they cannot be attacked by open invective, so they are enveloped in an honorable covering. We are speaking here about the secret sins of those in power. When they sin and others know it, they also know that they should be reproved, lest if the preachers are silent they might seem to have approved of the sin, and if it grows it becomes an example for others, unless the priest's tongue cut it short. Accordingly Holy Church through her preachers reproves some wicked deeds under the dispensation of invective, and she moves her lips as though to spare, but in sparing she does not spare, because she does not keep silence from the general invective against sin, although she does keep from direct invective. The next verse:

VI. 8. *What shall I do? If I speak, my pain will not stop. If I keep silence, it will not go away.* Everybody knows how well this line fits blessed Job's character, but suppose we treat him as a type of Holy Church. When she speaks her pain never ceases, because she never sees the wicked correcting themselves at her preaching. When she is silent her pain never leaves her, because if she silently turns away, her very silence causes her to groan the more, because in her silence she sees the sins of the insolent increase. The next verse:

VII. 9. *Now that my pain oppresses me, all my limbs are reduced to nothing.* Her pain depresses Holy Church when she sees the malice of wicked people increase, and while the numbers of depraved people grow even her weaker members are incited to follow their wicked example. So he is right to add, *all my limbs are reduced to nothing.* Just as strong people, you see,

*1 Cor 12:23-24

*Job 16:7

*Job 16:8

are ordinarily signified by bones, so are weak people by limbs. The members of the church, accordingly, are brought to nothing when by imitating the depraved whose numbers increase in the world, all the weak ones become weaker. They see how evil people thrive, and they often fall away even from the condition of faith in their desire for worldly goods. They are brought to nothing, as it were, because when they abandon the abiding essence of God and fall in love with passing things, they are directed to non-being. Job is right to say, "Now," because the time of the church's suffering is obviously now, whereas the time of joy follows hereafter. It often happens that Holy Church not only has to suffer disbelievers and adversaries from outside her borders, but she also barely survives the ambushes and adversity of those she has within her. So blessed Job aptly follows up with the following words:

*Job 16:9   VIII. 10. *My wrinkles bear witness against me.** What do wrinkles mean except duplicity? The wrinkles of Holy Church are therefore all those who live double lives in her, who cry out *faith* with their voices but deny it with their works. Of course they see that faith is honorable among the great ones of this world in time of peace, so they lie and say they are faithful. But when Holy Church is buffeted by sudden storms of adversity, they there and then display how their treacherous minds work. Holy Church, however, does not have such wrinkles in her chosen ones, because they obviously do not know how to display one thing externally and hold something else internally. That is why the illustrious preacher says, *That he might reveal his glorious church,*
*Eph 5:27   *unwrinkled and unstained.** She who lacks both shameful deeds and double speech definitely has neither spot nor wrinkle. But at the present time within the bosom of faith she contains many who are also base, so when a

time of persecution arrives, she suffers as enemies those whom she seemed previously to nourish with words of preaching. Let her say accordingly, *My wrinkles bear witness against me.* In other words, "Even those attack me with rebukes who are now members of my body, and they do not amend the malice and duplicity that is in them." So he again rightly adds,

IX. 11. *A liar stands up to face me and contradicts me.** Even in the time of her peace Holy Church suffers liars, while there are many of her members who do not believe in the promise of eternal life and yet falsely aver that they are faithful. While they do not presume to contradict her preaching openly, she endures liars, not face to face, but as it were behind her back. When the time comes for an outbreak of malice, however, the present fearful detractor turns to face her with open contradiction and with open mouth resists the words of true faith. Nevertheless we must realize that when we suffer in this way from unspiritual people, it is not so much they themselves who fiercely conspire for our death, but rather the evil spirit who governs their minds. It is just as Paul says: *Our struggle is not against flesh and blood, but against the principalities and powers and against the rulers of the world of this darkness.** So here also, while he is speaking of liars, Job immediately turns to the description of the master of liars and rightly speaks the following words:

X. 12. *He has gathered up his fury against me, and he has threateningly growled and bared his teeth against me. My enemy has glared at me with frightful eyes.** What else are all the wicked but members of the devil? He therefore acts through them, and whatever actions are in their hearts he has put there for them to need to act. Even now the devil is furious against Holy Church, but his fury is scattered, because he causes hidden tempta-

*Job 16:9

*Eph 6:12

*Job 16:10

tions in individuals. But when he attacks her openly with a persecution, he gathers up his fury against her, and he concentrates his whole attention on the attack against her. In this time of peace, however, his members do not have any united force against the elect, because they do not feel as strong as they would like to be to set his malice afoot. On the other hand, when they perceive that they are at liberty for perverse behavior, they attack her all the more boldly the more they are massed together in unanimity against her. So Job is right to say here, *He has gathered up his fury against me.* He goes on to describe this fury more at length: *He has threateningly growled and bared his teeth against me.* He then goes on to say, *My enemy has glared at me with frightful eyes.* Unquestionably that ancient enemy of the church growls and bares his teeth against her and glares at her with frightful eyes, because he sets his horrible designs afoot through some, and he provides these designs through others.

13. The teeth of this enemy are the persecutors and murderers of good people, who mangle the church's members while they afflict her elect with persecutions. The eyes of this enemy are those who arrange the evil things to happen to her and who incite her persecutors by their counsel with savagery against her. Her ancient enemy accordingly growls and bares his teeth against her when he hounds the lives of good people through those in her who practice base cruelty. He glares at her with frightful eyes, because he keeps on seeking evil by means of depraved counsel, with which he afflicts her still more grievously. Just as Truth incarnate in his preaching chose the poor, the ignorant, and the simple-minded, so contrariwise will that condemned man, whom the apostate angel will raise up at the end of the world to preach his false doctrines, choose the sharp-witted, the double-minded, and those who are

smart with the knowledge of this world. That is why Isaiah says, *Woe to the land of noisy wings across the rivers of Ethiopia, which sends ambassadors to the sea in papyrus boats on the water.*   *Isa 18:1-2

That condemned land is surely the condemned person who is called the noise of wings, because those who proudly fly in the sky of thought give forth the sound of the same perverse man in their preaching. That land is rightly stated to be located across the rivers of Ethiopia, since Ethiopia, as you know, is the home of a black population, and this world, because every person it nourishes is a sinner, is like Ethiopia the home of a black population. But this condemned land is, we are told, across the rivers of Ethiopia, because that condemned man is so intensely wicked that his sin far transcends the sins of all sinners. He sends ambassadors to the sea, because he scatters his preachers over the whole world. Concerning these Job rightly adds that they were sent *in papyrus boats on the water.*

As you know, paper is made from papyrus. So what does papyrus mean here, if not worldly knowledge? Papyrus boats are therefore the hearts of worldly teachers. The sending of ambassadors, then, in papyrus boats on the water means to put the preaching into the brains of unspiritual wise people and to call the sailing people to guilt. Those whom Isaiah accordingly designates by means of papyrus boats, Job signifies by means of eyes, obviously because they see in an unspiritual manner. Concerning these he adds the following:

XI. 14. *They opened their mouths against me and reproached me.*   *Job 16:11 Base people open their mouths in reproach when they preach their evil errors without fear and when they ridicule the preaching of true faith. Concerning them we must realize that they specifically persecute those in Holy Church, those who they perceive will profit many, and who harass the life out of carnal people with words of correction and make them change and become spiritual in the church's body. So he adds,

XII. 15. *They struck me on the cheek; they contented themselves with my pain.** The church's cheek is certainly holy preachers, just as Jeremiah, playing the role of Judea, says, *She wept bitterly in the night, and her tears were on her cheek.** In the church's adversity those are more likely to mourn who know how to castigate the life of the flesh by their preaching. It is unquestionably through them that Holy Church strikes the sinners to clean them from their vices and in a way absorbs them to make them her members. So he who was the first preacher, the church's cheek in a way, was told, *Slaughter and eat.**

So also Samson took the jawbone of an ass* and slew the enemy, because our Redeemer took the preachers' simplicity and patience in the hand of his power and put to death the life of the flesh, doing away with vices. Moreover the jawbone was thrown down on the ground, and after some time water flowed out of it, because the bodies of preachers, having been put to death, showed great miracles to the people. Accordingly depraved men strike the church on the cheek when they persecute the good preachers. Since these same depraved men consider that they have done something important in putting the preachers to death, after the blow to the cheek Job continues, *They contented themselves with my pain.* That pain surely contents them that particularly chastens the church's mind. The next verse:

XIII. 16. *God has confined me in evil company, and he has put me in the power of the wicked.** The people of the elect are confined in evil company when their flesh is temporarily given up to the persecutions of the ancient enemy. They are not delivered to a spirit but to

*Job 16:11

*Lam 1:2

*Acts 10:13

*see
Judg 15:16

*Job 16:12

the power of the wicked. Because they cannot reach the spirit directly, they are incited all the more fiercely against the flesh. But when the people of Holy Church start to endure serious adversity, and when she sees her weak members fall away to base behavior, she recalls to mind the time of her peace, when she fed her faithful with the richness of her preaching. So he adds astutely,

XIV. 17. *I who was once rich was suddenly broke.*   *Job 16:13
Because he maintained that he was suddenly broke, he signified the improvident mind of weak individuals. They do not know how to foresee coming evils, which they find all the more grievous the more unexpectedly they are undergone. Sudden adversity, however, does not happen to people with strong minds, because such evils are foreseen before they happen to them. Nevertheless that is what Holy Church suffers at the present time when certain of her members fall away, because they are sometimes worn down by sudden vices after having tasted the riches of her teaching. This happens so that they might be crushed by evils, as if they had never eaten the food of the word. The next verse:

XV. 18. *He seized my neck, broke me, and set me up as his target.*   *Job 16:13
Just as in evil people the neck signifies pride, so in good people it signifies the raising of liberty. Accordingly, sometimes even pride is used instead of authority in the raising of a standard. So the Lord promises Holy Church through the prophet, *I will make you the pride of the ages.*   *Isa 60:15
Because in the time of persecution certain weak souls do not dare to proclaim openly the truth they know, Job says appropriately of this enemy, *He seized my neck and broke me.* It is possible, however, that by the word *neck* Job signifies those who in the time of peace put themselves forward more than they should and take advantage of the opportunity of defending righteousness to do the bidding of the vice of pride. These people feel the

adversity in the time of persecution more keenly, precisely because they boasted of prosperity. Of them it is rightly said, *He seized my neck and broke me.* In other words, he has tamed the pride I felt in my weaker members by the blows of his conviction.

He set me up as his target. A target is ordinarily set up for the shooting of arrows. The faithful people are therefore set up as a target for their enemy, who always attacks them with his own blows and afflicts them with his persecutions. The one who suffers constant trouble in this life is set up as a target and receives the blows of the striker. When the illustrious preacher endured the misfortune of persecution and groaned under persecution from adversaries, he comforted the tender minds of his disciples concerning his afflictions with these words: *You already know that they are our lot.*[*] It is as if he freely said, "Why do you wonder about our injuries during this time? If we seek eternal happiness, we must suffer blows in the present time." The next verse:

*1 Thess 3:3

XVI. 19. *He surrounded me with his spears, and he accompanied the wound to my loins; he showed no mercy; he poured out my entrails on the ground.*[*] These words would have seemed to fit blessed Job literally, inasmuch as we hear, *He surrounded me with his spears, and he accompanied the wound to my loins; he showed no mercy.* Something is added, however, that we never read about him: *He poured out my entrails on the ground.* In this case, since we cannot find the latter phrase literally, whereas the former words do agree with his story, we must search out the spiritual sense.

*Job 16:14

Holy Church is surrounded by her enemy's lances when she is attacked in her members by spears of temptation hurled by the cunning foe. Moreover, he is right to say that we are *surrounded* by these lances, because the ancient enemy attacks us with the wounds of his temptations from every side. While gluttony is restrained, you see, in order that lust may be controlled, he often strikes the mind with the sting of vainglory. On the other hand, if the body is not held in check with the distress of abstinence, the mind is incited by the fire of lust. When we try to preserve a stringent economy, we fall into stinginess, but if we give away our possessions freely, we are often led to avarice, because we want to gather again what we have given away.

Accordingly, since the ancient enemy's spears are attacking us on every side, we are rightly told here, *He surrounded me with his spears.* The shrewd enemy surely promotes every sin, but it is we who let ourselves be persuaded to commit sin, so he fittingly adds, *He accompanied the wound to my loins.* Lust certainly resides in the loins. Therefore he who wanted to rid his heart of the pleasure of lust preached as follows: *Gird up the loins of your minds.** Consequently, since the   *1 Pet 1:13
ancient enemy entices the faithful people to lust, it is undoubtedly in the loins that he strikes.

Note well, however, that he did not simply say *wounded*, but *accompanied the wound to my loins.* Just as it is usually one who speaks, you see, but conversation is said of two or perhaps many, so also, since the ancient enemy does not urge us to sin without involving our will, he is by no means said to wound our loins, but to accompany the wound, because that which he maliciously suggests to us we follow up by performing it by our own will. In a way we wound ourselves together with him, because we are led to perform an evil action by involving our own free will.

There follows, *He showed no mercy.* In other words, he did not waver. *He poured out my entrails on the ground.* What else should we take Holy Church's entrails to mean but the minds of those who hold some of her mysteries in themselves and who are ministers of her interior sacraments? The ancient adversary, however, draws away certain ones from among the faithful, those who seemed to minister to the hidden sacraments, to secular pursuits; when this happens, he undoubtedly pours out her entrails on the ground, since he tramples them down in the meanest realities, those who formerly lay hidden in secret spiritual actions. The next verse:

*Job 16:15

XVII. 20. *Injury upon injury has struck me.** In her weak members Holy Church suffers wound upon wound when sin is added to sin, so that guilt might be piled up to an immense degree. The person whom avarice urges to robbery, robbery leads to deceit, so that once the crime has been committed, it may even be defended by the aid of falsehood. What proceeding is this if not the infliction of a wound upon a wound? That is why the prophet also says, with reason, *They overflow with curses, lying, manslaughter, theft, and adultery, and blood follows blood.** The word *blood*, you know, often signifies sin. So the one who wants to be free of sin cries out with repentance, *Deliver me from blood.** Blood therefore follows blood when sin piles up sin. Since therefore, when wound is added to wound, the power of the ancient enemy against us increases alarmingly, he is right to add,

*Hos 4:2

*Ps 50:16

*Job 16:15

XVIII. 21. *He rushes against me like a giant.** It is unquestionably easy to resist the enemy, if we do not keep consenting to him by giving in to him often or even once. If, on the other hand, the soul has formed the habit of being subject to his persuasion, the more often it subjects itself to him the more unbearable he becomes, to the point that it cannot resist him, because the evil adversary absolutely fights the defeated soul by perverse custom, just like a giant. Even so Holy Church often does reclaim the minds of the faithful to repentance even after the committing of sins, and she purifies sins of deed by virtue of voluntary sorrow. So Job rightly adds, XIX. 22. *I have sewn sackcloth over my skin, and I have covered my flesh with ashes.** What should we understand by sackcloth and ashes but repentance, and what by skin and flesh but a sin of the flesh? Accordingly, when some people return to repentance after a backsliding of the flesh, it is as though sackcloth were sewn onto the skin; moreover, the flesh is covered with ashes, because a sin of the flesh is covered up by repentance, lest the inflexible judge should examine it for the purpose of recompense. When, consequently, Holy Church induces her weak members to abandon sin and leads them to the cure of repentance, she undoubtedly helps them with her tears, so that they may be strengthened to receive the grace of their Creator. Through her strong members she mourns what she did not do, but, as it were, she did do in her fragile members. So he again rightly adds,

XX. 23. *My face is swollen with tears.** Holy Church's face is possessed by those who hold seats of government and who, being preeminent, seem to be the kind who would make faithful people honorable, even if something deformed lay hidden in their bodies. Those placed at the head really do mourn the sins of the weak among the people, and they agonize for the backsliding of others, as if they were their own. When they see certain ones come back after sinning to seek forgiveness, while others persist in evildoing, they often wonder at almighty God's hidden judgments, which they cannot penetrate. They are astonished at that which they do not understand. So he is right to add,

XXI. 24. *My eyelids are closed.** They are rightly called eyelids who stay awake to keep watch over the footpaths. Since, however, not even those charged with

*Job 16:16
LXX

*Job 16:17
LXX

*Job 16:17
LXX

watching understand the hidden judgments of God, the eyelids of Holy Church are closed. Still, as I remember having often said, Job is the type of Holy Church, and he sometimes speaks with the voice of the Head, sometimes of the members. So while he is speaking of the members, he immediately raises his voice to speak the words of the Head. So he again adds,

XXII. 25. *This is what I suffered when there was no* *Job 16:18 LXX* *evil on my hands, and I prayed pure prayers to God.** He bore his sufferings, and there was no evil in his hands. *Isa 53:9* *He did not sin, and no deception was heard from Him.** Nevertheless he put up with the suffering of the cross for our redemption. He alone of all men could lift up pure prayers to God, and he prayed for his persecutors even while suffering his passion, in these words: *Father,* *Luke 23:34* *forgive them; they do not know what they are doing.** What words or what thoughts could be a purer prayer than the offering of merciful intercession for those on whose account he suffered pain? So it happened that the blood of our Redeemer, poured out in fury by his persecutors, the believers later drank, and they proclaimed him Son of God. Concerning this same blood, Job now wisely adds,

XXIII. 26. *Let not the earth cover my blood, nor let* *Job 16:19* *there be a hiding place in it for my cries.** When the first man sinned he was told, *You are dust, and to dust you* *Gen 3:19* *shall return.** The said earth did not hide the Redeemer's blood, because all sinners receive the price of their redemption and proclaim it, giving praise; to as many of his fellows as they can they make it known. Neither did the earth hide his blood, because Holy Church has already proclaimed the mystery of her redemption in every part of the world. Take notice what follows: *Do* *not let there be a hiding place in it for my cries.* The blood of redemption that it receives is itself the cry of the Redeemer. That is why Paul says for his part, *The sprinkling of the blood that speaks better than Abel's.* *Heb 12:24 Of Abel's blood it had been said, *The voice of your brother's blood is crying to me from the earth.* *Gen 4:10

Nevertheless the blood of Jesus speaks better than Abel's, because Abel's blood asked for the death of his fratricide brother, but the Lord's blood obtained the life of his persecutors. In order accordingly that the sacraments of the Lord's passion might not be without effect in us, we should imitate what we receive and proclaim to others what we venerate. His cries find a hiding place in us, you see, if concerning what our mind believes our tongue is silent. So in order that his cries may not be hidden in us, it remains for all of us in our own small way to make known the mystery of his coming to life to our neighbors. We must turn our mind's eyes to the hour of the Lord's passion, when the persecuting Jews grew hostile and the disciples fled in fear. He who seemed to die according to the flesh was certainly not believed in as God. So Job rightly adds,

XXIV. 27. *Behold, my witness is in heaven, and he who knows me dwells on high.* *Job 16:20 LXX He whose faith was shaken on earth had a heavenly witness. The Son's witness is unquestionably the Father, of whom he says in the gospel, *The Father who sent me bears his own witness about me.* *John 5:37 The Father is indeed rightly called the knower, because he always works with the Son with the same will and the same counsel. He is his witness, because *No one knows the Son except the Father.* *Matt 11:27 Accordingly he had high in heaven a witness who knew him precisely then when those who saw him dying according to the flesh could not perceive the power of his divinity. Although men and women did not know it, the

Mediator between God and men knew in death that the Father was working together with him. This fact may also be assigned to the voice of his Body.

Holy Church, you see, endures the adversity of the present life, in order that heavenly grace may lead her on to eternal rewards. She despises death in her flesh, because she looks forward to the glory of resurrection. What she suffers is transitory, what she expects eternal. Of these eternal good things moreover she has no doubt, because she already has truthful testimony about them in the glory of her Redeemer. She surely gazes on the resurrection of the flesh in her mind, and her faith is greatly strengthened, because she sees that what is already done in her Head will happen beyond any doubt also in his Body, which in fact she is. The psalmist saw that the church would always remain in complete perfection, so he describes her with the title of moon, saying, *She is the eternally perfect moon.**

*Ps 88:38 LXX

Since the Lord's resurrection confirms her hope in the resurrection, he adds, *She has a faithful witness in heaven.* In order that she might not waver concerning her own resurrection, she has him who is already in heaven, who rose from the dead, as a witness. Consequently let the faithful people, even as they suffer adversity and are virtually worn out by terrible persecutions, lift up their heart to the hope of the glory that is to come, trusting in the resurrection of their Redeemer, and say, *Behold, my witness is in heaven, and he who knows me dwells on high.* Job is right to use the verb *knows*, because the Lord knows our nature not only as the one who created it, but also as the one who assumed it. His knowing our nature means that he took it upon himself. That is also what the psalmist said, *He knows what we are made of.** Why should we wonder at the fact that he is said to know in particular what we are

*Ps 102:14

made of when there is nothing that he does not know? But his knowing what we are made of means that he took it unto himself out of love.

28. This citation, however, while it fits blessed Job perfectly, can also be used for every one of us. Everyone, you see, craves human praise for what he does and seeks an earthly witness. Those who hasten to please almighty God with their actions, however, know they have a witness in heaven. Besides, it often happens that the very good works that we do are the subject of reprehension by careless people. The one however who has a heavenly witness should not fear human reproaches. So Job again adds,

XXV. 29. *My friends are long-winded, but my eyes pour out tears to God.* What else is meant by the word *eye* but the intention of the heart? It is written, *If your eye is simple, your whole body will be full of light.* When anything is done with a good intention, the act that follows such an intention will hardly be dark in God's sight. When friends are long-winded, that is, when faithful associates even become detractors, the eye must pour out tears to God, inasmuch as our intention overflows in compunction of intimate love and lifts itself up all the more keenly to internal reality the more it is forced to retire inside itself through the external insults it suffers, lest it lose itself externally. The next verse:

*Job 16:21 LXX

*Matt 6:22

XXVI. 30. *Would that a man could go to judgment with God, just as another man goes to judgment with his fellow man!* We always know very well that we are sinners, yet while we are often subject to trials, we are unaware of the sin for which we are suffering yet another trial. So we question ourselves in closer detail in the hope that we may somehow find out the reason for our present trial. Still, when the reason often remains hidden from us, our blindness becomes a burden to us, and our suffering

*Job 16:22 LXX

causes us still more anguish. Whenever people on the other hand go to judgment with their fellows, they announce their claim and understand the counterclaim; they make their move when they please and understand the move made against them. Those however who have been touched by divine censure indeed feel the blow but do not know the reason for it, even as they tell what they feel.

That which is told against them, though, they do not know, since they certainly groan under the lash, but God does not openly declare the reason for the punishing blow. That is why we are told here, *Would that a man could go to judgment with God, just as another man goes to judgment with his fellow man!* It is as if he said openly, "Just as all my words are heard, I would hear what is said of me." That however is impossible in this life, because there is a great chasm, namely, our powerlessness, between the eyes of our heart and the contemplation of God's simplicity. But we will then contemplate the purity of him who sees through us now when, having left our powerlessness behind, we finally come into the grace of interior contemplation that Paul

*1 Cor 13:12   speaks about: *Then I shall know, just as I am known.** So blessed Job knows that this contemplation cannot be had perfectly here, and while he groans at the blindness of the present life, he is comforted by the knowledge of its brevity. So he says,

XXVII. 31. *See how brief are the presently passing years, and I am walking on the path by which I shall*

*Job 16:23   *not return.** All passing things are brief, even if their end
LXX   may seem to be delayed. We walk the path of death, and we will not retrace our steps. Not that we are not led back to the life of the flesh by the resurrection, but that we do not return to the toil of this mortal life, not even to win its rewards again. The next verse:

XXVIII. 32. *My spirit will be weakened.** The spirit is weakened by the fear of judgment, because the closer the minds of the elect find themselves to be to the Last Judgment, the more frightfully they tremble at their own self-questioning. If they ever find any self-indulgent thoughts in themselves, they annihilate them with ardent penance; nor do they allow their thoughts to develop any sensual pleasure, because they judge and punish themselves all the more strictly the more immediate their expectation of the intransigent Judge. So it happens that they always think their end is near. The minds of reprobate sinners, on the other hand, multiply their acts of wickedness, precisely because they think they will continue their life here. The spirits of the just are therefore weakened, but those of the wicked grow in density. Because they grow fat by pride, they suffer no weakness of spirit. The just, on the other hand, consider the brevity of this life, so they escape the sins of pride and impurity. So he adds,

XXIX. 33. *My days will be shortened, and all that is left for me is the tomb.** If people consider what they will be like in death, they are always fainthearted in action, and when in their own eyes their life is already virtually over, then they are really alive in the eyes of their Maker. They want nothing transitory, they go against all the desires of the present life, and they consider themselves already virtually dead, since they are by no means ignorant of the fact that they will die. The perfect life is an imitation of death, and when the just carefully act this way, they avoid the snares of sin. That is why we find it written, *In all your works remember your last end, and you will never sin.** So blessed Job sees that his days are shortened, and he figures that only the tomb is left for him, so he rightly adds,

*Job 17:1

*Job 17:1

*Eccl 7:40

XXX. 34. *I have not sinned, and my eye abides in*

*Job 17:2

bitterness.[*] He might as well have said, "I have done no wrong, and I have been whipped." At this point, however, it comes to mind that he does confess his sins in numerous passages in this story, so why does he now deny that he has sinned? Still, a reason does immediately come to mind, in that his sin was not so great as to have deserved punishment, nor could he on the other hand be without sin. The Judge, as you know, praises and strikes him, he who also testifies that his blows were not intended to punish guilt but to increase merit. Again, Job himself, whom the Judge praised, does not deny that he was not without some sin, and it was precisely for that reason that he was praised, namely, that he did not deny his sin. But I think that we discuss this matter better if we consider these words of Job as spoken by our Head. Our Redeemer came to free us, he who did not sin but suffered its bitterness; he received the punishment for our guilt without being guilty himself. He is the one in whose voice Job adds,

XXXI. 35. *Deliver me and place me at your side, and*

*Job 17:3

let anyone's hand fight me.[*] He it is, you see, who did not sin either in thought or deed; he abode in bitterness through his passion, he was freed through the resurrection, and he was placed at the Father's side through the ascension, since of course he sits at God's right hand in heaven. Moreover, since after the glory of the ascension Judea was moved to persecute his disciples, Job rightly adds, *Let anyone's hand fight me*. Then indeed the fury of the persecutors grew fierce against the Lord's members, and then the flame of cruelty was lighted against the lives of the faithful. But where should the wicked go, and what should they do, when he whom they persecuted on earth was already sitting in heaven? About them he adds the following words:

XXXII. 36. *You have distanced their hearts from
discipline.** Obviously if they had known how to retain   *Job 17:4
discipline, they would never have despised the precepts
of our Redeemer, because the very mortality of their
flesh would have urged them toward the love of eternal life. The very fact, you see, that we are subject to
mortality in this life is already the sting of discipline.
What are these facts, namely, that we suffer heat and
cold, hunger and thirst, that we are subject to sickness
and eventually even death: what else are they but the
sting of sin? There are those, however, who put up with
these pains and yet are far from turning their minds to
fear their author. That is why we are now rightly told,
You have distanced their hearts from discipline. Even
if their bodies are subject to discipline, their hearts are
not so subject, since everybody is disciplined, but not
everybody is led to humility of mind. This is not said as
if the almighty and merciful God himself distanced the
human heart from discipline; rather, as Judge he allows
men and women to remain where they have fallen by
their own volition, just as we say in the Lord's Prayer,
Lead us not into temptation.* That is, do not allow us   *Matt 6:13
ever to be led astray. The next verse:

XXXIII. 37. *Therefore they will not be exalted.** If   *Job 17:4
their hearts were subject to discipline, they would desire
the things that are above, and they would not long to
obtain transitory goods. Therefore, since their hearts
are not subject to discipline, it is rightly said of them,
Therefore they will not be exalted. As long as they are
released into base desires, they always want earthly
goods, and their hearts are never lifted up to heavenly
joys. They would undoubtedly be exalted if they lifted
up their minds to the hope of the eternal homeland.
Those however who never try to conduct their lives by
discipline always wallow in base things through desire

and, what is worse, flaunt themselves in so wallowing, because they are proud on account of transitory things. They can be proud, but they can never be exalted, because they sink deeper in the base mud the more they make themselves proud. Accordingly the heart without discipline cannot be exalted, because the human mind, to the extent that it is wrongly lifted up, is pressed down into the base mud, and so on the other hand the mind that is rightly bent low is lifted up to the heights. The next verse:

XXXIV. 38. *He promises booty to his cronies, and*
*the eyes of his sons will fail.** After blessed Job has passed sentence on the multitude of the wicked, that is, on the body of the ancient enemy, he turns straightway to their leader himself, that is, to the head of all the damned. In short he turns from the plural to the singular number to pass sentence on him. So absolutely united into one body are the devil and all the evildoers that the name of the head often recalls the body, and the name of the body recalls the head. The name of the head recalls the body when it is said of the depraved individual, *One of you is a devil.** On the other hand, the name of the body recalls the head when it is said of the apostate angel himself, *An enemy has done this.** This very prince of all the depraved then has cronies as well as sons. Who are his cronies if not those apostate angels who fell with him from the seat of the heavenly homeland? What other sons does he have but those depraved people who are begotten by his perverse suggestions in the practice of evil? That is why the unfaithful ones are told by the voice of Truth, *Your father is the devil.**

39. This perverse author of error accordingly promises his cronies booty, because he promises the evil spirits depraved souls to grab at the end. *The eyes of his sons will fail*, since as long as he entices humans

*Job 17:5

*John 6:71

*Matt 13:28

*John 8:44

to hope only for earthly goods, he makes them love the things they cannot hold on to for very long. Nor can the intensity of depraved love endure, when both that which is loved and the one who loves are doomed to fail swiftly. The word *cronies* can also mean all the most cruel people who are already full of every kind of wickedness; *sons* on the other hand can mean those who are still deluded by the devil's deceitful promises to such an extent that they are urged to go on increasing their depravity. As for the former, he already has for cronies in virtue of their malice those who cannot increase further in perdition, while he nurses the latter as his sons with his promises, so that they may become worse. The eyes of his sons will fail, however, since the intensity of depravity collapses when they abandon all they desire here, and there they groan in their endless suffering. The next verse:

XXXV. 40. *He made me a byword for the crowd and an example for them.** Let blessed Job say this on his own behalf, and let him speak with the voice of all the elect. It is beyond question that everyone who is harassed by trials becomes in a way a byword for the crowd, because all fools, as long as they want to curse somebody, take as their curse a comparison with those who suffer a temporary trial, and they wish the same penalty on their adversaries that they notice was the lot of the just. So it happens that the law-abiding person becomes an example for those whose thinking is off base, while the penalty of the just is thought to be condemnation, and the glory that awaits them is not foreseen by any expectation of faith. The next verse:

XXXVI. 41. *My eye has darkened from indignation, and my limbs have been virtually brought to nothing.** The eye darkens from indignation when even those in the Lord's Body—that is, in the church—those who have the

*Job 17:6

*Job 17:7

light of truth, while they notice that they continue to be despised and scorned by depraved people are troubled by wonder at the hidden judgment of God; they cannot penetrate God's mystery or understand why perverse people are allowed to prevail against the guiltlessness of good people. Who would not be astounded when Herodias obtains from the drunken king by means of her daughter's dance that the head of the friend of the bridegroom, of the prophet who is more than a prophet, should be presented to him on a platter in front of his guests?

But while the just are darkened from indignation, the weak often fall headlong into infidelity. So he adds, *My limbs have been virtually brought to nothing.* The word *limbs* often expresses the extreme softness of the weak, who, when they see the wicked flourish while the righteous suffer, are sometimes brought to the point that they are sorry for ever having begun the good path, and in this way they fall into evildoing more swiftly, as if the good path they had started had injured their lives. The words he spoke, however, *My eye has darkened from indignation*, he explains in the next paragraph with more lucid words:

XXXVII. 42. *The just man will be surprised at this, and the blameless man will be stirred up against the* ^{*Job 17:8} *hypocrite.** The word *blameless* in this passage is taken to mean the just who are not yet perfect. They are still beginners on the good path, and even if they cannot hurt anyone, they are still incapable of perfect behavior themselves. When the hearts of little ones notice how the wicked flourish in this life, they are on fire with the flames of envy. We envy others who possess the good things of this life all the more as we ourselves have less contempt for those goods. Since the whole world cannot be possessed by everybody at once, one lacks what the other has.

So blameless people are stirred up against the hypocrite when they envy the pretender to honor, even when
they themselves would never hurt anyone. If, however,
we take the blameless people in this passage to mean
those who are perfectly on the good path, the blameless
ones are incensed against hypocrites when they notice
that they flourish, while the blameless ones feel contempt for the hypocrites and their good fortune together.
They preach the correct path, and they declare to other
people how contemptible those hypocrites are to the
extent that they see how anxiously the hypocrites go
after those things that they cannot keep very long. In
that sense Job also adds,

XXXVIII. 43. *The just man will hold to his course,
and he will add courage to his purity of life.*[*] Having
noticed the hypocrites, the just hold to their course, because while they see the hypocrites obtain the goods of
this world with crooked intent, they themselves hold
on all the more tightly to love of heaven, knowing that
the eternal reward will not be denied to good desires
as long as passing goods are not denied to those with
depraved and deceitful hearts. On this account the just
add courage to purity of life, because when they see
perverse people obtain worldly honor, they carry on
their good works to the point of perfection, and they
despise passing things all the more nobly the more they
see the abundance of them that even the evil possess.

They consider how contemptible are those things
that almighty God even bestows on crooked people.
If they were really so important, you see, the Creator
would never give them to his adversaries. So the just
consider that it is beneath them to want those good
things in which they see the evil abound; rather, they
direct their minds to the reception of heavenly things,
which cannot be common ground with the just and with

*Job 17:9

the reprobate sinners. So after the external pursuits of evil, Job goes on to describe the internal pursuits of the good and speaks words of exhortation:

XXXIX. 44. *Therefore change your ways and come, all of you.** This is the exhortation especially addressed to all the elect whom he calls to eternal life. They are invited to eternal life in two ways, that they may change their ways, and that they may come: they change their ways by believing, and they come by means of good works, or at least they change their ways by abandoning evil, and they come by doing what is good, just as it is written, *Leave evil and do good.** What follows gives cause for wonder:

XL. 45. *May I not find one wise man among you!** How is it that he calls them to wisdom and then prefers not to think them wise, unless they cannot come to true wisdom because they are deceived by reliance on their own false wisdom? It is written of them, *Woe to you who are wise in your own eyes and prudent according to your own lights.** They are also told, *Do not be wise in your own conceits.** That is why that illustrious preacher wanted those whom he had found wise according to the flesh to become foolish first, in order that they might perceive true wisdom, when he said, *If any of you seems to be worldly wise, let him become a fool, that he may be wise.** For his own part Truth himself said, *I praise you, Father, Lord of heaven and earth, because you have hidden these things from those that are wise and prudent and have revealed them to babies.** Since, accordingly, those who are wise in their own eyes cannot come to true wisdom, blessed Job rightly desires the conversion of his hearers and hopes that no wise person may be found among them. It is as though he told them openly, "Learn to be fools in your own eyes, in order that you might be truly wise according to God." The next verse:

*Job 17:10

*Ps 36:27

*Job 17:10

*Isa 5:21

*Rom 12:16

*1 Cor 3:18

*Matt 11:25

XLI. 46. *My days have passed away, and my thoughts have scattered, wrenching my heart.* Holy Church of the elect watches her lifetime passing through days and nights. She is accustomed to spend her nights in adversity and her days in prosperity. It is as though light rose for her in peace and tranquility, and night fell in the pain of persecution. When she returns to harsh persecution, which increases against her after the enjoyment of peace and quiet, she admits that her days have passed away. She, however, tends to be pressed hard by concerns during these days that are all the more serious to the extent that she figures on searching questions being asked her concerning that very peace and quiet by the Judge. Sometimes, you see, she considers the profit of souls during times of peace and quiet, but sometimes her concern extends to the disposition of worldly goods.

These dispositions of worldly actions are obviously all the more difficult for careful minds the more preoccupation with them pulls them away even a little from heavenly contemplation. So after he admits, either with his own voice or that of the universal church, that his days have passed away, he straightway adds with reason, *My thoughts have scattered, wrenching my heart.* When worldly happiness passes from the minds of righteous people, the solicitude for earthly business is also removed from them, and that is what seemed to wrench their thoughts. As long as they want to be always ready to discern the things above, by the very fact that they sometimes let go to attend to base thoughts because of worldly concerns, they feel wrenched. So it happens that the adversity of persecution is itself turned into high exultation and joy, because tranquility of heart is regained. So he rightly adds,

XLII. 47. *They turned night into day.* Scattered thoughts have turned night into day, because it is

*Job 17:11

*Job 17:12

sometimes more pleasant for the just to suffer wrong through adversity than in prosperity to be worn out by the solicitude for worldly business. Yet they are more careful, and they know how to rise above adversity and how to shine in prosperity, so he rightly adds,

*Job 17:12   XLIII. 48. *Yet again I hope for light after darkness.*
We hope for light after darkness either in the sense that after the night of the present time we glimpse the light of eternity, or in the sense that even here adversity alternates with prosperity, in such a way that they never stop succeeding one another. So it happens both that night is suspected during the light and light is foreseen in the night, just as it is written, *During the good times do not*
Eccl 11:27   forget evil, and during evil times remember the good.
But now that we have been redeemed by the grace of our Creator, we have that heavenly reward that when we are taken away from our house of flesh, we are immediately led to that heavenly prize. Our Creator and Redeemer broke into the prison of hell and led from there the souls of the just, so he will not let us go to that place from which he descended to free those others.

Those, you see, who had come into this world before his own coming, no matter how holy their lives were, when they left the body could by no means be received in the heavenly homeland straightway, because he had not yet come who would open the prison of hell by going down there and settling the souls of the just in their now-eternal home. So blessed Job, both in the affliction he suffers and in his knowledge that the reward of the just is delayed, rightly adds,

XLIV. 49. *If I endure, hell is my home, and I make*
Job 17:13   my bed in the darkness. The ancient saints were able to endure adversity, and yet when they left their bodies they were unable to leave the cells of hell, because he had not yet come who would descend to hell without

sin, so that he might free from sin those who were held
there. At that time humans made their bed in the darkness, when by listening to the persuasion of the shrewd
foe they abandoned the light of justice. In those same
cells of hell the souls of the just were also held without
torture, because they still went there for original sin,
even though they had no penalty to pay for their own
deeds, so to have made their beds in the darkness means
to have prepared their resting places in hell. It was terrible weariness for the chosen ones after their bodily
death not yet to see the Creator's face. It is no mistake
on blessed Job's part to call this weariness darkness.
Since this state of affairs has its source in the penalty
of weakness, he rightly goes on to speak about that
very weakness:

XLV. 50. *To rottenness I said, "You are my father,"
and to worms, "You are my mother and my sister."* *   *Job 17:14
How is it that he told rottenness, *You are my father*, if
it is not that every person from the beginning down to
the present is already spoiled? That is why he adds, *And
to worms, "You are my mother and sister,"* obviously
because we come into this world both from rottenness
and with it. As far as the corruptible matter of flesh is
concerned, our mother and sister are worms, since we
have issued from rottenness, and we have come with
rottenness that we carry. But if the passage is to be interpreted spiritually, it is not unjustified to call mother by
the name of nature and sister by that of habit, since we
exist from the former and with the latter. Our mother and
sister are worms, because we are urged by corruptible
nature and perverse habit, like worms, in a way, and our
minds are gnawed by insistent thoughts. The nature of
flesh is corrupt and its habits perverse, and because they
initiate so many concerns in our weak hearts, they—
mother and sister—are rightly called worms.

Insistent concerns wound our souls. Just men and women never stop carefully thinking about and taking counsel about what they should do, or looking ahead and wondering where they are being led after the present life. Those who were among the elect before the coming of the Lord knew that they were laboring in the present life, and yet they could not yet receive the reward of heaven after the present life, so their hearts were harassed with many thoughts. They awaited the grace of their Redeemer, and yet they could not reach it while living in the flesh. So he rightly adds,

*Job 17:15   XLVI. 51. *So where now is my expectation?* * What could the expectation of the just be, if not the just and justifying God, who would descend to the pains of the human race of his own free will and free the captives of death by the power of his justice? They never stopped awaiting his presence with anxious reflection; they knew he would be coming sometime, but they wanted him to come quickly. So Job does not say, "Where is my expectation," but *Where now is my expectation?* By the addition of *now* he shows that he earnestly desired the one who was to come sometime to come swiftly. The next verse:

*Job 17:15   XLVII. 52. *Who takes notice of my patience?* * He expresses the desire wherewith he who is clothed with flesh wants quickly to be redeemed and recalled from hell to heaven. It was really the lot of very few people to consider such thoughts or to be able to weigh carefully the troubles of the present life and the time of waiting that follows death. The just who lived before the coming of our Redeemer groaned, because they had both of these misfortunes to suffer. So he is right to say, *Who takes notice of my patience?* He who could take account of patience is of course not absent, but because he does not answer swiftly, he, God, is in a way said not to consider the delay.

Those who lived here below from the beginning of the world felt that redemption of the human race was delayed, but it happens at the end of the world. They were separated by a long period of time from the heavenly reward, as Truth himself bore witness: *Many prophets and kings yearned to see what you are seeing, yet they saw it not.** So when Job says here, *Who takes notice of my patience?* the yearning of earnest desire is clear. It is not, as we have said, that God does not take account of the patience of the just, but in a way he is said not to take it seriously, in that he doesn't seem to be in a hurry to answer such wishes and desires, but rather to seem to delay the granting of the grace of his dispensation for a longer time. Accordingly let Job say, *Who takes notice of my patience?* since what is brief to the dispenser is long for the lover. So still thinking about what this delay deprives him of, he repeats what he has already said. He feels that he is about to descend to hell, and he groans and intones words of pain, saying,

*Luke 10:24

XLVIII. 53. *My whole being is going down to the deepest place in hell.** Since it is clear that the just are held not in the torture chambers of hell but in the higher chamber of repose, an important question arises for us here: how it can be that blessed Job makes such an assertion here, namely, *My whole being is going down to the deepest place in hell.* If Job was going down to hell before the coming of the Mediator between God and humankind, it is clear that he was not going to descend to the deepest place in hell. Or does he call those higher chambers of hell the deepest place in hell?

*Job 17:16

As far as the highest heaven is concerned, you see, this atmospheric space here can already be called hell, and not without reason. Consequently, when the apostate angels were thrown down from the heavenly court and landed in this shadowy air, as the apostle Peter says,

God did not spare the sinful angels, but he cast them down to the confines of the nether world and delivered *2 Pet 2:4 *them to hell to be kept there for torture at the Judgment.** If, therefore, as far as the highest heaven is concerned, this shadowy air is hell, then as far as this high sky is concerned, the earth that lies below can also be thought of as hell and pit. Now then, concerning the earth and the regions of hell that are above the other chambers of hell, in this passage it is not improper to designate them by the words *the deepest place in hell*, since that which the atmosphere is to heaven, the earth is to the atmosphere and the higher chambers of hell are to the earth.

54. What he adds, however, is strange: *My whole being is going down.* If, you see, only the soul was to descend to hell, how is it that the holy man states here that his whole being is going down, unless he sees himself whole there where he knows his complete reward will be? That part of himself that he abandons on earth without sensation, until he regains it incorrupt at the resurrection, he does not feel as part of himself. So he states that his whole being is going down to the deepest part of hell, where he sees his soul going down alone, since he is whole there where he can feel what he receives. Or certainly his whole being descends to hell because the recompense of all his labor was as though all he has done descended there, and he finds his reward of repose there from all his work. Accordingly that very repose he awaits is also mentioned, when he goes on to say,

XLIX. 55. *Do you think that at least there my rest* *Job 17:16 *will be found?** With these emphatic words Job both expresses his desire and yet signifies that he is still in doubt: will he indeed receive that rest, or will just as many trials follow his consecrated works by the secret Judgment of the heavenly Judge? After the trials of the present time will still more tortures remain to follow? Concerning this matter we must carefully ponder with much fear what people among us now are sure of their eternal rest, if the one whose virtue was proclaimed by the Judge himself who struck him is still worried about his eternal rest. *If the just man is barely saved, where will the wicked and the sinner appear?* Blessed Job, you see, knew that he was going to rest after his trials, but in order that he might smite our hearts with fear, he appeared to doubt his recompense of eternal rest when he said, *Do you think?* This was obviously done so that we might remember with what dread we should fear the coming Judgment, when he who was praised by the witness borne by the Judge still did not, in his own words, feel safe concerning the reward of Judgment.

*1 Pet 4:18

BOOK 14

I. 1. In the second part of this work I showed how almighty God used the life of blessed Job as an example so that he might correct the minds of those who lived under the law; he did not know the law, and yet he kept it. He followed the precepts of life without having received them in writing. His behavior was first praised by the witness of God, and he was afterward allowed to be tested by the devil's plots, that he might reveal through temptation and tribulation the extent of his early progress in time of tranquility. The enemy of the human race, whose own behavior was bad, knew of Job's praise by the witness of God, and yet he demanded that he be tempted. When he had failed to lay him low by means of the loss of all his possessions or by striking him with so much bereavement, he provoked his wife against him as a goad of evil persuasion, so that he might at least wear him down through household conversation, him whom he could never manage to tire out through so many tormenting messages.

When, however, he could not obtain reinforcement with the help of the woman against this second victim sitting on a dung heap as he first did against Adam in Paradise, he turned to other means of temptation. He would bring in his friends as though to comfort Job and then provoke their minds to the harshness of angry speech. Thus harsh words together with trials might finally prevail over the man whose patience no trial had conquered. But the sly enemy himself who plotted to deceive the holy man suffered the deception that he had plotted, because for as many opportunities of ruin as he placed before the holy man, he offered him just as many means of victory.

Against distress the holy man certainly held on to patience, and against words he held on to wisdom. He calmly endured the painful blows of the lash, and he wisely curbed the foolishness of bad advice. But since in his sufferings and in his learned speeches he typifies the church, as we have already repeatedly said, his friends who sometimes speak wisely and sometimes foolishly correctly prefigure the heretics, and since they are the holy man's friends, much that they say about the sinners is right on target. But because they play the role of heretics, they often slip up and let themselves digress, and they strike the breast of the holy man with the darts of their words. Yet in their very blows against his invincible mind they become weary. Accordingly we must prudently distinguish in their words both their correct understanding of sinners and that which sounds silly in their attacks on blessed Job.

II. 2. *Bildad the Shuhite answered and said, "Is there no end of the words you blurt out? Think first, and then we will speak."* * All the heretics think that Holy Church is proud in certain thoughts, but they also suppose that she does not even think certain thoughts. That is why Bildad the Shuhite fabricates, as it were, the notion that blessed Job has vented proud thoughts, he who, he says, blurts out words. But Bildad indicates with how much pride he was himself puffed up when he supposes that blessed Job spoke what he did not think about. Since all the heretics complain of Holy Church's contempt and lack of esteem for them, he is right to add,

*Job 18:1-2

III. 3. *Why are we reckoned as dumb beasts, and why do we appear vile in your sight?* * It is characteristic of the human mind to suppose that the thing that it does is done to itself. Those who habitually despise

*Job 18:3

the behavior of good people think it is they who are the object of contempt. Concerning those matters that can be rationally understood, the church makes known against the heretics that their additions are not reasonable, so the heretics suppose that in the judgment of the church they are reckoned as dumb beasts, from which supposition of disdain they immediately break out in scorn and are provoked to insult the church. So he adds,

*Job 18:4   IV. 4. *Why do you lose your soul in your madness?** The heretics consider the fervor of righteousness or the spiritual grace of holy preaching to be not tangible goodness, but the frenzy of madness. They obviously suppose that the souls of the faithful are lost by such madness, because inasmuch as they perceive the church's zeal to be against themselves, they suppose her life to be lost. The next verse:

*Job 18:4   V. 5. *Will the earth be abandoned because of you?** They think they worship God everywhere themselves, and they think they have occupied the whole world by themselves. What does it mean to say, *Will the earth be abandoned because of you?* but that which they often tell the faithful, namely, that if what you say is true, then all the earth has been abandoned by God, as we by sheer magnitude of numbers now hold. But Holy Universal Church preaches that God can only be truly worshiped within her borders, adding that all those who are outside those borders will never be saved. Contrary to this, the heretics who confidently say they can be saved even outside her profess that God's help is theirs and present everywhere. That is why they say, *Will the earth be abandoned because of you?* In other words, will everyone outside you never be saved? So he goes on to say,

*Job 18:4   VI. 6. *Rocks will be transported from their place.** The heretics' call rocks those people whom they esteem as outstanding among human beings by their sublime perceptions, whom they positively boast about as their teachers. So when Holy Church strives to gather any headstrong preachers inside the bosom of correct faith, what else does she do but transport rocks out of their accustomed place, in order that those who hold the true doctrine may humbly lie down within her, those who previously stood rigidly in their headstrong attitude? But the heretics absolutely oppose such a proceeding, and they resist the transportation of rocks from their accustomed place at her word, because they obviously deny that those who taught false doctrines with a proud heart when they were among them could now come to her humbly and acknowledge what is true.

7. When the heretics notice that some of those who belong to Holy Church are troubled by poverty or other trials, they soon lift themselves up as proud judges, and whatever adversity they consider to have overtaken the faithful, they impute that misfortune to their sins, unaware as they are that the condition of people's present life does not in any sense prove that their actions have been blameworthy. In fact good things often happen to bad people and bad to good, because the true good is kept for good people in eternity for their reward, and true evil for bad people for their eternal recompense. Bildad accordingly typically represents the heretics who pride themselves because of their prosperity in the present life; he undoubtedly boasts about blessed Job's trials; he speaks as it were with the voice of the heretics and derides the insults of the just while eloquently holding forth against the practitioners of impiety. Yet he does not know how wrong he is to say such things against the just man, as he continues speaking:

VII. 8. *Will not the light of the dishonest man go out, or the flame of his fire stop burning bright?* * If he   *Job 18:5

declares these words as a description of the present life he is deceived, both because the light of prosperity is often discerned in the house of the dishonest and because the darkness of obscurity and poverty often covers the honest man. If, however, his speech is intended to show what dishonest people suffer at the end, he is right to say, *Will not the light of the dishonest man go out, or the flame of his fire stop burning bright?* But even if it could be rightly said about the dishonest man, it should not have been said about the holy man, who is subject to trials. But we are considering the muscular strength of his opinions, so let us measure how forcefully he casts his dart and stop looking at the one at whom he aims his cast, knowing for certain that he strikes a rock with ineffectual thrusts. So let him say, *Will not the light of the dishonest man go out?* because dishonest men have their light too, which is obviously the prosperity of the present life. But the light of the dishonest man will go out, because the prosperity of this passing life, along with that life itself, will come to an end. So he astutely adds, *or the flame of his fire stop burning bright?*

9. All dishonest people, you see, have their own flame of fire, which they enkindle in their heart with the ardor of worldly desires when they burn sometimes with these passions and sometimes with those, and they further inflame their thoughts with the various enticements of the world. If fire has no flame, however, it by no means shines with a spreading light. The flame of fire is therefore its beauty or external power that proceeds from its internal heat, because what people anxiously desire to obtain in this world, they often gain possession of as the finishing touch of their own perdition. So whether they gain supreme power or an increase of wealth, it is with external honors, as it were, that they shine. But the flame of their fire will not burn bright

when on the day of their departure all external beauty is taken away, and with only their internal heat they will be burnt up. Accordingly the flame is taken away from the fire when external glory is separated from internal heat. The just have their flame of fire too, but it is undoubtedly a flame that burns brightly, obviously because their desires shine out in good works. The flame of the wicked ones, however, certainly does not shine, because their desires are evil, and they are drawn away into darkness. So Bildad proceeds,

VIII. 10. *The light will go out in his tent.** If we should often take darkness to mean distress, we should similarly also take light to mean joy. So the light in his tent goes out because he lives in a bad conscience, where the joy born of worldly goods fails him. So Bildad is right to add, *The lamp which hangs over him will be extinguished.** If I may speak of the customary practice, the light of a lamp is placed in a clay vessel. The light in the vessel is then joy in the flesh. The lamp that hangs over him is put out because when retribution for their crimes catches up with the wicked, self-indulgent joy in their mind is put to flight. Concerning this lamp Bildad does not say (and rightly so) that it is with him, but rather that it hangs over him, because worldly joy takes possession of the mind of the wicked person and so engrosses him in pleasure that it is above him and not with him.

*Job 18:6

*Job 18:6

As for the just, even when they are prosperous in the present life, they know how to trample that prosperity underfoot, so that whatever goods cheer them, they may transcend them with the counsel of dignity and go beyond them under the guidance of virtue. Accordingly the lamp of the wicked, which hangs over them, will be extinguished, because their joy quickly fails them, joy that possesses them fully in this life. Joy now wrongly inflates them with pleasure, but the penalty afterward confines them in punishment. So Bildad again adds,

*Job 18:7   IX. 11. *The footsteps of his vigor will shrink.** Now it is as if the footsteps of his vigor changed as often as he did violence with his physical prowess. But the footsteps of his vigor will shrink, because the energy of his malice, which he now displays in his pleasures, the penalty later confines. The next verse:

*Job 18:7   X. 12. *His own plan will cast him down headlong.** All evil people now have a plan to strive after present goods, to despair of what is eternal, to do what is unjust, and to deride justice. But when the Judge of both the just and the unjust comes, all impious people will be cast headlong by their own plan, because they chose to think perverse thoughts, so they will be overwhelmed by the darkness of eternal punishment. Those whom worldly honor exalts here, endless punishment there beats down. Those who have enjoyed their pleasures here will be tortured there with uninterrupted vengeance. It often happens too, that the very prosperity of this world that impious people so longingly desire binds their course in such a way that even should they want to return to the practice of good works, they are unable, because those who are afraid of giving offense to the lovers of this world cannot do what is right. So it happens that through the honor that the impious strive for through sin, their sins abound still more, and this is what Bildad gives expression to by means of the following words:

*Job 18:8   XI. 13. *He has put his own feet in the net, and he walks in its meshes.** Those who put their feet in the net do not get out when they want to; so also those who cast themselves into sin do not come up again as soon as they want to. Those who walk in the meshes of the net get their steps entangled as they walk, and when they try to free themselves for walking they are instead hindered from walking. It often happens, you see, that the people who are prevailed on by the delights of this world and stretch out their hand for glory and honor succeed in attaining their desire and rejoice in having attained what they sought. We of course want the worldly goods we do not have, whereas we grow tired of those we do have; in this way, people learn how vile those things are for which they longed by seizing them.

So when they recover their judgment, they look around to see how they can without blame get rid of what they know they acquired with blame, but that very dignity that has entangled them holds them, and they cannot rid themselves of it without more blame, as they have not reached it without blame. Accordingly they have put their feet in the net, and they walk in its meshes, because when they try to free themselves, then they really know how strong are the bonds by which they are held. Nor do we really know that we are tied until we try to get out and we try to lift up our feet, as it were. So he elucidates this very restraint by adding, *The sole of his foot will be held in the snare.*[*] His end obviously will be tied in sin. Since when the enemy of the human race ties up anyone's life in guilt he anxiously pants for his death, Bildad is right to add,

XII. 14. *Thirst blazes up against him.*[*] Our ancient enemy unquestionably ensnares the sinner's life in sin, because he thirsts for the drink of his death. It could, however, also be understood differently. When the perverse mind notices that it has fallen into sin, it tries in a kind of surface level of thought to evade the snares of sin, but it fears neither alarm nor human reproach, so it chooses eternal death rather than suffer any adversity in time. So it abandons itself completely to vice, to which it is already bound by one sin. Its life is therefore enmeshed in guilt to its very end, and its foot is held

*Job 18:9

*Job 18:9

fast in the snare. Because sinners, inasmuch as they consider themselves held fast by evil, despair of their return therefrom, in that desperation they burn all the more fiercely for the satisfaction of their worldly desires, and so their mind seethes with desires. The soul already entangled in former sins is enticed to commit even greater ones.

That is why Bildad adds, *Thirst blazes up against him.* In his mind indeed thirst blazes up against him, because evildoing is a habit with him, and he is violently inflamed to drink up more of it. Surely the thirst of the impious person is covetousness for the goods of this world. Our Redeemer, you know, cured the man afflicted with dropsy in front of the Pharisee's house,* and as he was haranguing them about covetousness, we are told, *The greedy Pharisees heard all this, and they scoffed at him.** What does it mean that the man with dropsy was cured in front of the Pharisee's house, unless it is this: the sickness of one man's body expresses the sickness of another man's heart? As for the man with dropsy, the more he drinks, the more he thirsts, because any man who is covetous increases his thirst by drinking, because as soon as he gets what he wants, he eagerly desires to grasp at more. He who in obtaining goes after more has a thirst that increases from drinking. The next verse:

XIII. 15. *His trap is hidden in the ground, and his snare is on the path.** A trap is hidden in the ground when guilt is hidden underneath worldly advantages. The enemy in disguise unquestionably shows the human mind how desirable earthly profit is, and there he hides the trap of sin; in order that he might capture the soul, he lets people see indeed all they can desire, and yet they certainly do not see the trap of sin in which they place

*see Luke 14:1-4

*Luke 16:14

*Job 18:10

their foot. The snare gets its name from the deceiver.[1] The snare is then placed upon the path by the ancient enemy, when in an action in this world that the mind desires the snare of sin is prepared, a snare that obviously would not easily deceive if it could be seen. The snare is certainly put down in such a way that, while the bait appears, the snare itself is never seen by the passerby.

Guilty profit and unlawful prosperity in this world, you see, are just like the bait in a trap. Accordingly, when covetous people desire gain, it is as though the foot of their mind touches an unseen snare. Accordingly guilty honor, or guilty riches, or guilty safety, or even guilty worldly life are often offered to the soul, and they appear to the weak mind like bait, but it does not see the snare. It sees and desires only the bait, through which it is trapped and made a captive of unseen guilt.

There are certain mannerisms, you see, that are related to certain vices. Harsh conduct, for example, is usually connected with cruelty or pride. Flattering behavior, or behavior that is more pleasant than is seemly, is sometimes connected with lust and dissipation. Consequently the enemy of the human race considers the behavior of all persons and what vice they are in position for, and he faces them all with those vices to which he knows their minds are most apt to incline, so that he may propose to those of agreeable or pleasant disposition usually lust, but sometimes vainglory, but to harsh minds anger, pride, or cruelty. There he places the snare where he perceives the mind's path to lie, because

---

[1] There is a wordplay in the Latin that is impossible to convey in English. The word for snare is *decipula*, possibly from the root of the verb *decipio, decipere*, which means "to deceive"; the snare does indeed deceive.

there he inserts the danger of deception where he finds
the road of kindred thought. Since perverse individuals are afraid to suffer themselves anything that they
do to others, and they figure that the traps they lay for
everybody they can are equally laid for them by those
others, Bildad rightly adds,

*Job 18:11   XIV. 16. *Dread will frighten him on every side.*
He supposes that everybody is against him to the same
extent that he tries to be against everybody. How this
dread reveals itself in his actions is implied in his next
*Job 18:11   words: *It will trip up his feet.* If his feet are tripped up,
he cannot of course walk freely. As long as his feet are
impeded, he cannot go anywhere. So perverse desires
lead to worse actions, but worse actions confine the
person in fear, and this fear obviously impedes his feet,
keeping them from moving on to a good action. It often
happens moreover that people are afraid to be good,
lest they themselves should suffer from perverse people
what they remember having done to good people. As
long as they are afraid to suffer what they have done,
dread and suspicion are on every side, and it is as if
they had their feet impeded, as they are entangled in
fear. They succeed in doing nothing with hands free, because in any good work they lose ground wherever they
exceed the evil that they had desired. The next verse:

XV. 17. *Let his strength be diminished by famine,*
*Job 18:12   *and may hunger invade his ribs.* It is the habit of Holy
Scripture, it seems, to pray for the future that it foresees,
obviously not with the intention of cursing, but of fore-
telling. Because every person, you see, is a composite
of soul and body, each one is a mixture of weakness
and strength. From that part where the rational spirit is
ensconced, a person is not incongruously called strong,
and from that part wherein one is flesh, one is weak.
Our strength is our rational soul, which has the power

of reason to resist the vices that fight against us. That is why blessed Job said earlier, *You have strengthened him a little, in order that he might cross over into eternity.*[*] From our rational soul we indeed have the gift of living in eternity. The strength of this wicked man is therefore diminished by famine, because his soul is not refreshed by any internal food. The prophet spoke of this very famine when he said, *I will send famine on earth, not a famine of bread or a dearth of water, but a famine of hearing God's word.*[*]

*Job 14:20

*Amos 8:11

18. Bildad is right to add, *May hunger invade his ribs.* As you know, the ribs encircle the entrails, in order that their solidity may protect what lies within. Anyone's ribs are his soul's senses, which protect his hidden thoughts. Hunger then invades the ribs when all spiritual food has been taken away, the mind's senses fail, and they cannot govern or protect the thoughts. Hunger invades the wicked person's ribs, because internal famine diminishes his mind's senses, so that they can by no means govern his thoughts. As long as the mind's senses remain dull, the thoughts escape to the outside, and with the ribs weakened, as it were, the entrails, which could have remained healthy while hidden in secret, are spilled out. So it happens that with the thoughts scattered outside, the deceived soul longs for the appearance of external honors and loves nothing except what looks beautiful outside, against which deception he again adds correctly,

XVI. 19. *Let it devour the beauty of his skin, and let firstborn death consume his arms.*[*] The beauty of the skin is worldly honor, which is longed for externally and whose appearance, as it were, takes its place in the skin. By the word for arms, however, is not unsuitably expressed external works, because the body performs these works with the arms. What else is death but sin,

*Job 18:13

which kills the soul as far as its interior life is concerned? That is why it is written, *Blessed and holy is he who takes part in the first resurrection.* The one will rise with joy later on in his flesh who while still in this life rose from the death of the soul. If accordingly death is sin, firstborn death is not unsuitably understood as pride, since it is written, *Pride is the beginning of all sin.* So firstborn death devours the beauty of his skin and his arms, because pride trips up the wicked man's boasting or his actions.

He could, of course, even in this life be famous without guilt, if he had never been proud. He could be commended by the Judgment of his Creator for some of his works, unless pride tripped him up in the Creator's eyes on account of these very works. Actually we often see rich people who could have had money and fame without guilt, if they had wanted to have them with humility. Instead they are proud of their property, they become pompous with fame, they scorn others, and they place all the confidence of their life in that very abundance of possessions. That is why a certain rich man said, *Soul, you have many possessions stored up for many years. Take it easy. Eat, drink, and enjoy yourself.* When the heavenly Judge looks at these thoughts of theirs, he tears them away because of this very confidence. So here also Bildad correctly adds,

XVII. 20. *Let his confidence be ripped away from his tent, and let death trample upon him like a king.* By the word *death* in this passage is meant the enemy of the human race himself, who brought death upon us. Through his attendant, as it were, is expressed what John is told, *His name is death.* This very death tramples upon the impious man like a king on the very day of his death, because the one the enemy deceived at first with enticing persuasion, he seizes violently at the

*Rev 20:6

*Sir 10:15
LXX

*Luke 12:19

*Job 18:14

*Rev 6:8

end and drags away to punishment; the more forcefully
he bound him to evil actions, the more harshly he now
presses him down to the earth. Here also he tramples
upon the mind of the reprobate while he possesses it, because as often as he urged pleasures upon it, just as often
he put the feet of his tyrannical domination upon it.

21. If, on the other hand, we should understand by
the word *death* not the devil himself but sin, for which
reprobates are carried away to death, such death is certainly like a king in trampling upon the mind when it
takes possession of that unresisting mind. It is impossible, you see, for a person in this life to be without
temptation to sin, but it is one thing to resist temptation
to sin and something else to serve it as a master. Any
wicked person, however, because he cannot resist the
persuasion of sin, has no fear of being subject to its
mastery, so it is rightly said of him, *Let death trample
upon him like a king*.

The apostle undoubtedly banished the kingdom of
this death from the hearts of his disciples when he said,
Do not let sin rule in your mortal bodies. He did not say,   *Rom 6:12
"Do not let it be," but "Do not let it rule." It is impossible, you see, for there to be no sin, but it is possible for
sin not to rule over the hearts of good people. So when
any guilt strikes the heart of a wicked person, it finds
no resistance in him and brings him under its dominion.
Accordingly it is well said, *Let his confidence be ripped
away from his tent, and let ruin trample upon him like a
king*. His confidence is ripped away from the earth when
any crooked person who had prepared for himself many
possessions in this life according to his own wishes is cut
off by a sudden death. *Let death trample upon him like a
king*, either because he is smothered by vices in this life
or because at the moment of death he is torn away into
punishment and thus given over to the power of demons.

Such is the order of things in the minds of reprobate sinners, and on that account, even when there is no occasion for the committing of sin, thoughts and desires of so doing are not absent from their hearts by any means. Since they always follow the devil in their actions, they are very much his slaves in their thoughts. Consequently sin is first in the thought and afterward in action. That is why the daughter of Babylon is told, *Get down and sit in the dust, virgin daughter of Babylon; sit on the earth.*[*] All dust is earth, you see, but not all earth is dust. So what should we understand by dust but thoughts that keep flying around insolently and quietly in the mind, blinding its eyes? What is meant by earth but earthly actions? Since the minds of reprobate sinners are first thrown down to think depraved thoughts and later to do them, the daughter of Babylon, who lowered herself from the discernment of internal rectitude, is rightly told in a stunning sentence to sit first in the dust and then on the earth, because if she had not lowered herself in thought, she would not have been stuck in evil actions. The next verse:

*Isa 47:1

XVIII. 22. *Let the companions of him who is not dwell in his tent.*[*] In other words, let the apostate angels converse through their bad thoughts in the mind of him who is not, that companion of theirs who is not, precisely because he broke away from the sovereign Essence. Every day his failing increases, and he progresses further in nonbeing once he fell away from him who truly is, since he lost well-being, even if he did not lose his essential nature. Yet again Bildad expresses the same thoughts of the wicked man still more precisely when he adds,

*Job 18:15

XIX. 23. *Let sulphur be sprinkled in his tent.*[*] What else is sulphur but a fostering of fire? It coaxes a flame in such a way that it produces a most foul stench. Accord-

*Job 18:15

ingly what do we understand by sulphur, unless it be a sin of the flesh? The latter fills the mind with impure thoughts that resemble foul odors to such an extent that they ignite eternal fires. While the cloud of its rotten smell is growing in the mind of the reprobate, it is, as it were, feeding the flames that will later consume it. Actually sacred history itself testifies that we should understand the foul smell of the flesh by the word *sulphur*, since it reports that the Lord rained down fire and sulphur against Sodom. When he had decided, you see, to punish Sodom's sins of the flesh, he distinguished the stain of that sin by the very quality of its punishment. Sulphur indeed has the bad odor that belongs to the heat of fire. Accordingly, since they burned with perverse desires from the bad smell of the flesh, it was fitting that they should perish from the twin punishments of fire and sulphur, inasmuch as they learned from a just punishment what they had done out of unjust desire. This sulphur is therefore sprinkled in the tent of the wicked man whenever the perverse pleasure of the flesh dominates his mind, and since depraved thoughts endlessly possess his mind and forbid him to bear the fruit of good works, Bildad rightly adds,

XX. 24. *Let his roots dry up below, and let his harvest above be ruined.** What else is meant by the word *roots*, which are hidden from sight and bear grain openly, but thoughts, which while unseen in the heart produce visible works? So the word *harvest* signifies the open working that the hidden root obviously produces. Concerning any wicked person, thoughts first dry up, and later good actions fail. So Bildad is right to say, *Let his roots dry up below, and let his harvest above be ruined.*

When any depraved people, you see, place their thoughts in the meanest objects and disregard the desire of the joy of eternal freshness, what else do they do but let

*Job 18:16

their roots dry up below? Their harvest above is ruined, because all their works are reckoned as nothing by the sovereign Judge, even if they should seem good in human eyes. The roots therefore are below and the harvest above, because here at first we engage our good thoughts, so that we may one day deserve to receive the fruit of good works in the eternal retribution. As for all evil people, on the other hand, who abandon good thoughts and involve themselves in those things that are external, their roots are dried up below. The harvest above, however, is ruined, because the one who remains barren here below is called to no reward after this life is over. The next verse:

XXI. 25. *Let his memory pass away from the earth, and let not his name be honored in the streets.** We ought to notice here that Bildad the Shuhite speaks about any and every wicked man in such a way that his words may be secretly applied to the head of all the wicked people. The head of the wicked is unquestionably the devil. He himself, having in the last days entered into that vessel of perdition, will be called *Antichrist.* He will try to publicize his own name far and wide, and everyone today imitates him when he tries to extend the memory of his own worldly renown with honor and praise, and when he basks in a transitory reputation. These words should accordingly be understood with regard to any and every wicked person in such a way that they could also be related to that head of the wicked himself in a special way.

Let him say then, *Let his memory pass away from the earth, and let not his name be honored in the streets. Streets* is a Greek word that has special reference to breadth.[2] The Antichrist will try to establish his own

*Job 18:17

---

[2] The Greek word is πλατυσ, an adjective that means "broad." *Platea* is the Latin word, directly transliterated from the Greek, meaning "street."

memory on earth when he wishes to retain temporal glory, if possible, forever. His joy is for his name to be honored in the streets when he extends his evildoing far and wide. Since, however, his wickedness is not allowed to prevail for very long, let him say, *Let his memory pass away from the earth, and let not his name be honored in the streets.* In other words, let him quickly lose his worldly power and fame, and let all merrymaking for his name cease, which would have spread far and wide in the brief prosperity of the present time. The next verse:

XXII. 26. *God will drive him from light into darkness.** He is led from light into darkness, the one who for being honored in the present life is condemned to eternal punishment. So Bildad clarifies his meaning: *And transfer him out of the world.** Out of the world is he transferred at the appearance of the sovereign Judge, when he is taken from this world where he maliciously boasted. He will be condemned at the arrival of the end of the world with all his cronies, so he again rightly adds, *His seed will not be found, nor will he have descendants among his people, nor will there be any remnants in his regions.** It is surely written, *The Lord Jesus will slay him with the breath of his mouth and destroy him by the brightness of his coming.**

Since consequently his wickedness is terminated along with the present state of the world, there will be nothing left of his posterity in his people, because he himself along with his people will be driven away to punishment, and all the wicked who were born of his perverse persuasion in evil actions will be struck down by eternal ruin together with their head at the brightness of the Lord's coming. None of his posterity will be left in the world, because the strict Judge will put an end to his iniquity along with the very end of the world. That

*Job 18:18

*Job 18:18

*Job 18:19

*2 Thess 2:8

all this should be directly understood of the Antichrist
we are taught by the following verse:

XXIII. 27. *The last of men will be astounded at*
*Job 18:20 *his days, and shudders will invade the first of them.**
So violent will be the evil unleashed against the just at
that time that a not meager trembling will seize even
the hearts of the elect. So it is written, *So that even the*
*Matt 24:24 *elect, if it were possible, might be led into error.** These
words were not spoken, be it noted, because the elect
were going to fall, but because they were going to be
disturbed by dreadful alarm. We are informed here that
both the latest elect and the first will be maintaining the
conflict for righteousness against the Antichrist at that
time, because both those elect who are found at the end
of the world will have to die a bodily death and those
as well who have come forth from the first ages of the
world. Enoch, remember, and Elijah will be recalled to
the public, and they will be exposed to his fierce cruelty
and again suffer in their mortal flesh.

The last of humans are astounded at his strength
flexed with such enormous energy, and the first of them
are afraid. Because even if he is lifted up with the boast
of pride and therefore they scorn his worldly power, yet
because they are themselves still clothed with mortal
flesh, in which they can suffer for a time that punishment that they bravely bear, they nevertheless tremble
with fear. The upshot is that in them at one and the same
time there is constancy due to their inner strength and
also fear due to the flesh, because even though they
are among the elect, of such a kind that they cannot be
overcome by torture, yet because they are human they
also fear the torture that they overcome.

Let him say then, *The last of men will be astounded
at his days, and shudders will invade the first of them.*
He is obviously going to demonstrate such enormous

signs, you see, at that time, and he will perform cruel and harsh deeds of such a kind that he will cause astonishment in those whom he finds at the end of the world, and he will strike the forefathers who have been kept for his capture with the pain of bodily death. So since Bildad has spoken at length about all the wicked people or about the very head of the wicked himself, he follows up now with a general definition and adds,

XXIV. 28. *These then are the tents of the wicked, and this the place of him who does not know God.** He had already said earlier, *God will drive him from light into darkness, and transfer him out of the world.** After having added his misfortunes, he continues, *These then are the tents of the wicked and this the place of him who does not know God.* Obviously he is aiming at the fact that those who now commend themselves on not knowing God will then reach their own tents, when their own wickedness drowns them in punishment, and those who while boasting here of the false light of justice held a place not their own will someday find in darkness their own place. Perverse people, you see, do everything by pretense, and they try to usurp a place that does not belong to them, that is, the glorious name of the just. They reach their own place, however, when as the just desert of their wickedness they are tortured in eternal fire.

Here below, you see, in everything that they do, they fulfill their desire of receiving praise, imagining good works for themselves and enlarging the cavity of their minds for avarice. Accordingly, let the wicked go here and now and build their own houses, let them strut in all their pomp, let them spread their glorious name and multiply their estates, let them enjoy their abundant wealth. When, however, they reach eternal punishment, they will straightway recognize those as the tents of the wicked and this as the place of the one who does not

*Job 18:21

*Job 18:18

know God. All this Bildad had said rightly, but he did not know the one to whom he was speaking. The heart of the just man is gravely wounded when an opinion based on an unjust evaluation is stated against him. That is why blessed Job forthwith answers and says,

XXV. 29. *How long will you keep wounding my soul* *Job 19:2 *and wearying me with your words?* * The speeches of the holy man, as I have often said already, are sometimes to be taken as spoken in his own name, sometimes as spoken by the Head, and sometimes in his role as type of the universal church. The souls of the just are intensely wounded, you see, when they hurl severe judgments against good people, who do not know how to live well, and in their words they claim for themselves that justice that in practice they assault. So blessed Job himself answers his friends, who, as we have often said already, play the role of heretics: *How long will you keep wounding my soul and wearying me with your words?* Good people get tired of the words of the wicked when their words pile up against them, while they relax in their perverse faith or depraved behavior. The next verse:

*Job 19:3   XXVI. 30. *Ten times already you have upset me.* * We have counted the number of speeches given by Job's friends, and at this point we find that they have spoken five times. Since, however, he has listened to their insults five times, to which he has himself responded five times, he declares that he has been upset ten times, because his strife has been grievously borne, during which he has been reproached in vain, and he has been upset, because they would not listen to his words of teaching. So he was silent while listening, and when he spoke he was not listened to; consequently his strife was grievous, because he listened patiently and spoke to them without effect, so that he felt pain in his heart. That is why he said earlier, *What shall I* *do? If I speak, my pain will not stop. If I keep silence, it will not go away.** If, however, we refer these words to the type of Holy Church that Job is, it is clear that her great joy is to keep the Ten Commandments. Perverse people, however, upset her ten times, because through all their sins and by their depraved behavior they violate the Ten Commandments, and they upset good people as often as they resist God's word in their actions. The next verse: *Job 16:7

XXVII. 31. *You are not ashamed of oppressing me.** There are those whom sudden malice instigates to commit unjust acts but whom human respect causes to draw back. It often happens too that because they are externally ashamed, they return to their internal selves and assume an internal judgment seat against themselves, because if they are afraid to do evil because of a person, how much more because of God who sees all should they avoid the desire of evildoing? In such an event it happens that they correct greater evil through lesser good, namely, internal sin through external shame. There are others again who, after they have scorned God in their minds, spurn human judgment still more; all the evil their little heart desires they go ahead boldly and do without a trace of shame. Their hidden malice instigates them to do evil, and no obvious shame holds them back, just as it is said about some evil judge, *He neither feared God nor respected man.** That is also why we are told of certain sinners with shameless faces, *They proclaimed their sin like Sodom.** Accordingly the adversaries of Holy Church are frequently so bold that neither the fear of God nor shame before people holds them back from evildoing. So blessed Job rightly says of them, *You are not ashamed of oppressing me*, because even if it is depravity to wish what is evil, it is still worse not to be ashamed of wanting evil. The next verse: *Job 19:3

*Luke 18:2

*Isa 3:9

XXVIII. 32. *Certainly, even if I knew it not, my igno-*
Job 19:4   rance would be mine.* It is a peculiarity of the heretics
that the vain haughtiness of their knowledge gives them
cause for pride, that they often deride the simplicity of
those who believe rightly, and that they count as nothing
the meritorious life of humble people. Holy Church, on
the other hand, in all that she wisely discerns, humbly
See 1 Cor 8:1 bows her head lest knowledge should puff up, lest she
should become proud because of the investigation of
hidden things, lest she should presume to search out
See Sir 3:22   anything that is beyond her powers. She makes it a point
to know nothing about those things that she is unable to
investigate, and this strategy is better for her than boldly
to define those things that she does not understand. It is
written, of course, *Just as it is unwise for anyone to eat*
too much honey, he who investigates grandeur is over-
Prov 25:27   whelmed by its glory.* If more honey is consumed, you
see, than is expedient, the sweetness that delights the
mouth ruins the life of the one who consumes it.

The investigation of grandeur is sweet too, but the
one who wants to study it more than human knowledge
allows is overwhelmed by the bright glory of majesty.
Just like honey that is consumed excessively, the inves-
tigator's understanding fails and is ruined. That which is
for us is said to be with us; on the other hand, that which
is against us is said to be not with us. Accordingly, since
the heretic's knowledge puffs up his heart but the awareness of their ignorance humbles the faithful, let blessed
Job say with his own voice, and let him also say with
the confession of the entire church, *Certainly, even if I*
knew it not, my ignorance would be mine. It is as if the
heretics were told to their face, "All your knowledge
is not with you, because it is against you, as long as it
lifts you up with stupid pride. My ignorance, however,
is with me, because it is for me, as long as I do not dare

investigate anything about God with pride but do keep myself humbly in the truth." Because, then, the heretics seek to know these very things and seize on them for the sole purpose of pride, so that they may appear learned against the humble faithful, he is right to add, XXIX. 33. *You, however, are provoked against me.** *Job 19:5 Perhaps it is easier to explain these words if we show how they apply to blessed Job's friends in a special way. It is indeed they who find the just man struck down, and they should have looked inside themselves and by no means have disparaged him with angry words. They should instead have wept for themselves, because if he who had served so well had been struck down in such a way, what punishing stroke did they deserve who had not been good servants? Of them he rightly says, *You, however, are provoked against me.* It is as if he told them to their face, "You ought to have been provoked against yourselves because of my discomfiture." This is the correct procedure of provocation: namely, that we are first provoked against ourselves, and afterward against bad people.

The one who is provoked against good people is swollen by pride. We are provoked against ourselves when we admit our own evil deeds and apply to ourselves the strict retribution of repentance; we are provoked when we by no means overlook our sins and do not favor ourselves with any flattering thoughts. If we first censure ourselves strictly for our own evil deeds, then we can justly be provoked also against someone else's evil deeds for that person's profit, so that those things we punish ourselves for we may likewise overcome in others by exposing them.

34. This kind of provocation, however, the wicked do not know; instead they acquit themselves and attack others. They favor themselves in their own consciousness

with the soft caresses of flattery, and they are provoked against the lives of good people with stern harshness. That is why blessed Job's friends, who are waxing proud about his trials, are now rightly told, *You, however, are provoked against me*. In other words, they are abandoning their own self-accusation and angrily charging Job in their severe judgment. Those who do not judge themselves first, you see, do not know how to judge another person correctly. Even if they know by hearsay, perhaps, how to make a correct judgment, nevertheless they cannot judge correctly what another person deserves when the awareness of their own innocence offers no standard of judgment.

That is why when some people set an ambush for our Lord and led an adulterous woman to him, they were told, *Let him who is without sin among you be the first to stone her.** Obviously they had gone forth to punish somebody else's sins and forgotten their own. They were then recalled to their own inner self-awareness, so that they might first amend their own sins and then reprove those of other people. That is why, when the tribe of Benjamin had fallen into a sin of the flesh, the whole people of Israel gathered together and wanted to avenge the crime, but Israel's army was itself defeated in battle once and again. After God was consulted about whether they should have gone to avenge the crime, he ordered that it be done. So the people of Israel proceeded according to the command of the divine voice, but they again lost the battle twice. Then finally they defeated the sinful tribe so completely that they almost died out.*

How is it that Israel is aroused to the point of avenging the crime yet is at first defeated, unless those through whom the sins of others are punished must first be purified themselves so that when those who hasten to correct the vices of others are already pure they may come for vengeance? Accordingly it is necessary that when God's

*John 8:7

*see Judg
19–20

scrutiny ceases to take revenge on us, our own internal conscience should reprove us; it should rise up against us and urge us to tears of repentance. Nor should she be arrogant against good people and meek toward herself, but stern against herself and humble toward all good people. Consequently proud accusers are here rightly told, *You, however, are provoked against me, and you charge me with my own acts of disgrace.* All the arrogant people, you see, consider temporal misfortune serious disgrace, and they believe anyone to be hateful to God to the exact degree that they see him brought low through the blows of misfortune. They look for nothing either in his behavior or in his actions, but whomever they see struck down in this life they suppose to be already condemned by God's judgment. So blessed Job gives utterance now to the following wise words:

XXX. 35. *You charge me with my own acts of disgrace.* It is because they had known he was a just man before his misfortunes that they now judge him unjust because of his very misfortunes. The heretics often make the same judgment with regard to certain members of the church whom they see subject to misfortunes; it is written of God, they say, that *He beats every son he receives.* They suppose that the troubles endured by the faithful have no other cause but sin, so they think they are just themselves, because they have been abandoned in their own perverse attitude, which has stiffened without blows. The next verse:

XXXI. 36. *At least will you understand now that it is not with impartial justice that God has afflicted me?* O how harsh is the sound of the just person's voice when he is troubled by misfortune! Yet it is not pride but sorrow that is expressed. Still, he is not a just person if he abandons justice in sorrow. The heart of blessed Job, however, was meek, and even when his voice was harsh,

*Job 19:5

*Heb 12:6

*Job 19:6

he did not sin. If we say he did sin while speaking in this way, we assume the fulfillment of the devil's words when he promised, *Touch his flesh and bones, and then* watch *him curse you to your face.*

*Job 2:5

A serious question arises here: did Job not sin when he said, *At least will you understand now that it is not with impartial justice that God has afflicted me?* If we say Job is right, then we say that God has done what is unjust, something that is unspeakable. If, on the other hand, he did sin, the devil has proven about him what he promised. Accordingly we must construe the matter as follows: God acted rightly toward blessed Job, and blessed Job, on the other hand, did not lie when he said he was struck by God unjustly; consequently the ancient enemy lied when he predicted Job would be caught in a sin.

Sometimes, therefore, the words of good people are thought to be perverse, because their internal understanding is not taken into account. Blessed Job had paid attention to his own life, and he weighed the trials he suffered, and he saw as unjust that he should undergo such trials in return for such a life. So when he says he was not dealt with out of impartial justice, he has spoken openly what the Lord had said about his adversary in secret, namely, *You incited me against him, to cause him*

*Job 2:3

affliction for no reason at all. What God says, namely, that he afflicted blessed Job for no reason at all, blessed Job now declares, namely, that he was not afflicted by God with impartial justice. How then has he sinned, when he departed in nothing from the judgment of his Creator?

37. Perhaps, however, someone could say that we are praising ourselves on our own account, just as the Judge had praised us in secret, and we cannot do so without sin. There is no doubt that the one whom the

just Judge praises is praiseworthy. If, however, that one praised himself, his righteousness is no longer held to be praiseworthy. This is obviously rightly said if what the just Judge declared with impartial judgment, the one who is being discussed should afterward presume to say of himself out of a proud heart. After all, if his thinking remains humble while he also inquires after the reason for the pain, he said rightly and truly of himself that he no more forsook justice than he was at variance with truth.

38. So also the apostle Paul reported many things about himself that showed his courage, in order that his disciples might be edified, but in telling them about these exploits he did nothing wrong, because he did not retreat from the course of truth, or from sure testimony, or from a humble heart. Blessed Job accordingly knows his own life to be righteous, so he can say that his affliction is not caused by just judgment. In this statement he does not sin, and he does not disagree with the Creator, since he whom God struck down in vain also declares himself afflicted by no just judgment. Yet again, however, another question arises, which I remember having answered already at the beginning of this book, namely, that if almighty God does nothing in vain, why does he say that he afflicted blessed Job in vain?

I said then that our just Creator did not heal any vices of blessed Job by all those misfortunes, but rather increased his merit. What he did, then, was just, because it increased the good man's merit. It did not seem just, however, because it was thought to punish the causes of sin. Blessed Job, however, thought his sins were wiped out because of these trials, not that his merits were increased, and on that account he calls the judgment unjust, because he focuses on his life and trials. Well, if his life and trials are weighed carefully, that was not just, as I have said, which blessed Job thought happened to him through misdirected anger. If, however, we pay attention to the Judge's mercy and consider that through the trials endured by the just man the merits of his life are heaped up, the judgment was just, or rather merciful. Accordingly Job spoke the truth when he thought of his life and trials, while God at the same time did not afflict Job out of unjust judgment but piled up merits for him using his trials.

Besides that, the devil did not deliver what he promised, because with the words that sound so harsh blessed Job did not forsake true judgment or a humble heart. Yet perhaps we understand these words of the afflicted Job less well if we do not know the decision of the Judge. When he passed sentence between the two parties, he told Job's friends, *You have not spoken the truth before* *Job 42:7 *me, like my servant Job.* Who could be such a simpleton as to allow that blessed Job had sinned in his speech, when it has been declared by the voice of the Judge himself that he spoke well? Furthermore, if we apply his words to the person of Holy Church, they will not be incongruous with her weakest members. During the days of persecution of the church those members carefully weigh both her merits and her trials, and they see the prosperity of unrighteous people on the one hand and the deaths of the righteous on the other, and they conclude that none of this is just. Yet we again hear the voice of the blessed man:

*Job 19:6   XXXII. 39. *He surrounded me with blows.* To be struck with blows is unquestionably one thing, and to be surrounded by them something else. We are struck with blows when, even though certain things pain us, we still have consolation. But when our affliction is so severe that our soul cannot recover its composure from any kind of consolation, we are no longer simply struck by blows but really surrounded by them, because no matter which way we turn we find the whip of trials. Paul was certainly surrounded by trials when he said, *There is battle outside, fear inside.** He was surrounded by blows when he said, *Perils from my people, perils from the Gentiles, perils in the city, perils in the desert,** and other dangers that he reckons up so he can prove that there was no rest for him anywhere. So when Holy Church is so completely surrounded by the blows of her trials, her weak members also are reduced to a state of faintheartedness, in such a way that they think themselves already desperate, because they seem to be slow to get a hearing. Continuing to follow the same typology, the blessed man rightly adds again,

*2 Cor 7:5

*2 Cor 11:26

XXXIII. 40. *Behold, I will cry out for the violence I have suffered, and none will listen; I will cry aloud, and none will judge.** Almighty God knows what can be profitable for us, and he pretends not to hear the voice of the sufferers so that he may increase the profit, that he may purify our lives with pain, and that peaceful tranquility that cannot be found here may be sought elsewhere. Yet some even of the faithful do not understand this way of distributing favor. It is by such persons that we are to understand these words: *Behold, I will cry out for the violence I have suffered, and none will listen; I will cry out, and none will judge.* None will judge, we are told, when he who is pretends not to judge, because there is none to judge our case against the adversary except him. Nor is this without judgment, namely, the fact that the judgment is delayed, because even while blessed Job was saying these things, both the holy man's merits and the adversary's penalty were increasing. It belongs to the Judge, therefore, to delay the awaited judgment. That judgment that God internally arranges is one thing, however, and the decision that the soul, worn out by

*Job 19:7

trials as it is, strives for externally is something else. So he again adds, weakened by blows,

XXXIV. 41. *He has blocked my path, and I can-* *Job 19:8 *not go on; my track he has darkened.** He saw his path blocked by blows of the whip when, wishing to cross over to safety, he could not evade the whip. Seeing that he was being buffeted, although he could find nothing in his life deserving blows, he saw the footpath of his heart darkened by ignorance, and he could not discern the reason for the blows. All this is not incongruously applied to the weak members of Holy Church as well, when they remember their misdeeds and are prevented from doing good works as well; having become fearful because of their own weakness, they do not presume bravely to undertake any good deed to counteract the bad. Those who remember how weak all their actions are fear to undertake anything great and good. When they often do not know if their choices are good, it is as though darkness fell on their path, and they shake with fear.

It often happens that the soul loses certitude about its own actions to such an extent that it is really ignorant as to what is virtue and what is sin. The soul then finds darkness on its path, and whatever it wants to do, it has no idea what to choose. Since, therefore, we often sin by weakness and sometimes by ignorance, the weak members of Holy Church say, *He has blocked my path, and I cannot go on.* Those however who are in the dark as to what good work they should choose add, *My track he has darkened.* To see the good we should choose and be unable to do it is the penalty of sin; the greater penalty of sin, however, is not to see the good we ought to choose. Against both of these twists we hear the psalmist's voice say, *The Lord is my light and my help; whom should I* *Ps 26:1 *fear?** Against the darkness of ignorance he is light, and

against weakness he is help. The Lord shows us when
we should desire action, and he bestows strength to do
what he has shown us. The next verse:

XXXV. 42. *He has robbed me of my dignity, and he
has taken away the crown from my head.** There is no
doubt that all this corresponds with the person of the
blessed man who finds himself afflicted. So since the
historical sense is clear, we need not explain the words literally. We should however investigate their hidden meaning. He says, *He has robbed me of my dignity.* Now every
person's dignity is justice. Just as a garment covers the
body against the cold, so justice protects us from death.
So justice is not unsuitably compared to a garment, as
the prophet says: *Let your priests put on justice.** Since in
the time of her affliction Holy Church loses in her weak
members this garment of justice that protects her in God's
sight, she can rightly say, *He has robbed me of my dignity.*

In other words, justice is taken away from the weak
ones, justice that could not be taken from them if it had
clung to their inmost heart, but since like a garment it
hung externally, it could be taken. In that case we should
ask how they could be called members of Holy Church
if they could lose justice, which they seemed to hold.
We must realize then that her weak members do often
lose justice temporarily. When they later return to repentance after recognizing their sin, they then cling more
tightly than they thought possible to that same justice
that they had lost. So he again adds, *He has taken away
the crown from my head.* Just as the head is the primary
part of the body, so in the internal person the mind is of
primary importance. The crown is the reward of victory
and is fitted from above, in order that the one who has
contended might receive the prize.

Since, however, many of those who are beset by
adversity by no means persevere in the struggle, in them

*Job 19:9

*Ps 131:9

Holy Church as it were loses a crown from her head. The crown on the head is unquestionably the reward from above in the mind. There are many others who, while they suffer adversity, neglect the thought of the reward from above, and they cannot reach the final victory. In them accordingly the crown is taken away from the head, because the heavenly spiritual reward is taken away from the thought of the mind, in order that they might still desire external tranquility and not be on the lookout for the eternal reward that they used to think about.

43. On the other hand, the head of the faithful is certainly taken to mean the priests, and not without reason, because they are the first rank of the Lord's members. That is why the prophet says the head and the tail should be cut off,* where obviously the prophet means by the words *head* and *tail* priests and reprobate prophets respectively. The crown is taken off the head, then, when even they who seemed to be preeminent in this body of the church abandon the prize of the heavenly reward. When the leaders fail, you see, the whole army that followed them is also cut down. So immediately after the loss of the officers, Job goes on to speak of the general shake-up of the church and adds,

XXXVI. 44. *He has ruined me on every side, and I am perishing; he has taken away my hope, as if I were an uprooted tree.** The church is, as it were, being pulled down on every side, and she perishes in her weak members when those members that seemed solid collapse and when the crown is taken off her head, that is, when the eternal rewards are being neglected, even by those in charge. He is right to add concerning the weak members who are falling, *He has taken away my hope, as if I were an uprooted tree.* It is the wind, of course, that knocks the tree over. Those who are terrified by threats

*see
Isa 9:14-15

*Job 19:10

to the point of giving in to injustice, what else are they but trees that suffer a blast of wind and lose their state of rectitude? It is as though they lost hope because of the wind when they give in to the threats and persuasion of depraved people and abandon the eternal reward for which they hoped. It often happens too, that people fear a penalty and abandon justice, and by a judgment of God it then happens that even as they abandon justice, they do not escape the penalty that they feared, so that those who feared their mind's destruction least also have to suffer diseases of the flesh, which they did fear. So Job again adds,

XXXVII. 45. *The wrath of God has been kindled against me, and he has regarded me as his enemy.** The illustrious preacher has certainly borne witness and taught us that God is faithful, that he will not permit us to be tempted beyond what we can bear, and that he will provide with the temptation an issue by which we can bear it.* The prophet also says in the Lord's name, *I struck you with an enemy's blow, a cruel punishment.** The one therefore who is struck in such a way that his prowess is overpowered by the blow, the Lord no longer strikes for discipline like a son, but like an enemy in anger. When, accordingly, trials surpass our power of endurance, it is very much to be feared that our sins require that the Lord should strike us, no longer like a father disciplining his son, but as the Lord when he strikes out at his enemies. Furthermore, it also happens that the evil spirits persuade the hearts of afflicted ones concerning many things, and while they endure external trials, they plant evil thoughts in their minds; so after speaking of the wrath of God, Job adds,

XXXVIII. 46. *With him came his thieves, and they made themselves a path through me.** His thieves are evil spirits whose occupation is to bring about the deaths of

*Job 19:11

*see 1 Cor 10:13
*Jer 30:14

*Job 19:12

humans. They make themselves a path in the hearts of afflicted people, and while these latter endure external hardship, they never stop injecting evil thoughts into their minds, about which Job again adds, *They encamp and encircle my tent.** They encamp and encircle our tent when they surround the mind on every side with their temptations. They urge the mind with their worst suggestions at one time to mourn over temporary losses, at another to lose hope concerning eternity, at another to rush into impatience or to hurl blasphemous words at God.

*Job 19:12

These words, as I have already said, fit blessed Job even according to the literal sense. When he brought all the evils he had suffered before his mind's eye, he did not reckon himself a son subject to correction, but rather an enemy who had been struck down. The thieves made themselves a path through him, because the evil spirits received permission to buffet him. They encamped and encircled his tent, because when his property was stolen and his children killed, they also bruised his whole body with wounds. But what is most amazing is that when he mentions thieves he adds *his*. Why is this? Obviously he wanted to emphasize that the thieves in question were God's. In this matter, if the will of the evil spirits is distinguished from their power, why they are called God's thieves is elucidated. Evil spirits unquestionably never stop sighing for ways to hurt us. Of themselves, however, they have the depraved will, but power to hurt they have not, unless God wills to permit it. Although they desire to injure us unlawfully, they cannot injure anyone unless the Lord permits it for a just cause. Since, therefore, the unjust will is in them, and the just power as well as the thieves themselves are said to be God's, their desire to inflict evil unjustly belongs to them, and it belongs to God to let them fulfill their desire for a just cause.

Now since, as I have often said already, the holy man before us in the throes of suffering sometimes speaks with his own voice, sometimes with that of the church, and sometimes with that of our Redeemer, and he often tells his own story in such a way that he may typically relate what concerns Holy Church and what concerns our Redeemer, we may put aside for the moment the concern for the story in itself, so that we may in the following paragraphs show how it refers to the life of our Redeemer. The next verse:

XXXIX. 47. *He has made my brothers distant from me, and my acquaintances have abandoned me like strangers; my relatives have left me, and those who once knew me have forgotten me.** We shall explain these words better if we bring forward the witness of John, who said, *He came to his own people, and his own did not accept him.** His brothers became distant from him, and his acquaintances went away. Him whom the Hebrews who kept the law knew how to prophesy, the same Hebrews in no sense recognized when he was present. So he is right to say, *My relatives have left me, and those who once knew me have forgotten me.* The Jews were his relatives according to the flesh; they knew him through the law's instruction, yet they as it were forgot him whom they had prophesied, since they both proclaimed that he would become incarnate by the words of the law and, after he had become incarnate, denied him with faithless words. The next verse:

XL. 48. *The tenants in my house and my handmaids treated me as a stranger.** The tenants of God's house were the priests whose supposed origin in the service of God was already held to be a duty and condition of life. Handmaids are not improbably understood to be the souls of Levites who serve before the inmost sanctuary familiarly, like the slaves of a family who serve in the

*Job 19:13-14

*John 1:11

*Job 19:15

intimate bedchamber. Let him accordingly say about the priests who serve with diligent care, let him say about the Levites, obedient ministers in the innermost room of God's house, *The tenants in my house and my handmaids treated me as a stranger.* They had, you see, long foretold the incarnation of the Lord in the words of the law, but they refused to recognize and venerate him. He reveals still more openly that he was not recognized by them in their perverse willfulness when he adds,

*Job 19:15   XLI. 49. *I was like a stranger in their eyes.** While he went unrecognized by the synagogue, our Redeemer was a stranger in his own house. That is what the prophet openly proclaims: *Why are you going to be like a settler on the earth, like a traveler who turns aside to tarry?*

*Jer 14:8   He who is not listened to as the Lord is no owner of a field, but supposedly a settler. He who as a traveler only turned aside to tarry took a few men from Judea to continue the calling of the Gentiles and went on to finish his journey. Accordingly he was a stranger in their eyes, because they only knew what they could see with their own eyes, so they could not understand that which was in the Lord, since they could not see it. As long as they scorned visible flesh, they did not reach invisible majesty. Let him then say it with reason: *I was like a stranger in their eyes.* Concerning this people he again astutely adds,

XLII. 50. *I called my servant, and he did not an-*

*Job 19:16   *swer.** What were the Jewish people but a servant who obeyed God, not with filial love but with servile fear? Against this error Paul tells us, *You have not received a spirit of servitude, that you should still live in fear, but you have received a spirit of adoption as sons, whereby*

*Rom 8:15   *we cry, "Abba, Father."** This servant, consequently, the Lord called, because having loaded him with gifts, he eagerly led him to himself as if he were lifting up his voice. But the servant did not answer, because he disdained to bring forth works that were worthy of God's gifts. God calls us, you see, when he anticipates us with gifts; we respond to his call when we serve him in a way befitting our perception of his gifts. Since therefore he anticipated the Jewish people with so many gifts, let Job say, *I called my servant.* But since that people also showed contempt for him after so many gifts, let him add, *and he did not answer.* The next verse:

XLIII. 51. *With my own mouth I entreated him.** It is as if he said openly, "I am he who before my incarnation sent him so many precepts to fulfill through the prophets; I became incarnate and came to him, and with my own mouth I entreated him." That is why Matthew, when he described how he issued his instructions on the mountain, said, *He opened his mouth and said.** He might have said outright, "Then he opened his mouth, he who had previously opened the prophets' mouths." That is why the bride also, in her desire for the Bridegroom's presence, said of him, *Let him kiss me with the kiss of his mouth.** Holy Church undoubtedly learned as many precepts from his preaching, as it were, as she received kisses from his mouth. He said well, *I entreated,* because when he was revealed in the flesh and humbly gave the commandments of life, he called the proud servant, as it were, in order that he might live. So he rightly adds,

XLIV. 52. *My wife trembled at my breath.** Who else do we take the Lord's wife to be but the synagogue, whose understanding is subjected to him in the carnal covenant of the law? The breath, however, belongs to the flesh, but the unfaithful people understood the Lord's flesh carnally, because they thought him to be a mere man. His wife trembled at his breath, because the synagogue was terrified to believe him to be God, him

*Job 19:16

*Matt 5:2

*Song 1:1

*Job 19:17

who looked to them like a man. When they heard the words of his mouth in a bodily fashion, they refused to understand the hidden divinity in him, and they did not believe him to be the Creator who looked like a creature. The carnal wife therefore trembled at the carnal breath, since she was given over to carnal understanding, and she did not recognize the mystery of his incarnation. The next verse:

*Job 19:17   XLV. 53. *I entreated the sons of my womb.** God is not confined by the form of a body, so when the members of a body, such as hands, eyes, and womb, are named, it is so that the effects of his power may be traced out by such words for bodily members. He is surely said to have eyes, because he sees all things; he is described as having hands, because he does all things; in the womb, however, is conceived the offspring that is brought forth into this life. What then should we take God's womb to be, if not his plan in which before the ages we were conceived and predestined, in order that we might be created in time and brought forth? Accordingly, God who remains before the ages entreated the sons of his womb, because he came humbly in his incarnation to call those whom he created by divine power. But because in the very flesh in which he appeared he was despised in their estimation, he adds,

*Job 19:18   XLVI. 54. *Fools also looked down on me.** With the wise falling away from the true faith, it is rightly added concerning the fools as well, that while the Scribes and Pharisees despise the Lord, the throng of people also follow the lead of their unbelief, those who, because they saw a man, scorned the preaching of the Redeemer of the world. Now by the word for fools is often meant those who are poor among the people. That is why Jeremiah says, *I said, "Perhaps it is only the poor and foolish who do not know the way of the Lord and the*

judgments of their God." * But, having left behind the
worldly wise and the rich, our Redeemer had come to
seek the poor and foolish. So now, as if to aggravate the
pain, he says, *Fools also looked down on me.* He might
as well have said outright, "They also have despised
me, those for whose healing I took up the foolishness
of this preaching."

 It is indeed written, *In God's wisdom the world did
not know God through wisdom, so it has pleased God
to save those who believe through the foolishness of our
preaching.* * The word of God is certainly wisdom, but
the foolishness of this wisdom is called the flesh of the
Word, in order that whereas none of the carnal people
could reach the wisdom of God through the prudence of
their flesh, through the foolishness of preaching—that
is, through the flesh of the Word—they might be healed.
Accordingly he says, *Fools also looked down on me.* It
is as if he said openly, "By them too I was despised, for
whose sake I was not afraid to be judged a fool." When
the people of the Jews saw the Redeemer's miracles,
they honored him because of the signs, saying, *He is the
Christ.* * When they saw him weak and lowly, they disdained to believe he was the Creator, and they said, *He
is not; rather he misleads the crowd.* * So he rightly adds,

 XLVII. 55. *When I drew back from them, they hu-
miliated me.* * It is indeed as though the Lord drew near
to the hearts of the people when he showed them miracles, and as though he again drew back when he showed
them no sign. But when the Lord drew back they slan-
dered him, and when his miracles stopped they refused
to venture faith in him. But what is strange in his having
to endure such treatment from the people, when even
those who seemed to be teachers of the law behaved
worse? They maintained by the words of the prophets
that he was to become incarnate, they saw him incarnate,

*Jer 5:4

*1 Cor 1:21

*John 7:26,
41

*John 7:12

*Job 19:18

and yet they were cut off from him by a dividing wall of faithlessness. Concerning them he has more to say:

XLVIII. 56. *My former counselors hated me, and he whom I loved the most turned away from me.* It is clear to everybody that God needs no counselors, God who indeed grants wise counsel to human counselors. About which fact it is also written, *Who has known the mind of the Lord, or who has been his counselor?* But just as when bread or clothing is given to the needy, the Lord testifies that it is he who has received it, it is the same with counsel; when any ignorant person is given correct counsel, he whose member that person is who is thus taught also receives that counsel. All we faithful ones are members of our Redeemer, and just as he is cared for in us through compassion and generosity, so he is helped in us through counsel and teaching.

*Job 19:19

*Isa 40:13;
Rom 11:34;
see 1 Cor 2:16

The scribes and doctors of the law, accordingly, who were accustomed to teach the people how to live, what else were they but counselors of our coming Redeemer? Nevertheless, when they saw the incarnate Lord, they separated many people from faith in him by their counsel, despite the fact that formerly they seemed to have taught many through the words of the prophets to believe in the mystery of his incarnation. Since, therefore, it is he whom God loves most, who draws more people to the love of God, he again adds concerning the very same group of teachers of the law and Pharisees, *He whom I loved the most turned away from me.* That very group was persuaded by unbelief to turn away from the true faith, the group that formerly served God in the labor of preaching and that God loved most; moreover, the throng of people followed them, not only in not believing in the Lord but also in persecuting him, and still further they were whipped on by ferocity to making

him suffer the passion. In that passion also the disciples'
hearts were confused. So he again adds,

XLIX. 57. *My flesh is consumed, and my bones have
clung to my skin.* By bones we mean the strength of the
body, and by flesh its weakness. Since Christ and the
church are one person, what do we mean by bones but
the Lord himself? What do we mean by flesh but the
disciples who were weakened at the time of his passion?
What do we mean by the skin that remains outside the
body's flesh but those holy women who served the Lord
in external ministries by looking after the needs of the
body? When his disciples, you see, though not yet steadfast, preached the true faith to the people, the flesh clung
to the bones. When the holy women prepared externally
whatever was necessary, like the skin they remained on
the body externally. When, however, the time had come
for the crucifixion, grave fear came upon the disciples
because of the persecution of the Jews, and they all fled,
but the women remained steadfast.

*Job 19:20

Accordingly, it is as though the flesh were consumed, and the Lord's bones clung to his skin, since
strength at the time of his passion, when the disciples
fled, came to the women who were close to him. Peter
certainly did remain steadfast for a while, but afterward in his terror he denied him. John also remained
steadfast, and to him in the very hour of the cross it was
said, *Here is your mother.* Yet even he could not stay
long, since it is also written of him, *A certain young man
followed him, wearing a muslin sheet over his naked
body, and they grabbed him, but he left the sheet in
their hands and ran away from them naked.* Even if
afterward, in order that he might hear the Redeemer's
words, he returned at the time of crucifixion, still he was
at first terrified and fled.

*John 19:27

*Mark
14:51-52

The women, however, are mentioned not merely to have not been afraid and to have not fled, but even to have remained until his burial. Let him say it then: *My flesh is consumed, and my bones have clung to my skin.* In other words, "Those who should have clung more closely to my strength were consumed by fear at the time of my passion. Those, however, whom I made external ministers, I found faithful enough to cling to me during my passion without fear." It clearly follows that these words were spoken to indicate a mystery, since he goes on to say,

*Job 19:20   L. 58. *My lips only are left around my teeth.** What else do we have around our teeth except lips, even if we have not been flogged? But on the other hand, what is meant by lips but speech, and what by teeth except the holy apostles? They have been placed in this body of the church in order that they might sting the lives of carnal people with a view to their correction and might break the hardness of their stubborn hearts. That is why that prince of the apostles, who was like a tooth placed in the

*Acts 10:13;   church's body, was told, *Slaughter and eat.** In the hour
11:7   of his passion, however, these teeth* before the fear of
*i.e., the   death lost the sting of correction, lost confidence in their
apostles   own strength, and lost the facility of any kind of activity.

So true was this that the two apostles walking on the road after his death and resurrection were saying in conversation, *We were hoping that he was the one to re-*

*Luke 24:21   *deem Israel.** So he is right to say here, *My lips only are left around my teeth.* They still talked about him, but no longer did they believe in him. Only their lips, therefore, had remained around their teeth, because they had lost the power of doing good works, and they retained only the words of conversation about him. They had lost the sting of correction, but they had the exercise of speech. Their lips only were left around their teeth, because they still knew how to talk, yet they were afraid to preach him anymore, or to correct the vices of the unfaithful. So having finished holding forth in the name of the Head, blessed Job returns to his own words and says,

LI. 59. *Take pity on me, take pity on me, at least you my friends, because the Lord's hand has touched me.**Job 19:21 The minds of the saints generally have this characteristic, that when they suffer something unjustly from their adversaries, they are moved not so much to wrath as to entreaty. If they could gently restrain their perversity, they would prefer entreaty to anger. So he is right to say here, *Take pity on me, take pity on me, at least you my friends, because the Lord's hand has touched me.* Look, they are the ones whom he regards when he sees himself attacked by insults and whom he calls friends. To the minds of good people, you see, even that which seems to be contrary is transformed into something favorable. All perverse people, then, are either converted by the charm of good people to reconciliation and by that very fact become friends and good people themselves, or they persevere in malice and become friends in this way also, even if unwillingly, because if the good people have sinned in any way, the perverse ones, even if unknowingly, purify them by their persecution.

We should take notice as well that the blessed man is publicly in accordance with and renders spoken testimony to what has happened secretly in God's presence. It was undoubtedly Satan who struck him down, yet he did not attribute the blow to Satan himself but counted himself touched by God's hand, even as Satan himself had said, *Just reach out and touch his flesh and bones, and then watch him curse you to your face!* The holy man knew very well by the very fact that Satan had moved against him with a perverse will that he had power not of himself, but from the Lord. The next verse:

LII. 60. *Why do you persecute me like God, and why* *fill yourselves with my flesh?*[*] It is not inconsistent with a pious way of speaking for people to say they are being persecuted by God. There is such a thing as a good persecutor, just as God says of himself through the prophet's words: *Him who secretly slanders his neighbor I* *did persecute.*[*] But when any of the saints are allowed to suffer trials, they know that it is by an internal dispensation that they suffer persecution for sins that they have committed. When the cruel minds of persecutors desire the power of striking others, however, they are instigated not by eagerness to purify but by the fire of envy against the lives of good people. And they certainly do this, because almighty God allows them to do it.

Whereas, however, there is one cause that is set afoot through them in common with God, it is not the same will that is served in that cause, because while almighty God produces purification in his love, the depravity of the unjust people ferociously employs malice. So when he says, *Why do you persecute me like God?* he relates that action to an external blow but not to an internal intention, because even if they set in motion externally what God arranged to be done, their desire is not at one with God when they act, with God who wills that good people should be purified by affliction.

It can however be understood differently. Almighty God is all the more just in striking down the vices of others to the extent that he has no vices in himself. People, however, when they strike others for the sake of discipline, should strike the weaknesses of others in such a way that they might also be able to turn their eyes on their own weaknesses, so that by reflecting on themselves they might know how to spare others when they strike, since they know very well that they deserve blows themselves. That is why it is here said, *Why do*

*Job 19:22

*Ps 100:5

you persecute me like God? He might have said more
clearly, "You are chastising me for my weaknesses, as
if you yourselves, like God, had no weaknesses." So
we ought to consider whether perchance there are those
who are in need of harsh correction; if so, then severe
penalties should be administered by us, when God's
hand lets go the whip. When divine chastisement is
present, however, no longer should chastisement but
comfort be our concern, lest if we add words of rebuke
to pain, we add one blow to another.

61. He is wise to add, *Why fill yourselves with my
flesh?* He whose mind hungers for the discomfiture
of his neighbors undoubtedly wants to be filled with
somebody else's flesh. We should realize as well that
they who nibble at the lives of others by detraction fill
themselves with their flesh too. That is why Solomon
says, *Do not attend drinking parties, nor eat with those
who put out flesh for consumption.** Putting out flesh for   *Prov 23:20
consumption is unquestionably to mention our neigh-
bors' vices turn by turn in derogatory conversation, the
penalty for which is forthwith also mentioned in the
same place: *Because those taking their ease in drink
and giving pledges will be consumed, and they will be
covered with rags in their sleep.**   *Prov 23:21

They take their ease in drink who get drunk on the
scandal of somebody else's life. Giving pledges, however, is what everyone does for his share at a banquet;
so also in conversation he offers words of detraction.
Both those who take their ease in drink and those who
give pledges will be consumed, since it is written, *All
detractors will be eradicated.** They will be covered   *Prov 15:5
with rags in their sleep, because one's own death will
find out in contempt the one who is devoid of any good
works, whose drunken detraction kept busy here searching out the crimes in somebody else's life.

But it is not fitting that all the harshness that blessed Job suffered should be passed over in silence, nor that the darkness of ignorance should conceal it from human knowledge. His sufferings are as good for edification for the preservation of patience as they are for the knowledge of his patient acts by the inspiration of divine grace. So blessed Job also wishes the trials he suffered to be brought forward as an example, so he forthwith adds,

LIII. 62. *Who will grant me that my words be written down? Who will allow them to be inscribed on a tablet with a steel pen or on a leaden plate or at least sculpted* in stone?* All that happened to that oppressed man the oppressed Jewish people knew, because they had been taught by the vigorous declaration of the fathers, and it had been written down with steel pen on leaden plates. The hard hearts of the Gentiles also knew it, however, and what does this mean but that it is engraved in stone? Remember too that anything written on lead is quickly obliterated, because the metal does not hold an impression. As for stone, it takes a long time for letters to be inscribed on it, but they are difficult to remove.

*Job 19:23-24

Now then the leaden plate can symbolize Judea, and it is fitting, since she received God's precepts without labor and quickly lost them. Rightly also are the Gentiles symbolized by stone, for they could only with difficulty receive the words of Holy Scripture for their observance, but once received they stoutly kept them. What does the iron pen signify but God's strong declaration? That is why the prophet says, *The sin of Judea is written with an iron pen on a diamond fingernail.** The nail is an end of the body, and diamond is the hardest stone, so hard that it cannot be cut with steel. The iron pen then signifies a strong declaration, and the diamond fingernail the eternal end. So Judea's sin is said to be

*Jer 17:1

written with a steel pen on a diamond fingernail, and it means that the guilt of the Jews through God's strong declaration is reserved for an unending end.

63. We are correct also in taking the leaden plate to mean those whom heavy avarice weighs down, who are told by the scolding prophet, *Sons of men, how long will your hearts be heavy?** The nature of lead is heaviness and weight, and it signifies the sin of avarice in a special way, which makes the mind it infects so heavy that it can never desire to be lifted up to the heights. That is why it is written in the prophecy of Zechariah, *"Lift up your eyes and see. What is that going out?" And I said, "What is it?" He said, "It is an amphora going out." He spoke again: "It is their eye in the whole earth." It seemed to hold a leaden cover, and a woman seemed to be sitting in the middle of it. He said, "She is impiety." He forced her down inside the amphora. Then he replaced the leaden cover on its mouth.**

*Ps 4:3

*Zech 5:5-8

After this vision of the amphora, the woman, and the leaden cover, in order that he might demonstrate more clearly what he had learned, the prophet also added the following: *I again lifted up my eyes, and I saw two women going out; a spirit was in their wings, and they had wings like those of a kite; they lifted up the amphora between heaven and earth. I said to the angel who spoke to me, "Where are they taking the amphora?" He answered, "To build a house for it in the land of Shinar."** We gain nothing by the prophet's testimony that we bring forward to explain lead if we do not also repeat and expose it. He says then, *"Lift up your eyes and see. What is that going out?" And I said, "What is it?" He said, "It is an amphora going out."*

*Babylon; Zech 5:9-11

God wants to show the prophet the human race and by what principal sin it lapsed, so he signifies, as it were, the open mouth of avarice by means of the image of an amphora. Avarice is indeed like an amphora, which keeps the mouth of its heart open all around. He goes on to say, *It is their eye in the whole earth.* We see a lot of people with dull minds, who, nevertheless, as we also see, are clever in the doing of evil, as the prophet bears witness: *They are wise enough to do evil, but how to do good they do not know.** Their minds are dull indeed, yet concerning their own desires they are aroused by the spur of avarice. Those also who have no eyes for seeing good things are alerted to vigilance by the thought of reward in order to do evil. So he is right to say about this very avarice, *"It is their eye in the whole earth."* *It seemed to hold a leaden cover.*

*Jer 4:22

What is the leaden cover, if not the weight of sin from the same avarice? *A woman seemed to be sitting in the middle of it.* Lest we should by chance be in doubt concerning the woman, the angel added in the same breath, as the text continues, *He said, "She is impiety."* *He forced her down inside the amphora.* Impiety is forced down inside the amphora, because of course impiety is always kept inside avarice. *Then he replaced the leaden cover on its mouth.* The leaden cover is placed over the woman's mouth, because impiety is obviously weighed down by the gravity of its own sin of avarice. If she did not play around with base pursuits, you see, she would not remain impious toward God and neighbor.

64. *I again lifted up my eyes, and I saw two women going out; a spirit was in their wings.* What else do we take these two women to mean but the two principal vices, namely, pride and vainglory, which beyond any doubt are linked with impiety? They have, we are told, a spirit in their wings, because they serve Satan's will in their actions. The prophet assuredly calls him a spirit about whom Solomon said, *If the spirit of one wielding power rises above you, do not let yourself be moved.** The Lord, for

*Eccl 10:4

his part, says in the gospel, *When an unclean spirit goes out of a man, he wanders in dry and waterless places.* A *Matt 12:43 spirit is in their wings, because pride and vainglory is in all they do, and they are subservient to Satan's will.

They had wings like those of a kite. The kite is always naturally eager to set an ambush for chickens. These women, then, have wings like those of a kite, because their actions beyond any doubt resemble those of the devil, who always lies in wait for the lives of little ones. *They lifted up the amphora between heaven and earth.* It is a characteristic of pride and vainglory that the person whose thoughts they infect they extol beyond all others. Sometimes through striving for possessions, sometimes through the longing for dignity, the one whom they have once captured they lift up as though to the highest honors. The one who is between heaven and earth, however, both abandons the lowest places and never reaches the highest.

65. Accordingly these women lift up the amphora between heaven and earth, because pride and vainglory lift up the mind that is captured by its longing for honors in such a way that, full of scorn, it virtually abandons its neighbors and haughtily makes for the heights. When such as these grow proud, they both mentally transcend their companions and still do not join those citizens who are above. It is called an amphora lifted up between heaven and earth, because any avaricious person through pride and vainglory both scorns neighbors close by and never reaches the things that are above and beyond. Such people, therefore, are held between heaven and earth, because they neither embrace equality with their brothers here below through charity nor yet manage to reach the heights by self-exaltation.

I said to the angel who spoke to me, "Where are they taking the amphora?" He answered, "To build a

*Babylon *house for it in the land of Shinar." * A house is built for this same amphora in the land of Shinar. Shinar indeed is called their stench. Now, a sweet smell comes from virtue, as Paul attests, saying, *He reveals the sweet odor of his knowledge everywhere through us, because we* *2 Cor 2:14-15 *are the sweet odor of Christ toward God.* On the other hand, a foul smell comes from vice: *Covetousness is the* *1 Tim 6:10 *root of all evil.* So since all evils are born from avarice, it is fitting that the house of avarice be built in stench. Remember too that Shinar is an exceedingly broad valley in which some proud men had started building a tower, but when the languages were divided, the tower was destroyed. Now this tower was called Babylon because of the aforesaid confusion of minds and languages. Nor is it unfitting that the amphora of avarice should be put there, where Babylon, that is, confusion, is built, since it is certain that from avarice and impiety all evils come forth, so this avarice and impiety are rightly said to dwell in confusion.

66. I have slightly digressed, in order that I might show how the weight of sin is symbolized by the leaden plate. The words of blessed Job, however, apply equally well to Holy Church, who guards the two testaments of Holy Writ. She pleads that her words be written down a second time, saying, *Who will grant me that my words be written down? Who will allow them to be inscribed on a tablet?* These words are spoken with forceful purpose, sometimes to hearts weighed down by avarice, but sometimes to hard hearts as well, so she writes with steel pen on a leaden plate, or at least on stone. Well, we are right in saying that blessed Job uses the words of our Redeemer and his church, if we find something openly spoken by blessed Job about our Redeemer. By what right should we believe, then, that he intimated something figuratively about him, if he did not openly

show it in clear words? But let him now say openly what he thinks about him and remove every doubt from our minds. The next verse:

LIV. 67. *I know that my Redeemer lives.* He who no   *Job 19:25
longer says *Creator* but *Redeemer* openly proclaims him who, after he created all things, in order that he might free us from captivity, appeared among us clothed with flesh and freed us from eternal death by his passion. We should also notice the great faith with which Job commits himself to the power of the divinity of Christ, of whom Paul says, *Although he was crucified in weakness, he lives by the power of God.* Job said, *I know that my*   *2 Cor 13:4
Redeemer lives. He could say in clearer words, "Every unfaithful person would know him: scourged, derided, struck with the palm of the hand, crowned with thorns, mocked with spittle, crucified, and dead. I, however, believe in him with unwavering faith, him who lives after death, and with full voice I confess that my Redeemer lives, who died at the hands of impure men." But through his resurrection, blessed Job, what is your confidence in the resurrection of your own flesh? We beg you to confess that openly with your voice. The next verse:

LV. 68. *And on the last day I will rise from the earth.*   *Job 19:25
Obviously the resurrection that he reveals in himself, he is one day going to bring about in us. Unquestionably the resurrection that he reveals in himself he promised to us, because the members follow the glory of their Head. Accordingly our Redeemer accepted death in order that we might not fear death. He revealed the resurrection, in order that we might have confidence in the possibility of our own resurrection. That is why he did not will his death to exceed three days, lest if his own resurrection were delayed, ours would be entirely hopeless. The prophet rightly said of him, *He drinks from the*

*Ps 109:7

stream on the wayside, so he will lift up his head.* It is as though he deigned to drink from the stream of our pain, not at a rest stop but on the road, he who tasted death temporarily, that is, for three days, and in that death that he tasted he by no means remained like us until the end of the world. So when he rose on the third day, he showed what would follow in his Body that is the church. He demonstrated by his own example what he promised to bestow, that just as the faithful realized that he had risen, they might hope for the prize of their own resurrection at the end of the world.

See how we remain in dust after our body's death until the end of the world, whereas he waxed vigorous on the third day after the dryness of death and showed us the power of his divinity by the very freshness of his flesh. That is the truth that Moses displayed when he *see Num 17:1-8 put the twelve rods in the tent.* Aaron's priesthood, you see, originated in the tribe of Levi, and it was scorned, and that tribe was considered unworthy to offer holocausts. Then the twelve rods for the twelve tribes were ordered to be put in the tent, and Levi's rod blossomed and proved its worth in Aaron's office. What is meant by this sign if not the following? All of us who lie in death until the end of the world, like the other rods, remain dry. Yes, while all the other rods remain dry, Levi's rod blossoms, because the body of the Lord, who is obviously our true priesthood, was left in the dryness of death and burst forth in the flower of resurrection.

By the flower Aaron's priesthood was rightly recognized, because our Redeemer, who was born of the tribes of Levi and Judah, was shown by the glory of resurrection to be our intercessor. Accordingly, see now how Aaron's rod blooms from aridity, but the rods of the twelve tribes remain dry, because now indeed the Lord's body lives after death, but our bodies are still made to wait for the glory of resurrection until the end of the world. That is why he cautiously introduces this very delay and says, *And on the last day I will rise from the earth.*

69. We have the hope, accordingly, of our resurrection, given the glory of our Head. Lest anyone should perhaps say, however, even in secret thought, that Jesus rose from the dead because he who is both God and man overcame that death by his divinity that he suffered in his humanity, whereas we, who are mere humans, cannot rise from the condemnation of death, it is well that in the very hour of his resurrection many bodies of saints rose as well, in order that he might show us both his own example and that of others who were like us in being mere humans and thus confirm our hope in the resurrection. Inasmuch as a person might of himself despair of ever receiving what the God-man had revealed in himself, he might presume it possible for him to receive it, since he realized that those who were doubtlessly mere humans had, in fact, received it.

70. There are those, however, who when they reflect that the soul separates from the body, which in turn dissolves into rottenness, which in turn resolves into dust, which in turn so confuses itself with the atoms that it could never be seen by human eyes, they consequently despair of the possibility of the resurrection. When they behold dry bones, they do not believe it possible for them to grow flesh again and to live afresh. If they do not obediently hold faith in the resurrection, they should certainly do so by reason. What does the world do every day but imitate our resurrection in its most basic components? Every day, moment by moment, this light of time certainly dies, as it were, what with the darkness of night drawing closer, and the visible light disappears; then it seems to rise every day, when the light that had vanished from our eyes reappears, while the darkness is again dispersed.

In the course of the seasons we notice the shrubs losing their green leaves and stop bringing forth fruit. Then suddenly we look, and the leaves are bursting forth from what looked like a dried-up tree, as if it were rising again; before long the fruit is growing, and the whole tree is clothed with new life and beauty. We never stop seeing the tiny seeds of trees being committed to the damp earth, and from there not long afterward we see huge forests rise and bring forth leaves and fruit. Accordingly, let us regard carefully the tiny seed of whatever tree you like, which falls upon the ground, in order that a tree might be produced from it, and let us imagine, if we can, where in such a tiny compass of that seed a tree of such immense size could have hidden, which came forth from it? Where was the wood, where the bark, where the green leaves, where the abundant fruit? Was there any of that to be seen in the seed when it fell to the ground?

Yet the hidden artisan and maker of all things brought it about in a wonderful way that the rough bark hid in that soft seed, that the hard physical strength was concealed in its tenderness, and that in its dryness was hidden abundant fruitfulness. Why should we wonder, then, if God should remake into a person, when he so wills, that most insubstantial dust, resolved into atoms and removed from our eyesight? Does he not remake the tiniest seeds into gigantic trees? Consequently, since we are rational creatures we should gather our hope of resurrection from the very substance and contemplation of nature.

Since, however, our use of reason has become dull, the Redeemer's grace has come forward as an example. Our Creator, you see, came and accepted death and revealed the resurrection, so that we, who have refused to hold the hope of resurrection by reason, might hold it by the help of his example. Let blessed Job then say, *I know that my Redeemer lives, and on the last day I will rise from the earth*. Whoever, then, despairs of the possibility of the power of the resurrection's being effective in his life should blush at the words of this man of faith who is a Gentile. He should also carefully estimate the heavy penalty that will be clapped on him if he still does not believe in his own resurrection when he knows that the Lord's resurrection has already taken place, if Job believed in his own resurrection while he hoped in the Lord's resurrection, which was still to happen.

71. Yet see how I hear *resurrection*, but I am still waiting for the effect of that resurrection. I believe that I am going to rise, but I want to hear how. I surely need to know whether perhaps it will be that I will rise in some other subtle or airy body, or in the one in which I die. But if I will rise in an airy body, it will no longer be I who rise. How is there a true resurrection if there cannot be true flesh? Simple reason supplies the fact that if there would not be true flesh, the resurrection would doubtless not be true. Nor is it right for us to call it resurrection when that which falls does not rise. But blessed Job, please remove our clouds of doubt, and since you have received the grace of the Holy Spirit, and you have begun to tell us about our hope of resurrection, show us clearly if our flesh really rises.

LVI. 72. *I will again be wrapped up in my own skin.** Since he openly says *skin*, all doubt about the true resurrection vanishes, because our body will not be intangible in that glorious resurrection, or more subtle than wind or air, as Eutychius, the bishop of the city of Constantinople, wrote. In that glorious resurrection our bodies will indeed be subtle through the effect of spiritual power, but tangible as well through their actual nature. That is why our Redeemer also, when his

*Job 19:26

disciples were in doubt about his resurrection, showed them his hands and his side and offered them his bones and flesh to be touched. *Feel me and see*, he said. *A spirit does not have flesh and bones, as you can see that I have.** When I found myself in the city of Constantinople with the aforementioned Eutychius, I confronted him with this witness of the truth of the gospel, and he said, "The Lord acted in this way precisely in order that he might remove any doubt concerning his resurrection from the disciples' hearts." I answered, "This is a great wonder that you construe, namely, that a doubt should arise for us there where the disciples' hearts were cured of doubt."

*Luke 24:39

What could we possibly say that is worse than this: that a doubt should arise for us concerning his true flesh from the fact that his disciples were brought back to faith and cured of all doubt? If, you see, the Lord is construed not to have what he displayed to the disciples, and by which their faith was confirmed, then is our faith brought to nothing.* Eutychius then added, "He had a tangible body when he displayed it, but after the disciples touched it and their hearts were confirmed, all that they could touch of the Lord was again reduced to a subtle substance." To which I replied, "It is written, *Christ rising from the dead dies no more. Death has no more power over him.** If, then, anything in his body could be changed after the resurrection, against the truly spoken witness of Paul, the Lord returned to death after the resurrection. Who would be such a presumptuous fool as to say such a thing, except one who denies the real resurrection of his flesh?"

*See 1 Cor 15:13-14

*Rom 6:9

Then he objected saying, "*When it is written, 'Flesh and blood cannot possess the kingdom of God,'* * by what account can we believe that flesh really rises?" To which I replied,

*1 Cor 15:50

Holy Scripture speaks about flesh in one way according to nature, and in another according to guilt or corruption. She certainly speaks about flesh according to nature when she says, *This is now bone of my bone and flesh of my flesh,** and *The Word was made flesh and lived among us.** However, she speaks about flesh according to guilt when she says, *My spirit will not remain in these men, since they are flesh.** The psalmist also says, *He remembered that they are flesh, a breath that passes never to return.** Paul also told his disciples, *You are not in the flesh, but you are in the spirit.**

It is not that they to whom the letter was sent were not in the flesh, but that they had conquered the passions and desires of the flesh, and because they were now free by the power of the spirit, they were not in the flesh. So the apostle Paul again says, *Flesh and blood cannot possess the kingdom of God.* Here he intends flesh to be understood according to guilt, not according to nature. So he immediately shows that it was flesh according to guilt that he was talking about when he adds, *Nor will corruption possess incorruption.** Accordingly, in the glory of that heavenly Kingdom there will be flesh according to nature, but there will not be flesh according to the desires and passions, because the sting of death will be overcome, and the flesh will reign in eternal incorruption.

73. To these words Eutychius also promptly answered that he agreed; nevertheless he still denied that a tangible body could rise. In the book he had written about the resurrection he also invoked the testimony of the apostle Paul, who said, *What you sow in the ground does not live again, unless it dies first, and what you sow is not the body that shall be, but a bare kernel.** He

*Gen 2:23
*John 1:14

*Gen 6:3

*Ps 77:39

*Rom 8:9

*1 Cor 15:50

*1 Cor 15:36-37

is quick to use this text to prove that flesh, tangible or not, will not be there, since the holy apostle in speaking of the glorious resurrection said that what is sown in the ground is not the body that is to be. I, however, am still quicker to answer that in saying, *what you sow is not the body that shall be, but a bare kernel*, the apostle Paul indicates what we see, namely, that the seed is born with stem and leaves, which is sown without stem and leaves. He consequently did not say that the seed grain that was before is missing when the glorious resurrection is added, simply that the aforesaid glory is there, which was not there before. Eutychius, however, while he denies that the real body rises, never says that what was not there before is now present, only that what was there is now absent.

*Eutychius and I

74. We* were locked together in a long argument over this matter, and we began to recoil in a serious rivalry when the emperor Tiberius Constantinus of holy memory granted him and me a secret audience, and he acknowledged the contention that raged between us. He weighed the arguments on both sides; he dismissed the book Eutychius had written about the resurrection, adding his own arguments against it, and he decreed that it should be consigned to the flames. Upon our leaving the emperor a grave illness overtook me, and illness and death overtook Eutychius himself. Upon his death, since there was almost no one who followed his teachings, I left things as they were and did not follow up, lest I should seem to be hurling words at dead ashes. While he was still alive and I lay ill with a high fever, however, whoever I was acquainted with who went to visit him, as I understood from their report, said that he held the skin of his hand before their eyes and said, "I confess that we will all arise with this flesh." This statement, as they alleged, he had formerly absolutely denied.

75. Let us, however, put aside such considerations and carefully examine blessed Job's speech to know if there will be a real resurrection and a real body in the resurrection. See, we already cannot doubt our hope of resurrection, since Job said, *And on the last day I will rise from the earth.* When he said, *I will again be wrapped up in my own skin,* he also took away any doubts we might have on the real reconstituting of our bodies. Finally, in order to take away all hesitation from our thoughts, he added,

76. *In my flesh I will see God.* Here is the resurrec-   *Job 19:26
tion, here the skin, here the flesh openly confessed in words. What is left, accordingly, on which our mind can still doubt? If, therefore, before the event of the Lord's resurrection, this holy man believed that flesh would be integrally reinstated, what will be the penalty of our doubts, if even after the example of the Redeemer the real resurrection of the flesh is not believed? If following the resurrection there is no tangible body, a different person certainly rises from the one that died, and that is a crime to speak of, let alone believe, if when I die another person rises. In view of this I beseech you, blessed Job, give us your opinion and remove from us our anxiety concerning this question. The next verse:

LVII. 77. *It is I myself who will see him, and my eyes will look upon him, not somebody else.* If, then,   *Job 19:27
as some followers of erroneous doctrine maintain, there will be no tangible body after the resurrection, but rather a delicate invisible body will be called flesh even if it is not the substance of flesh, it is certainly one person who dies and a different one who rises. Blessed Job, however, dismantles their argument with the voice of Truth, saying, *It is I myself who will see him, and my eyes will look upon him, not somebody else.* We follow blessed Job's faith, and we believe in the really tangible

body of our Redeemer after the resurrection. Consequently we affirm that our flesh after the resurrection
will be both the same and different: the same by nature
and different by glory, the same in truth and different
in power. It will be delicate, because incorruptible. It
will be tangible, because it will not lose the essential
reality of its nature. The holy man shows us with what
hope he holds that same confidence in the resurrection
and with how much certitude he awaits it, as he adds
the following words:

*Job 19:27   LVIII. 78. *This hope of mine rests in my bosom.**
We think we have nothing that is more secure than what
we hold in our bosom. He keeps his hope accordingly
resting in his bosom. He takes therefore for granted
that true certitude about the hope of resurrection. Since,
however, he has taken notice that the day of resurrection
is coming, even now he contradicts the deeds of evil
people, either with his own voice or as a type of the holy
universal church, and he foretells the Judgment that will
take place on the day of resurrection. He forthwith adds,

LIX. 79. *Why do you now say, "Let us persecute
him, and let us find simple words against him?" Run,
therefore, from the thrust of the sword, because the
sword is the avenger of evil, and know that judgment is*
*Job 19:28-29   *near.** In the first sentence he indeed reproves the acts of
the wicked, but in the second he takes notice of the pen-
alties forthcoming from divine Judgment. He says, *Why
do you now say, "Let us persecute him, and let us find
simple words against him."* When any perverse people
listen to a noble speech with evil intent, and when they
are desirous of finding in the tongue of a righteous person access for accusation, what else are they after but
simple words to use against him, words with which they
obviously would usurp the initiative in speaking and
wax eloquent in evil accusation against him?

The holy man, however, when he suffers such things from the wicked, does not grieve against them but for them, and he contradicts their wicked deliberations, showing them the evils they should run away from. He says, *Run, therefore, from the thrust of the sword, because the sword is the avenger of evil, and know that judgment is near.* All people who act wickedly, by the very fact that they scorn fear of such acts, do not know that there is a God who judges. If they knew that there were grounds for fear, they would not do the things that are liable to be punished.

There are many people, you see, who know very well that there is a Final Judgment as far as the word is concerned, but in their actions they show that they are ignorant of it. Those who do not fear it as they should do not yet realize with what a terrible whirlwind it is coming. If they knew how to weigh the burden of the dreadful scrutiny, they would be on their guard to fear the day of wrath. To run away from the thrust of the sword means to propitiate the verdict of that implacable scrutiny before it appears. Dread of the Judge can only be escaped before Judgment. It is not perceived now, but it is appeased by prayer. When therefore the Judge is seated for that dreadful scrutiny, when he can be seen and when he can no longer be appeased, inasmuch as he has already suffered the acts of the wicked too long, he will angrily requite everything at once. So it is necessary to fear the Judge now, when he is not yet pronouncing Judgment, when he waits long, and when he still puts up with the evil that he sees, lest when he once raises his hand to pass sentence, he should strike as implacably in Judgment as he waited at length before Judgment.

BOOK 15

The words of Zophar the Naamathite prove that blessed Job's friends could never be perverse. Zophar heard the dread of the coming Judgment from Job's mouth, and he forthwith put in,

I. 1. *On this account my different thoughts succeed one another, and my mind is pulled in different directions.** It is as if he said in plain words, "Because I behold the terrible Last Judgment, my disordered thoughts alarm me." The more terrible the soul considers the threat of Judgment, surely the more it is rent asunder by its thoughts. The mind is torn with different thoughts, terrified by anxiety as it is: now it remembers the evil it has done, now it remembers the good it has neglected to do, now it considers what is blameworthy in it, now it sees how lacking it still is in right conduct.

Blessed Job's friends, however, while they had learned from the constancy of his life how to live good lives, did not know how to weigh God's Judgment precisely, and they did not believe that any of the just could experience misfortune in this life. That is why they suspected that the same holy man was in fact evil, him whom they saw buffeted by trials, and this suspicion even led them to the point of stooping to rebuke him, in which rebuke, however, they stooped with a certain amount of respect, as it were. So Zophar adds the following:

II. 2. *I will listen to the teaching with which you reproach me, and the inspiration of my understanding will answer for me.** He might as well say it outright: "I hear your words well enough, but whether they were

*Job 20:2

*Job 20:3

truly spoken I detect with the help of the inspiration of
my own intelligence." Those friends, you see, scorn the
words he spoke, so they take in his teaching not as something helpful, but rather as an excuse for contention, in
order that they might criticize what they heard instead
of following it. After Zophar had as it were prefaced his
remarks with tact, he springs forth in what is now open
reproach against the blessed man and says,

III. 3. *This I know: that from the beginning when
man was placed upon the earth, commendation of the
wicked is of short duration, and the hypocrite's laugh
is as a moment.** It is now clear that because Zophar is   *Job 20:4-5
inflated by the inspiration of his own intelligence, he
only pronounces judgments on the wicked in order to
turn them around into rebukes of blessed Job. The one
whom he had first witnessed as a person who acted
justly and later as one who suffered punishment, Zophar
now esteems as nothing but a hypocrite, since what he
saw was obviously a righteous servant struck down by
a righteous God, a thing he believed to be impossible.
Let us however rehash those judgments of his that are
seemingly correct, even if not spoken with a right intention, and let us follow them up with careful thought;
condemning his false statements against blessed Job,
let us try to see how true they are if spoken against the
wicked.

He said, accordingly, *This I know: that from the
beginning when man was placed upon the earth commendation of the wicked is of short duration.* Since he
is going to speak about the brevity of the present life, he
recalls the eye of the heart to the first beginning, in order
that he may gather from past events the knowledge that
those who seem to be something as long as they exist
are really nothing. If, you see, we guide our mind's eye
from the very beginning of the human race to the time in

which we are now living, we see how brief everything is that can end. Let us suppose that some person lived out his life from the first day of creation until the present day; today, however, that life that seemed to be led for so long is over. Behold, the end is at hand, and already the past is as nothing, because all that time has passed away. There is no future in this world, because there remains not one moment of time, not even the shortest, for life. Where, then, is that long time that was found to be used up between the beginning and the end? It is as brief as though it never existed.

4. The wicked, of course, love the present life, and in this life beyond any doubt they arrogantly want to be praised. They are exalted by vocal applause, and they do not wish to be good but to be called good. The applause they seek they consider long lasting as long as they are seeking it, but they know it to have been brief once they are without it. At the end they unquestionably find out that what they loved was nothing. So Zophar rightly speaks against these wicked people: *This I know: that from the beginning when man was placed upon the earth commendation of the wicked is of short duration.* He is right to add as well, *and the hypocrite's laugh is as a moment.*

Hypocrites often pretend to be saints, yet they certainly have no fear of letting their wickedness be seen; they are honored by all, and the boast of holiness is allowed them by those who see what is external but cannot perceive what is internal. So it happens that they are merry in the first seat, cheerful in the first couch, proud of the first greeting, elevated by the respectful voices of their flatterers, and swollen with proud thoughts by the services of their subordinates. It is just as the voice of Truth tells us about such persons: *They do all their works in order to be seen by men. They broaden their phylacteries and lengthen their fringes. They love places of honor at banquets and first seats in synagogues and greetings at the marketplace and being called Rabbi by men.* *   *Matt 23:5-7

What is this merrymaking of theirs compared to eternity? When the moment of death breaks in, will it not be burnt up as though it had never been? The unrestrained gladness of that merrymaking has absolutely passed away, and the penalty remains; when the experience is lost, the sentence endures. So Zophar is right to say, *The hypocrite's laugh is as a moment.* In forming a period the pen is lifted as soon as it is put down, and there is no delay in moving it and writing a line. The hypocrite's laugh too is like a period, because it appears for a moment and then disappears forever. Just as a pen rests on a period and is lifted, so the hypocrite's laugh touches this life and is gone. On the same subject Zophar continues:

IV. 5. *Even if his pride should ascend to heaven and his head touch the clouds, just like a dunghill he will come to nothing in the end.* * The pride of hypocrites is   *Job 20:6-7
said to ascend even to heaven, when their souls seem to be exalted to the point of living a heavenly life. Their heads, as it were, touch the clouds as well, when their most important organ, that is, their intelligence, is believed to equal that of the older saints in its merits. Like a dunghill they will come to nothing in the end, because when they die they are led to torture, and since they are full of the excrement of vice, they are trampled upon by the evil spirits. Delight in the present life, you see, which lawless people consider to be the greatest good, the just regard as dung. That is why we find it written, *The lazy man is stoned with the dung of bulls.* *   *Sir 22:2 LXX

He who will not follow God becomes slothful as regards love of eternal life. As often as he is struck by the loss of earthly possessions, he is unquestionably discouraged on account of the things that righteous people disdain as so much excrement. He, accordingly, who is ruined by blows such as the loss of temporal goods, what is he subjected to but being whipped by the dung of bulls? The hypocrite then is rightly compared to a dunghill, because as long as he aims to have worldly honor, at one time his thoughts within himself cause his heart to expand, and at another he begrudges such honors to some or scoffs at others who really have them. He is full of so many vices, therefore, that in the sight of the eternal Judge it is as though his breast smelled like so much excrement. Let him say then, *Even if his pride should ascend to heaven and his head touch the clouds, just like a dunghill he will come to nothing in the end.* Even if he pretends to live a heavenly life, and even if he flaunts his intelligence as though it were the equal of that of the true preachers, just like a dunghill he will come to nothing in the end, because his soul will be condemned for the fetid odor of its vices. The next verse:

V. 6. *Those who have seen him will say, "Where is* *Job 20:7 *he?"* * The life of hypocrites is often found reprobate even by other people at the end, in order that it might then become plain by clearer signs what kind they were. Those accordingly who have seen him proud say of him when he is dead, *"Where is he?"* because he appears neither here, where he was proud, nor in eternal rest, where he was supposed to be. Concerning the brevity of his life Zophar again rightly adds,

VI. 7. *Like a dream which flits away he will not be* *Job 20:8 *found, and like a vision of the night he will go away.* * What is a hypocrite's life but a kind of vision or apparition that displays an image that does not exist in reality? It is rightly compared to a dream in which he loses all his dignity and prestige even while he still holds on to it. It often happens to certain poor people that in a nocturnal vision they are astonished that they have become rich: they see themselves honored, and they contemplate piles of money, armies of obedient servants, beautiful clothes, and an abundance of food displayed all around them. They rejoice that they have escaped want, with which they put up in the midst of sighs. They suddenly awake, however, and they find out how false was their rejoicing; they are sorry to be awake, because it is real want that keeps them awake.

Such are the minds of hypocrites, who while they act in one way display themselves to people in another, and they are praised for their very ostentation of holiness; moreover, they are preferred to many better people in the esteem of others, and while they wax proud in their secret internal thoughts, externally they display their humility. As long as they receive extravagant praise from other people, they even imagine that they are in God's sight such as they boast that people have come to know them. Therefore they also happen to presume that they are going to receive the reward of eternal life, and those who exult in human popularity here have no doubt whatever that they will have rest there. Meanwhile, however, the hidden hour of God's call creeps up, and when they close the eyes of flesh, open those of the mind, and immediately receive the eternal recompense, they see there that their affluence with regard to reputation for virtue was a dream. So it is rightly said of this hypocrite, *Like a vision of the night he will go away.* If, then, he sees himself for the moment as one rich in the esteem of people, it is a display of a phantom and has nothing to do with solid virtue. When, you see, his mind awakes in bodily death, he knows beyond any doubt that when he enjoyed human popularity he was dreaming. The next verse:

VII. 8. *The eye which had seen him will not see him, nor will his place be found anymore.** Where is the hypocrite's place if not the hearts of flatterers? There indeed he rests where he finds human applause. So the eye that had seen him will not see him, because the fool taken away by death is hidden from his friends who used to look at him with admiration. His place will not be found any more, because the tongues of flatterers will not follow him to Judgment with their applause. As long as he lives, however, he never stops teaching his followers his own behavior, and through his depraved actions and mistakes he gives birth to others who follow his example. Concerning them Zophar rightly adds,

*Job 20:9

VIII. 9. *His sons will be weakened by poverty.** It is written, *Wisdom will not enter the spiteful soul.** The psalmist also says, *Rich people have suffered want and hunger.** If, you see, this want and hunger of theirs meant external starvation, or if they lacked bread for the body, they were surely not rich. While they increase externally, however, internally they are empty, so they are said to be rich and in want at the same time, because they obviously never deserve to eat their fill of the bread of wisdom. The sons of this hypocrite accordingly will be weakened by poverty, because those who are born in hypocrisy by imitating him have no solidity in truth, and poverty of heart weakens them. The next verse:

*Job 20:10
*Wis 1:4
*Ps 33:11 LXX

IX. 10. *His hands will return their pain to him.** What meaning is intended by *hands*, if not works? Accordingly his hands will return their pain to him, since he will be justly condemned for his evil works. Zophar was right to say *return* instead of *give* because his evil works will win him eternal punishment, as though it were a debt to be repaid. Before he reaches eternal punishment, however, let him add more fully how he behaves himself here. The next verse:

*Job 20:10

X. 11. *His bones will be filled with the vices of his youth, and they will sleep with him in the dust.** The root of a bad beginning multiplies causes of guilt even by anticipation. Insofar as people begin to do evil, their habits are already worse, since what they have begun increases. What consequently is this hypocrite's youth, if not the beginning of his evil ways? In youth beyond any doubt passion already begins to burn. The hypocrite is young at the very time when he begins to long for and embrace the passion for honors, and the warm encouragement of his flatterers increases that passion in him, makes it stronger, and changes it into bones, as it were. The evil he began to do, you see, grows daily worse and harder by habit.

*Job 20:11

Let him then say, *His bones will be filled with the vices of his youth*, because the hard-grained habits of wickedness in him were formed by the vice of a bad beginning. That is why it is written, *The proverb goes: "The way of youth is such that even when he grows old it will not leave him."* * His bones will surely sleep in the dust with him, because his wicked habits endure in him all the way to the point where they pull him down to the dust of death. For his bones or vices to sleep with him in the dust means that they do not abandon him until they are dust, which in turn means that he never stops doing evil until he dies. His evil habits hold him fast after they have once started, and they continue to harden every day. With him they sleep in the dust, because they never leave him except at his death. There is, however, another way of understanding the matter.

*Prov 22:6

12. The hypocrite sometimes still has something strong and healthy in his actions, but as long as he pretends to have many good qualities that he in fact does not have, he loses even what he does have. That is why Zophar is right to say at this point, *His bones will be*

filled with the vices of his youth. Fickle and inconstant as he is, he does many things childishly, so even those things that he does in a manly fashion are weakened by vice. His bones will obviously sleep with him in the dust, because all his pretentious actions are like dust, so much so that if there is anything strong in him, it is emptied of all solidity. Through the assumption of virtue he loses even that which could have been virtue in him. For his bones to sleep with him in death, then, means that even if there are any good actions in him, they perish along with his evil actions. The next verse:

XI. 13. *When evil will be sweet in his mouth, he will hide it under his tongue.** Evil is sweet in the hypocrite's mouth, because the wickedness in his mind is pleasant to him. The mouth of the heart is its thought, about which we find it written, *Deceitful lips are in the heart, and in the heart they have spoken evil.** This evil that is sweet in the hypocrite's mouth is hidden beneath his tongue, because bitter malice hides in the mind, and it is covered up by superficial smooth talking. Evil, you see, would be on the tongue instead of beneath it, if the hypocrite spoke malice and depravity openly, but he is like many honest people when they take notice of certain men acting perversely, those who need to be disciplined with sharp rebukes; their tongues are harsh, while they hide kindness beneath the tongue of their minds. That is why the voice of the Bridegroom of Holy Church speaks, *Milk and honey are beneath your tongue.** Those, you see, who will not speak of the kindness in their minds openly to people who are badly disposed, but rather speak fiercely to them with a certain harshness, still insert among the harsh words a certain kindness, as if it were hidden. They obviously have kindness, not on their tongue but beneath their tongue. Because among the harsh words that they speak they insert something

*Job 20:12

*Ps 11:3

*Song 4:11

soft and kind, the mind of the saddened person can be restored by gentleness. In the same way perverse people harbor evil not on the tongue but beneath the tongue, and they pretend kind speech while they make perverse plots in their inward thoughts. That explains why Joab grasped Amasa's beard with his right hand and, reaching secretly for his sword with his left, poured out his entrails on the ground.* Grasping the beard with the right hand means to caress a person as it were out of kindness. On the other hand, the one who secretly attacks a person out of malice reaches for a sword with the left hand. That is why it is written about the very head of evildoers, *Distress and trouble are under his tongue.** The one who does not openly flaunt the evil he intends for those whose death he is plotting does not assert their pain and grief, but presses it down under his tongue. Concerning this hypocrite, Zophar again adds,

XII. 14. *He will save it and not abandon it; he will hide it in his throat.** The evil he loves he will save, because he does not punish it in himself by repentance. So Zophar adds, *He will not abandon it.* Obviously, if he wanted to abandon it, he would never save it but rather punish it. Instead he hides it in his throat, because he keeps it in mind in such a way that he never vocally reveals it. The next verse:

XIII. 15. *His bread in his belly will be turned into the venom of asps within him.** Like bread in the belly is the satisfaction of worldly pleasure in the mind. Accordingly let the hypocrite be filled now with the praise that is offered him, and let him enjoy his honors. His bread in his belly will be turned into the venom of asps within him, because the satisfaction of passing pleasure is turned into bitterness in the end when retribution arrives. Furthermore, what he thought here to be commendation and renown, there he knows to have been

*see
2 Sam 20:9

*Ps 9:28

*Job 20:13

*Job 20:14

the venom of asps, that is, the persuasion of evil spirits. At that time indeed wicked people see that they were infected with the poison of the ancient serpent, while they are being delivered to avenging flames and tortured along with the very one who persuaded them. This bread tastes different in the mouth from what it is like in the belly, because the joy of passing delight is sweet as long as it is still felt here, while it is being chewed, as it were, but it grows bitter in the belly, because when the joy is past, it is swallowed and becomes a penalty.

16. On the other hand, bread is not unsuitably taken for the understanding of Holy Scripture, which refreshes the mind and imparts to it the vitality necessary for good works. Even the hypocrite is often eager for instruction in the mysteries of Holy Scripture, not however in order that he might live by them, but rather that he might appear learned to others. His bread in his belly will be turned into the venom of asps within him, since, as long as he boasts of his knowledge of holy law, the water of life changes for him into a cup of poison; there he dies as a reprobate where he seemed to be learning how to live.

Nor is this an unsuitable interpretation, because the hypocrite does sometimes apply himself to the word of instruction for purposes of ostentation, and, blinded by God's judgment, he understands that very word wrongly, because his zeal was wrong. When he falls into the error of heresy it happens to him that he unfortunately dies from that bread, as if from the venom of asps, and he finds death in his own self-instruction, because in the words of life it was not life at all that he sought. It often happens, however, that even if the hypocrite understands the eloquent divine admonition correctly, because he never keeps it in practice, before the course of his present life is over he even loses that understanding, in order that he might lose the knowl-

edge that, while he had it, he refused to practice. The
next verse:

XIV. 17. *He will vomit the riches he has devoured,
and from his belly God will drag them out.* The hypocrite wants to know God's word, but not to do it. He
wants to speak intelligently, but not to live right. Because he does not act according to what he knows,
he loses even the knowledge, in order that, since he
does not join purity of action to his knowledge, having scorned the purity of good works, he might also
lose knowledge. Accordingly the riches of the holy law,
which he devoured by reading, he vomits by forgetting,
and God drags them out of his belly, because what he
refused to keep, God roots out of his memory through
just judgment, lest he should hold God's precepts only
on his tongue, precepts that he does not follow in his
life. That is why the prophet says, *God tells the sinner,*
"Why do you proclaim my justice and adopt my cove-
nant with your mouth?" If it should ever happen that
the hypocrite appeared to hold these words of doctrine
in his mouth until the end of his life, then he would be
condemned all the more firmly, in that even the evil
person is not at all deprived of God's good gift. It is
surely written, *It is for those who hold his command-*
ments in memory to do them. The one therefore who
holds God's commandments in memory but never does
them holds his sentence of condemnation in those words
of teaching.

18. That is why it is written in Zechariah: *"What do*
you see, Zechariah?" I said, "I see a flying scroll. Its
length is twenty cubits, and its breadth is ten cubits." He
said to me, "It is the curse pronounced over the whole
earth, because every thief, as it is written there, will be
judged." What is the flying scroll if not Holy Scripture,
which, while it is speaking of heavenly matters, alerts

*Job 20:15

*Ps 49:16

*Ps 102:18

*Zech 5:2-3

our attention to the highest region of the mind, because while we sense Holy Scripture to be above us, we avoid turning our attention to the lowest realities, concupiscence, in other words. We are told that the scroll's width is ten cubits, but its length twenty cubits.[1] The breadth of our action, you see, is single, and the patience of hope is stretched double, because for our good works here we have peace of mind, and there eternal joy is prepared for us.

Truth is our witness, who says, *Anyone who leaves houses or lands, etc., will receive a hundredfold in this world and will possess eternal life in the world to come.** The number one hundred unquestionably denotes perfection, the result of ten times ten. Accordingly that one receives the hundredfold who, already having nothing in this world, has attained such perfection of mind that he no longer seeks to possess anything. This perfection gains us double for what is single, so this scroll is rightly doubled in length to twenty cubits and made ten cubits longer.

*Matt 19:29

Since, moreover, these holy words mean eternal damnation for those who either refuse the knowledge of them or at least knowingly despise them, it is rightly said of this scroll, *It is the curse pronounced over the whole earth.* He also adds the reason for its being called a curse: *"Because every thief,"* as it is written there, *"will be judged."* So since the hypocrite scorns life ac-

---

[1] There is something wrong with the CCSL text here between lines 30 and 31. The words *Veritate attestante, quae ait: Si quis reliquerit domos* are repeated in line 33, which gives the full quotation. It would seem that these words have obliterated the sentence that continues with *mitas*, which is not a word, but a part of a word. I have supplied the missing words from Migne (PL 75:1089C), which gives *quia latitude operationis nostrae simpla est et longani[mitas]*, etc.

cording to the words of the law that he knows, and seeks support from its doctrine, he is judged a thief, because by the very fact that he speaks what is righteous, he steals praise for himself out of the life of the righteous. On the same subject Zophar rightly adds,

XV. 19. *He will suck the head of adders, and the tongue of a viper will kill him.* An adder is a small   *Job 20:16 snake, but a viper has a longer body. Adders bring forth eggs, and from the eggs their young are hatched; when vipers conceive young, however, they rage about in the womb, and when they have broken the walls thereof, they issue forth from the mother's body. That is why they are called vipers, since they are born forcefully. Vipers accordingly are born in such a way that they emerge violently, and they are brought forth with the mother's death.[2] What, then, is meant by the small adders, if not the hidden suggestions of the evil spirits who creep out in people's hearts with their persuasions, which are small at first? What is meant by the viper's tongue but a violent temptation from the devil? First he creeps up slowly, but then he strikes violently. He sucks the head of adders, because the hidden suggestion is small at first, when it rises in the heart, but the viper's tongue kills him, because after the mind is captivated, it is killed by the venom of a violent temptation.

The unclean spirits first speak to a person's heart with subtle counsels, and while they slowly persuade him, they are as it were spreading the venom of adders.

---

[2] The idea that vipers' young are brought forth alive in the womb was widespread in the ancient world. It is partly based on the etymology of the word, as Gregory points out. *Vipera* is from *vivi para*, literally "born alive." But the etymology moves in another direction as well, as Gregory also indicates: *vi para* meaning "born with force."

So it is written, *They hatch adders' eggs, and they weave spiders' webs. He who eats their eggs will die, and what* *Isa 59:5 *is hatched out will burst forth as a king.** For adders' eggs to be hatched by evil people means that the counsels of evil spirits that hide in their hearts are openly followed by evil deeds. To weave spiders' webs means to perform any work in this world for the sake of earthly concupiscence. Such works are unstable and weightless, and the wind of mortal life undoubtedly carries them away. He is right to add, *He who eats their eggs will die,* because those who take counsel from unclean spirits kill the life of the soul within them.

What is hatched out will burst forth as a king,[3] because the counsel of the evil spirit hidden in the heart is nursed and becomes full-grown evil. This king is the king of snakes. Who is the head of reprobates if not the Antichrist? What is hatched out, therefore, bursts forth as a king, because he who receives in himself the counsel of adders for nursing becomes a member of the wicked head and grows in the body of the Antichrist. We are told about this hypocrite, *He will suck the head of adders, and the tongue of a viper will kill him.* When he freely accepts the evil suggestion of the ancient foe, he is beaten and later gives himself over to his violent temptations. That is why he insinuated words of flattering persuasion into the man standing in Paradise also. Him whom he has once forced to consent he draws even now albeit unwillingly, and when he is almost beaten by the sensual pleasure of his own corruption, he kills him violently.

---

[3] To put in *basilisk* here, as some do, clarifies nothing. The Vulgate has *regulus,* which means literally "a petty king or a prince." *Basileus* is the Greek word for king. *Basilisk* is a mythological creature, sometimes represented as half man, half snake, sometimes as a serpent or dragon. See *Oxford English Dictionary,* s.v. *basilisk.*

Yet perhaps we can also construe these same facts using the contrary mode of interpretation. The adder, you see, kills by means of its quick-acting poison, but the viper more slowly; accordingly the adder symbolizes the sudden violent temptation, whereas the viper shows forth the slow daily temptation. So the former demonstrates death by sucking of its head, the latter by its tongue, because the sudden temptation often kills the unwary mind as soon as it sucks; the long-lasting temptation, however, which suggests depraved actions by long-continuing persuasion, is like a viper killing with its tongue. All hypocrites, you see, have been infected by the suggestions of unclean spirits as if by the venom of snakes, so they never consider the heavenly gifts of the Holy Spirit; rather they project their whole attention outwards to win applause, so Zophar is right to add,

XVI. 20. *Let him not see the streamlets run from the river, full of honey and butter.*[*] The Lord says in the gospel, *As for him who believes in me, as Scripture says, "Rivers of living water will flow out of his belly."*[*] The evangelist immediately adds, *He said this about the Spirit, which those who believed in him were to receive.* The streamlets from the river consequently denote the gifts of the Holy Spirit. Charity is a streamlet of the river, faith is a streamlet of the river, and hope is a streamlet of the river. Since, however, no hypocrite loves God or neighbor, because he seeks the passing honors of the world, he sees no streamlets from the river because he is not inundated by the waters of charity. As long as the hypocrite is after present gain, he scorns the future reward. Since he has no faith, he sees no streamlet from the river with his mind's eye. *Faith,* you see, *is the evidence of things unseen.*[*] As long as the hypocrite holds on to what he does see, he has no regard for hope in what is unseen. He does not see the streamlets from

*Job 20:17

*John 7:39

*Heb 11:1

the river through desire, because his whole attention is focused on what can be seen. It is written, *Who hopes for what he sees?** He would have seen the streamlets from the river if he had closed his eyes to the honors of the present world and opened them to love for the heavenly homeland.

*Rom 8:24

It is worth noticing as well that instead of *streams* he says *streamlets.** The streamlets from the river, you see, can be taken to mean those spiritual gifts that run so insensibly in the lover's mind from the heavenly source that they cannot be expressed by any tongue of flesh. The lover's mind is often full of so great a gift of contemplation that he is able to see what is ineffable. This very inundation of the Holy Spirit is a rushing river, which is gathered into the mind of one who contemplates, being poured in abundantly, and the soul is filled with much more than she is able to understand.

**rivulos fluminis,* as opposed to *rivos,* "streams"

We should realize as well that when the grace of the Holy Spirit is poured into us, it fills us at the same time with honey and butter. Honey, of course, falls from above, and butter is drawn from the milk of animals. So honey is from the air, and butter from flesh. The only-begotten Son of the most high Father is God over all, and he became man among all. When he filled us with the sweetness of his divinity and the mystery of his incarnation, he satisfied us with honey and butter at the same time. Since, accordingly, the Spirit of Christ gladdens the mind that it has filled with the sweetness of his divinity and faith in his incarnation, these streamlets of the rushing river are called streamlets of honey and butter together, because they both refresh the mind with sweetness from the high knowledge of God and anoint it with the mystery of his gifts from the grace of his incarnation. Because this hypocrite, however, is in possession of external approval, he does not receive these internal gifts, so Zophar goes on to add what punishment awaits him afterward:

XVII. 21. *He will pay for all that he has done, but he will not be consumed.** He pays in torture for those desires that he illicitly kept alive here; handed over to the flames of vengeance, he dies eternally, because he is kept eternally in the state of death. He is not consumed by death, because if the life of the dying one were consumed, his penalty would also be consumed with it. Rather, in order that he might be endlessly tortured, he is compelled to live endlessly in punishment, so that he whose life here was death in guilt might live his death there in punishment. Let Zophar then say, *He will pay for all that he has done, but he will not be consumed.* He is tortured but not ended; he both dies and lives; he gives out but continues; he eternally ends, but he is without an end. Such sufferings are too terrible even for the hearing thereof; how much more the undergoing of them! Nevertheless, the fullness of evil that is his exacts the result that he should never be without punishment, so he is right to add,

*Job 20:18

XVIII. 22. *According to his many deceptions, so shall he endure.** Those who found out many devices for evildoing will be tortured with fresh devices as a penalty. What they could not surmise here, they feel there when they are given over to vengeance. Consider the case of the chosen souls who are active in good works: they are sometimes eager to do more than the Lord deigns to command. Virginity of the flesh is never commanded, but sometimes praised. If it were commanded, then marriage would certainly then be considered a sinful act, yet many excel in the virtue of virginity to the point that they give more weight to compliance than the precept demands.

*Job 20:18

Such is often the case with crooked people, and with those who behave in a depraved manner as well, namely, that they get more out of the crooked actions they perform than they could get out of the base examples of habitual evildoers. That is why they are hit with the club of a more thoroughgoing retribution, because by themselves they found out more depraved actions, for which they deserved to be hit. So he is right to say, *According to his many deceptions, so shall he endure.* He would not find, you see, more evil to do if he did not first seek it, and he would not seek it unless he eagerly ran to do it. The overabundance of evil thoughts is consequently weighed in his torture, and he is given pain for the retribution he deserves.

Even though the pain is everlasting for all condemned sinners, yet they who have also found much more evil in their own desires receive more intense torture. Zophar, however, has introduced the penalty of this hypocrite, so he forthwith adds his crime, and it is not just any old crime that he lists, but the one that gives birth to all the others. It is certainly written, *Covetousness is the root of all evil.*[*1 Tim 6:10] He who is said to be the vassal of covetousness is therefore displayed beyond any doubt as the slave of all evil. So he adds,

XIX. 23. *He destroyed and stripped down the house of the poor man; he snatched it away and did not build it, and his belly was not satisfied.*[*Job 20:19-20] Those who overpower the poor person and grind him down destroy his house; they are not ashamed to despoil him through avarice. They snatch his house away and do not build it. It is as if Zophar said openly, "He who ought to build it instead snatches it away." The Lord is going to come on Judgment Day, and he is going to tell reprobate sinners, *I was hungry, and you gave me nothing to eat; I was thirsty, and you gave me no drink; I was a stranger, and you did not take me in; I was naked, and you did not clothe me,* etc.[*Matt 25:42-43] This indictment is followed by the sentence, *Depart*

*1 Tim 6:10

*Job 20:19-20

*Matt
25:42-43

from me, you accursed, into the eternal fire prepared for the devil and his angels.*   *Matt 25:41

If the one who is convicted of not having given is punished with so severe a penalty, what will be the penalty of the one who is convicted of having stolen? He snatched it away therefore and did not build it, because not only did he not give what was his own, but he also took what belonged to someone else. Zophar was right, then, to add, *His belly was not satisfied.* The evil person's belly is avarice, because it holds whatever is swallowed by perverse desire. It follows that avarice for the things one desires is not lessened, but rather increases. It is like fire that consumes the wood thrown upon it and increases in intensity, and where the flame seems momentarily to be suppressed, there it is seen slightly later to grow. When almighty God grows intensely angry with the avaricious soul, he often first permits it to have whatever it wants; then later he takes it away for retribution, where it has to endure eternal torture for all its satisfied desires. So Zophar adds,

XX. 24. *Once he has what he desired, he cannot go on possessing it.** It is the result of still greater wrath   *Job 20:20
when what is wrongly desired is granted, and then retribution follows immediately, because he also obtained what he desired while God was angry. So the psalmist says, when it is reported that the people have wrongly desired to eat flesh, *The food was still in their mouths when God's wrath rose against them, and he slew many of them.** Usually God's judgment appears later, when   *Ps 77:30-31
their evil desires are impeded from being fulfilled. The sooner evil desires are allowed fulfillment, the sooner they are normally punished. Where hypocrites, then, hastily gather more possessions, in order that they may gain power, there it quickly happens that they may not, because even bushes that grow slowly endure year by

year, whereas those that grow quickly in a short time
wither; it is as though they hurry up to be and end up
not being. The next verse:

*Job 20:21

XXI. 25. *Not even his food remains.** His food is
all that he has coveted with a base desire, but when
hypocrites have been struck down, not even their food
remains, because when they are themselves led to eternal recompense, they are dispossessed of all the goods
that they had here. So Zophar goes on, *Because nothing

*Job 20:21

*will be left of his goods.** If, you see, anything were left
for him of his goods, he would take with him what he
had possessed. But he tried to get everything, and he refused to fear the Judge, so when he was taken out of this
life, he went to the Judge naked. As far as this wicked
man is concerned, however, his penalty and the torture
awaiting him count for less in retribution if only he is
allowed freedom in this life. Yet there is no freedom in
guilt, because it is written, *Where the Spirit of the Lord

*2 Cor 3:17

*is, there is freedom,** and his guilt is often his penalty
for the base mind. So Zophar is right to add,

*Job 20:22

XXII. 26. *When he is satisfied, he will be cornered.**
At first, of course, he is eager to store up what he avari-
ciously desires, and when he has, as it were, brought together many things in a kind of belly of avarice, he is filled
and compressed, because as long as he is anxious about
his acquisitions and how to guard them, his very wealth
presses him in. The field of a certain rich man brought
him abundant yields, but he had no place to store so much
grain, so he said, *"What shall I do? I have nowhere to store
my crops!" Then he said, "I know what to do. I will tear

*Luke
12:17-18

*down my barns and build larger ones."** Accordingly, he
who, cornered by abundance, said, *What shall I do?* was,
as it were, pressed in by too much food and agitated.

Let us consider how intense were the longings with
which he earnestly desired that his field would bring

forth abundant fruit. See now how his wishes have
been satisfied, and the field has already produced abundant crops. But since his barns are insufficient to store
the crops, the well-supplied rich man is at a loss as to
what to do. O restriction born of plenty! The soul of
the avaricious man is cornered by his fruitful field. In
saying, *What shall I do*, he unquestionably declares
that he is cornered by the results of his desires, and he
is troubled by a kind of pack of material things. Zophar
is therefore right to say, *When he is satisfied, he will
be cornered.* The mind of the avaricious person, you
see, which first sought rest in abundance, is later more
wearily troubled about how to keep it. So Zophar also
adds here again,

XXIII. 27. *He will be agitated, and every pain will
rush upon him.** The first pain he had was the very ex-   *Job 20:22
haustion caused by his concupiscence: how he would
seize the objects of his ardent desire, how he would obtain this by flattery and that by terrorism. Yet once he has
obtained his desire and acquired its object, another pain
harasses him: how to guard with fear and agitation what
he well knows he has acquired with immense trouble.
On every side he fears lurking thieves, and he dreads
undergoing what he did to others. He is terrified lest another man stronger than he should wreak violence upon
him. When he sees a poor person, he suspects a thief. He
watches over the things he has collected with great dil-
igence, lest they be carelessly used up because of their
own inherent decline. In all these circumstances fear
itself is a penalty, and he unhappily suffers as much as
he fears to suffer. Besides, he is also led to hell, and he is
committed to eternal torture. Every pain therefore falls
upon him: first the penalty of concupiscence here, later
the trouble of standing guard, and then in hell, some
time or other, the penalty of retribution burns him up.

28. Composure of heart is a wonderful thing, not seeking what belongs to another but remaining satisfied every day. Furthermore, from this composure eternal rest too is born, because by means of good serene thought the transfer to eternal joys is made. On the other hand, reprobate sinners are worn out both here by their desires and there by torture; for them as well the trouble of pain is brought forth from their troubled thoughts, while from the heat of avarice they are dragged into the furnace of hell. Since also, as we have already said, the sooner any perverse people attain their desire the more easily they are often swept away to torture, Zophar adds the following wish:

XXIV. 29. *If only his belly might be filled, in order that God might let loose against him the fury of his* *Job 20:23 *wrath, and that he might rain his attacks upon him.** The Lord rains down his attacks upon this hypocrite when he strikes down his works with the sword of his judgments. For God to rain down his attacks means that he besets the life of the wicked from above with imperative judgments to their ruin. For God to rain down his attacks means that he strikes down the hearts of those who grow proud against him; it means that he lets loose against the barren mind the arrows of his judgments, as if they were so many drops of rain condensing. So when people are finally being dragged off to Judgment, they may at one time remember that they desired what was wrong and that it was still worse eagerly to collect what they desired, and at another time they may mourn the loss of what they collected; at last indeed they may sense the fire of retribution, which sight they held in contempt, lest they should foresee it and live a good life. The next verse:

XXV. 30. *He will flee the iron weapons and rush* *Job 20:24 *upon the bow of brass.** We must realize that avarice sometimes creeps up through pride, but sometimes through fear. There are those, you see, who want to appear stronger, and so they are provoked to grasp someone else's property. There are others again who are afraid that necessary support might be lacking to them, and they give free rein to their minds to covet; they go after the property of others when they suspect that their own cannot suffice. Anything necessary is not unreasonably called *iron*, because it tortures the life of the needy with the sore of sadness; such was the shattered life of him who was sold by his brothers and of whose dire state of need it is also written, *Iron pierced his soul.**

*Ps 104:18 LXX

What else are iron weapons but the needs of this life, which press hard upon us and threaten the life of the needy? Rust, of course, wears away iron; as for bronze, however, it is usually more difficult for it to wear away. Iron accordingly symbolizes the needs of the present life, which is passing away, but bronze the eternal doom. Since the mind of the unjust pays no heed to God's Judgment, it is rightly compared to a bow, because it strikes as it were from ambush while those who are struck are not alert. They will then flee the iron weapons and rush upon the bronze bow, because they fear the necessities of the present life and seize much wealth through avarice. In this way they make themselves liable to the intransigent blows of the Last Judgment. Although they flee the iron weapons, they are caught by arrows from the bronze bow, because they foolishly take precautions against the misfortunes of time but are struck down by the eternal sentence. Those therefore who run away from severe want here when they have guilt will find there the eternity of rightful recompense. Nevertheless, before this unjust man is dragged off to Judgment, Zophar inserts what he did here. He goes on,

*Job 20:25

XXVI. 31. *He is drawn forth and comes out of the sheath, and his bitterness is glowing.** This unjust man lies in wait to plunder his neighbors, but while he is plotting in his base thoughts, it is as though the sword were still in the sheath. When he wickedly achieves the evil he plotted, he comes out of the sheath, because he issues forth from his hidden thought through the injustice of an evil action. He is revealed in action just as he was when hidden in thought. Notice that Zophar said, *He is drawn forth and comes out of the sheath.* He is obviously drawn forth by the deceiver; he comes out on the other hand by his own initiative. There is no doubt but that the one who is drawn follows the one who draws him; he who comes out, on the other hand, seems to move according to his own will. Accordingly, he who is drawn forth both by the ancient enemy for any plots and equally by his own free will is bound by his own desires; he is said to be drawn forth and to come out of his sheath. The fact that he issues forth from his own base thoughts to perpetrate the most shameful acts is due both to that unclean spirit who suggested it and to his own wickedness who consented to it by his own free will.

32. The dreadful power of that unclean spirit is further shown when Zophar adds, *His bitterness is lightning.* When lightning suddenly strikes from the sky, our eyes are blinded by fright; its brightness surrounds us, and it strikes whatever is in its path. Such and so is obviously the case with the unjust when they take for themselves the honors of this world: when their power grows bright in this world, then it happens that they are struck down at the Last Judgment. For the lightning of the wicked means the brightness of the honors paid them in this life. Since the splendor of their dignity delivers them up to eternal punishment in hell, however, it is

rightly said, *His bitterness is lightning.* He who is glad
to make a hit for the moment as if with dread and brightness will for that reason endure eternal punishment.
It is indeed written about a certain rich man that
He feasted magnificently every day.* Magnificence,   *Luke 16:19
however, is one thing, but lightning is something else.
Magnificence of course does not strike, but when the
word *lightning* is used, it is a magnificence that strikes.
Those who are in positions of power hurt others, and
their power is not incongruously called lightning, because where they are extolled against good people as
if with the brightness of glory, the lives of good people
endure suffering.

XXVII. 33. *Dreadful entities come and go upon
him.** What are these dreadful entities that are named   *Job 20:25
here, if not evil spirits who must surely be feared and
fled from by righteous minds? Since, moreover, these
same evil spirits should be, each and every one of them,
believed to attach themselves to certain vices, and since
this perverse man seems indeed to abandon some vices
temporarily but to start committing others, then surely
upon him the dreadful entities come and go, because
some evils abandon the mind of the perverse man, while
others occupy it.

You may often see the wicked who are ensconced
in positions of worldly power violently moved to anger
and doing whatever that anger whispers to them; once
their fury subsides, lust forthwith deranges their mind.
When lust temporarily retires, pride immediately, as it
were, doubles for continence in their thinking; then, in
order that other people might fear these wicked people,
they want to look frightening. Yet when the situation
requires them to say something deceitfully, they turn
off their proud frightful appearance and coax their in-
terlocutor with gentle speech. If they stop looking like

proud people, they do not recoil from the appearance of deception. In their mind vices replace other vices, so it is rightly said of them, *Dreadful entities come and go upon him*, because as many vices as are fading away and succeeding one another in pressing upon his mind, just as many evil spirits derange his soul, as though going and coming. Yet although the things he does externally only show themselves partially, all these evils gather together at once in his mind. So Zophar adds,

XXVIII. 34. *All the darkness is hidden in his se-*
Job 20:26   cret places.* No matter what good acts the hypocrite flaunts externally, some of the darkness of his evil deeds shows up; nevertheless what does show up in his deeds is less than what still hides away in his thoughts. He who does not complete the entire performance at once holds everything hurtful concealed in his mind. All the darkness, accordingly, is said to be hidden in his secret places, because although he does not display all the evil that is in him, he still wants to bestow it all on his neighbors. Zophar follows up with the retribution that awaits a mind so base:

*Job 20:26   XXIX. 35. *An unkindled fire will devour him.** The fire of hell is described in few words in a very admirable way. Material fire, you see, requires material fuel in order to be kindled. When it is needed for service, that material fire is undoubtedly fed by piled-up wood. There can be no fire unless it is lit, nor can it continue to burn without being refueled. The fire of hell, on the other hand, although it is material, and it materially burns the reprobate sinners who are thrown into it, is not enkindled by any human initiative, nor is it fueled by wood, but once created it remains inextinguishable, and it needs no rekindling, nor does it lack heat. Zophar, then, is right to say about this unrighteous man, *An un-kindled fire will devour him*. Almighty God's justice, you see, knows everything beforehand, and he created the fire of hell at the very beginning of the world, which should start burning as a penalty for evildoers, but it will never stop burning, even without wood.

We must know for certain, however, that all reprobate sinners, because they have sinned with body and soul together, are tortured there with body and soul together. That is why the psalmist says, *You will make them like a blazing oven at the time when you are present; God will upset them in His wrath, and the fire will burn them up.** The oven burns within, but he whom the fire devours begins burning from the outer extremities. In order that Holy Scripture, therefore, might describe how the reprobate sinners burn both externally and internally, it proclaims that they are consumed by fire and that they are made like an oven, so that their bodies might be tortured by fire and their souls too might burn with pain. So here again, when we are told of this impious man, *An unkindled fire will devour him*, something about his spirit is immediately added:

XXX. 36. *He who is left in his tent will be shattered.** The tent of the impious man is his body, because he is glad to live in it, and if it were possible, he would choose never to leave it. As for the righteous people, they place their joy in the hope of heaven, and their citizenship is in heaven; although they are still in the flesh, it is as though they were no longer in the flesh, because they are nourished by no pleasure of the flesh. So some of them are told, *You, however, are not in the flesh, but in the spirit.** They were certainly still in the flesh who received the teaching and advice contained in these magisterial letters, but it was as though they were no longer in the flesh, and that means to have no love for the things of the flesh.

On the other hand, this unrighteous man put all his joy in the life of the flesh, so he lived in the tent of the

*Ps 20:10
LXX

*Job 20:26

*Rom 8:9

flesh. When he has received that flesh back at the resurrection, he will obviously burn with it in hell, to whose flames he will be delivered. Then he will want to be led away from it; then, if he could, he would try to avoid its torture; then he will start to wish to avoid what he loved. Because, however, he preferred that flesh to God, by God's Judgment it happens that with the flesh he will be more intensely tortured in the fire. Here, therefore, he does not wish to leave the flesh, but he is nonetheless taken away from it; there, on the other hand, he wants to leave it, but he is stuck with it on account of punishment. Accordingly, to add to his torture, he is reluctantly led from the body here, and there he unwillingly remains in the body. Since consequently his spirit, by wrongly loving the flesh more than itself, preferred it to itself, hereafter it wants to evade the flesh in its torment, but it cannot. So it is correctly said, *He who is left in his tent is shattered.* Concerning this indictment Zophar follows up immediately with the words,

XXXI. 37. *Heaven will expose his wickedness, and earth will rise up against him.** What do we understand by heaven if not the just, and what by earth if not sinners? So we ask in the Lord's Prayer, *Thy will be done on earth, as it is in heaven.** Obviously, just as the will of our Creator is done perfectly by all the just, so it should be done by us sinners as well. Of the just it is also written, *Heaven recounts the glory of God.** The sentence that is passed on sinful humankind is as follows: *You are dust, and to dust you shall return.** Heaven accordingly exposes the wickedness of this impious man who is conducted to that terrible Judgment, and earth rises up against him. Here he never had any mercy on good or bad people, but in that dreadful scrutiny, both the lives of good people and those of sinners condemn him, and that which hurts the just more than sinners is still more

*Job 20:27

*Matt 6:10

*Ps 18:2

*Gen 3:19

serious. That is why the prophet says, *Her blood is still in her midst; she poured it out on the clearest rock; she did not pour it out on the ground where it might be covered with dust.** *Ezek 24:7

He obviously indicates the sinners with the ground and the dust, but with the clearest rock he indicates the just, who are not disfigured by the crude marks of sinners. Blood is poured out on the clearest rock when the malice of a bloodthirsty mind rages in the affliction of the just person's soul. Since therefore it is more serious to afflict the just unrighteously than the unjust, it is still worse to hurt both the just and the unjust together. Since accordingly this evil man was obnoxious to both the just and the unjust together, *Heaven will expose his wickedness, and earth will rise up against him*, to indict and condemn him. The reason is that he both withstood those whose thoughts were of heaven and oppressed those whose minds were on base things.

On the other hand it is possible that earth signifies not sinners and base people, but those who are intent on worldly business and who finally reach eternal life by the aid of almsgiving and tears. Of them the psalmist, after he has declared that the Lord is coming for Judgment, says, *He summoned heaven above and earth, that he might judge his people.** The Lord assuredly *Ps 49:4 summons heaven above when those who have abandoned all their possessions and taken up the new form of heavenly life are called to sit in Judgment and come with him as judges.

Earth is also called above when those who had been obliged to concern themselves with worldly business would rather have sought heavenly gain than earthly in that business. Of them it is said, *I was a stranger, and you took me in; I was naked, and you dressed me.** *Matt 25:35-36 Heaven consequently exposes the wickedness of this

hypocrite, and earth rises up against him, since both
those who come with God as judges and those who are
freed by Judgment stand as witnesses against his evil
ways. Nothing therefore of what he has done is hidden
at the time of his condemnation. If indeed many of his
acts are now deceitfully hidden from people, nevertheless whatever lay hidden within his breast is exposed
on the day of his condemnation. So he is right to add,

XXXII. 38. *The seed of his house will be exposed,*
*Job 20:28   *and it will be dragged down on the day of God's wrath.*
The seed of his house is exposed at that time when all
the evil that was born in his conscience is brought to
light. It is true that for a while the hypocrite's house remains hidden, since although his works appear as a good
image, his motive is hidden. What he does is one thing,
but his motive is something else. When the Judge comes,
however, every person's conscience will be led out to
bear witness; that is why it is written, *The thoughts ac-*
*Rom 2:15   *cuse or even excuse one another.* Therefore the house
is exposed by the seed of the hypocrite, because the base
thoughts of his mind are uncovered. In the day of God's
wrath he is dragged away, because when the Judge's
wrath is revealed, he is delivered to the avenging flames
and removed from the Judge's presence.

He who refused the thought of heaven while he
lived, you see, is weighed down by the burden of his
sins, so he falls out of the Judge's sight into the bottom,
where he is punished. For now, however, the Judge looks
at the sinner and endures the sight; moreover, he awaits
the conversion of each one, because it is the time for
patience and not yet the day of wrath. Yet the hypocrite
remains immovable in this time of patience while he
sets afoot much evil, and no trials assail him. On the
day of wrath, however, he is taken away, because it is
the time for recompense, so he is seized for punishment

and removed from the sight of the eternal Judge. The next verse:

XXXIII. 39. *This is the lot of the impious man from God and the inheritance of his words from God.** If he had willed to live a good life when he was put on this earth, his lot from the Lord would be a share in the heavenly kingdom. But since he chose subjection to his base desires, he found his lot from the Lord to be torture, since he did not seek a share in the grace of the Lord himself. So he is right to say *the inheritance of his words from God.* He who is pulled down to the place of punishment, you see, for the many evils he has done, was perhaps believed to be not at all judged for the bad things he said. When, however, the inflexible Judgment of almighty God requires punishment from reprobate sinners for their wanton actions, he moves against them to the very limit of retribution for evil words, in order that those who are debtors for much evil when they are delivered for punishment might pay the last single coin of their debts.

*Job 20:29

The smaller sins are forgiven those, you see, who stringently weep for the greater ones they have committed. For those who bear a greater burden of guilt, on the other hand, even the lesser sins also bear down on them in hell. The saints, however, do not wish to receive their due portion from the Lord; rather they desire to have the Lord himself as their portion. That is why the prophet prays in the following words: *My portion is the Lord.** As for the wicked man, since he did not want to have the Lord himself as his portion, he found his portion outside the Lord in the fire, in order that, shut out from his presence because he did not have the desire of finding his joy in him, he might be tortured beneath him.

*Ps 118:57

Zophar has brought up all these points in order that through these truths he had spoken of against the hypocrite he might strike a blow against the life of blessed Job; he supposed that he who had been struck down by God had done all the good he had done without a simple heart. He believed that the one struck down by God must have displeased God. Even in this matter Job's friends play the role of the heretics; the latter, when they see anyone belonging to Holy Church doing good works yet sighing under the weight of trials, they suppose that there is no good quality in their good works; they think that those whom they see suffering under God's lash are bad people, obviously not knowing that *The trials of the righteous people are many** and that *He beats every son he receives.**

*Ps 33:20
*Heb 12:6

Blessed Job, however, like the holy universal church, who calmly puts up with the darts of words cast by base people and when she hears proud words does not abandon the course of her humility, with deep humility in his heart answers and says,

XXXIV. 40. *Hear my words, I beseech you, and do penance.** After he said, *Hear*, he added, *I beseech you.* He implies the depth of humility with which he spoke when he hears proud men lifting themselves up against him, so that he might recall their understanding to the teaching of salvation. The saints within the universal church, you see, are prepared not only to teach truth but also to put up with baseness. They do not fear mockery. So he adds,

*Job 21:2

XXXV. 41. *Bear with me, that I too may speak; after I have spoken, if you wish, you may mock me.** When good people speak, you see, there are two things that they intend to do in their speeches; obviously they primarily want to profit both themselves and their hearers or, if they cannot profit their hearers, to profit themselves alone. When the useful things they say are listened to carefully, then they profit both themselves

*Job 21:3

and their hearers. When however their hearers mock them, they have certainly done their best and absolved themselves from the guilt of silence. Let then blessed Job say, in order that he may profit both himself and his hearers, *Hear my words, I beseech you, and do penance.* On the other hand, in order that he may perform what is due, even if he cannot profit his hearers, he adds, *Bear with me, that I too may speak; after I have spoken, if you wish, you may mock me.*

It is noteworthy that, intending to add *do penance*, Job prefaced it with, *Hear*, but being ready to add *after I have spoken, if you wish, you may mock me*, he prefaced it with, *Bear with me.* The reason is that *to hear* is subject to a wish, whereas *to bear* means "not to wish." The friends then should hear if they want to be taught; if, however, they are ready to mock, they should bear with his words, since obviously for proud minds the teaching of humility is a grievous and heavy load. He continues,

XXXVI. 42. *Is my disputation against a man, that I should not rightly be sad?* * Every person who pleases God and displeases people has no reason for sadness. Regarding those however who please people and displease God, or who think they displease both God and other people, if they feel no sadness, their lives are far from the virtue of wisdom. Blessed Job thought he displeased God because of his trials, and for that reason he called his soul to sadness, since the one whom he feared to have displeased was not one to be despised. If, however, his dispute was with people concerning the merit of his life, he should by no means have been moved to sadness, but he was rendered uncertain about his previous life because of his present trials, so in these trials he rightly needed to be sad. So Job adds,

XXXVII. 43. *Pay attention to me and be astonished.* * In other words, reconsider what I have done and

*Job 21:4

*Job 21:5

wonder at the trials I am suffering. He again rightly

*Job 21:5
adds, *and place your finger over your mouth.** He might
as well say it openly: "You know the good I have done,
and you are considering the trials I suffer, so restrain
yourselves as well from misguided words and in my
trials dread your own losses." We certainly distinguish
something by means of our fingers, so discrimination is
not inappropriately indicated through the finger. That is
why the psalmist says, *Blessed is the Lord my God, who*
*Ps 143:1
*trains my hands for battle and my fingers for war.** By
hands he obviously means action, by *fingers* discrimination. Accordingly the finger is placed over the mouth
when the tongue is restrained through discrimination,
lest we should fall into a foolish error through speech.
That is why he says, *Place your finger over your mouth.*
In other words, "Link up the virtue of discrimination
with your speech, that you might distinguish with your
correct words about the hypocrite the one to whom they
should be said." The next verse:

XXXVIII. 44. *As for me, when I am mindful of my*
*Job 21:6
*trials, I tremble, and shivers strike at my flesh.** Blessed
Job's last speech shows that he had not forgotten his actions. In view of that fact, when he now tells his friends,
As for me, when I am mindful of my trials, I tremble,
and shivers strike at my flesh, it is all too clear that he
is speaking derisively. It is as if he said openly, "When I
remember that I have acted like a hypocrite, I am seized
with a shaking fit, and I forthwith weep with repentance." He avows that his flesh is seized with shivers
when he remembers it. In other words, the instability
of his work collapses in view of the fear of retribution.
Zophar, however, had had a lot to say about the speedy
damnation of the wicked, and his words were meant to
sting blessed Job's integrity, so the holy man adds the
following words against him:

XXXIX. 45. *Well, then, why do the wicked live on,* *supported and strengthened as they are by riches?* * If *Job 21:7 God's patience, you see, did not put up with them, they would never live so long in sin. They are supported by riches when they begin to grow powerful, but when they are allowed to remain so long in this life, they are strengthened. Their long lives also strengthen those whose property supports them in their arrogant power. Either that, or they are certainly said to be supported and strengthened because honors support them and possessions strengthen them. On the other hand, there are many who are both supported by honors and strengthened by riches; they attain their desires in this world, but they are deprived of progeny to take their place. For these people their power is itself a pain, when they consider how great their inheritance is and the lack of heirs to whom they might leave it. What good is it if they have everything but have no sons who might take their place? The next verse:

XL. 46. *Their seed remains with them.* * To increase *Job 21:8 the greatness of their happiness, along with their abundant property they are gifted with heirs as well. Moreover, lest any passing necessity should so much as remove from their eyes those in whom their soul exults, he says about this same seed of theirs that it *remains with them.* But what if they are given children who themselves are stricken with barrenness? In such a case their family is wiped out, just as it was feared it would be wiped out by the parents' sterility. He goes on: *A throng of relatives and* *descendants is in their sight.* * Look on the present life, *Job 21:8 look on their honors and riches, look at their children, and look at their grandchildren. What if some internal thought should obsess the mind, or some domestic quarrel break up the existing happiness and security? What is worldly prosperity, if there is no joy? The next verse:

XLI. 47. *Their houses are secure and peaceful, and God's rod is not over them.*[*] They are secure and peaceful, because they live in sin, they do what is lamentable, and they lose no happiness. The rod of God's discipline does not strike them, and the more guilt they heap up, the fewer blows they receive for their guilt.

*Job 21:9

Now we have heard how they prosper internally, so let us see what prosperity smiles upon them in the field. He goes on: *Cattle conceive and do not abort; the cow brings forth and does not lose her offspring.*[*] The usage in common speech is that the bull signifies the male sex and the cow the female, but the literary language makes use of the common gender; that is why he says now, *Cattle conceive and do not abort; the cow brings forth and does not lose her offspring.* For the owners of the herd the foremost joy is when there is no barrenness in the flock that conceives; the second is that the conceived fetus is brought to birth; the third is when the born calf is nursed and brought to maturity. In order accordingly that he might show that the wicked people had the entire fecundity of the flock, he asserts that they conceived and did not miscarry, brought forth and did not lose their own offspring. Happiness is of less account, however, if while the herd increases the herdsmen do not increase. So the fruitfulness of the family immediately follows that of the herd, as he continues,

*Job 21:10

XLII. 48. *Their children go out like flocks, and their babies exult and play.*[*] These words show us that just as they are granted more possessions to own, so also many children are born to guard them. Notice that he said, *Their babies exult and play.* Lest we should think that the very play of the babies in the house of the wicked is of small account, he adds, *They take up the timbrel and the harp, and they delight in the sound of musical instruments.*[*] It is as much as to say, "The masters are puffed

*Job 21:11

*Job 21:12

up with honors and riches, while the subjects delight in playacting." But, O blessed man, why do you tell us so much about the pleasures of wicked men? You have been describing them for a long time now in your speech, but now after so much, briefly tell us what you think: XLIII. 49. *They spend their days surrounded with good things, and in a moment they go down to hell.** See now, blessed man, how long you have been telling us about their happiness; how is it that you now assert that in a moment they go down to hell, unless because it is obvious that the whole length of time that the present life lasts is as a moment when it is abruptly ended? When anyone is brought to the end, he no longer holds anything of the past, because all his time has run out, and he has no future, because there is nothing left, not a single second out of an hour. Consequently the life that could be so drastically shortened was only a moment. As I have already said, in a moment we take up the pen and put it down again. So he, as it were, had life for a moment, he who received it and lost it.

*Job 21:13

This moment can also be understood in the sense that those who were long put up with as evildoers are often snatched away by a sudden death, so that they are not even allowed to weep over their sins before dying. But the life of the just is also ended by a sudden death sometimes, so it is better to take this moment as signifying their earthly life, so that whatever could have happened was swift. Blessed Job's friends, then, who, because they saw him suffer blows, believed him unjust, are rightly taught by this blessed man's speech about the prosperity and perdition of the unjust that prosperity in the present life is no proof of innocence; rather, many people are brought to eternal life through trials, and many others who are destined for unending punishment die without trials. About them Job again adds,

*Job 21:14 XLIV. 50. *They say to God, "Get away from us."* *
Not even fools would go so far as to say these words,
but refractory people tell God, "Go away," not in so
many words, but by their behavior. Those you see who
do what almighty God forbids, what else do they do
but close their minds against the Almighty? Just as the
thought of his precepts serves to bring him inside us, so
also disobedience to his commandments means to turn
him out from his dwelling in our hearts. They therefore
say, *Get away from us*, those who refuse to offer him
entrance into themselves and assail him by their evil
actions, even if they seem to praise him with words.
They say,

*Job 21:14 XLV. 51. *We do not want to know your ways,* * obviously because they disdain that knowledge. Because
Truth tells us, *The servant who does not know the master's will but does things that deserve a whipping will
be beaten less, and the servant who knows the will of*
*Luke
12:47-48 *his master but does not do it will be beaten more,* * there
are those who do not want to know what they should do
and think they will be beaten less if they do not know
what they ought to do. But it is one thing not to have
known and something else not to have wanted to know.
He does not know who wants to understand but cannot.
He however who, in order that he might not know, turns
away his ear from the voice of Truth, is not judged to be
the one who does not know, but the one who disdains.
God's way is peace; God's way is humility; God's way
is patience.

Since, however, wicked people disdain all these
virtues, they say, *We do not want to know your ways.*
While they are proud in this life, while they are puffed
up with dignity, while they go on grasping even for
what they do not have, they disdain God's ways in their
thoughts. Since God's way in this life was humility, this

God himself, our Lord and Redeemer, came to suffer reproach, insults, and passion, and he willingly put up with adversity in this world; he courageously avoided prosperity in order that he might teach us both to aim at the prosperity of eternal life and not to be terrified of adversity in this world. Since the wicked grasp at the glory of the present life, they run away from degradation, so it is reported that they said, *We do not want to know your ways.* Obviously they do not want to know what they disdain to do. What they say is expanded in the following words:

XLVI. 52. *Who is the Almighty, that we should serve him?* * The mind of humans is badly spread thin outside   *Job 21:15
of itself; it is so scattered among material objects that it can neither return to itself internally nor find the strength to think of him who is invisible. That is why people of flesh disdain spiritual commands, and because they do not see God physically, they are sometimes brought to the point that they even suspect he does not exist. That is why it is written, *The fool has said in his heart, "There is no God."* * That is also why it is said here, *Who is the*   *Ps 13:1
Almighty, that we should serve him?

People, you see, frequently prefer to serve those whom they see physically to serving God whom they do not see. All that they do reaches only as far as their eyes reach, and since their bodily eyes cannot reach as far as God, they either disdain to offer submission to him or, if they start to do so, they give it up. As we have said, they do not believe him to exist whom they do not see with their bodily eyes. But if they humbly sought God the Creator of all things, they would find in their hearts that he who is unseen is better than the thing that is seen. They are unquestionably fashioned from an invisible soul and a visible body, but if what is not seen is snatched away from them, what is seen thereupon undergoes corruption.

The eyes of flesh are open, but they can neither see nor feel anything. The sense of sight dies, because the indweller has gone. The house of flesh remains empty, because that invisible soul who used to look out of its windows has left it. Accordingly, all carnal beings ought to judge from their own makeup that invisible entities are superior to visible ones and through this ladder of reflection, so to speak, mount toward God, since he remains there where he is invisible, and he remains there in the highest place, where he can never be grasped. There are those, however, who have no doubt that he is God and that he is incomprehensible, yet they seek not him but external gifts. So since they obviously see that his servants do not have these gifts, they disdain to serve him. Such people add still more words as follows:

XLVII. 53. *What does it profit us, if we pray to him?* * When God is not sought in prayer, the soul is quicker to get tired of prayer; when everyone perhaps asks for those things that out of hidden judgment God refuses to grant, God likewise meets disdain, because he does not want to give people what they desire. The Lord, for his part, wants to be loved more than the things he has created, so he wants to be asked for eternal goods rather than those of earth, just as it is written, *Seek the kingdom of God and its justice and all these things will be added for you.* * He did not say, "will be given," but *will be added.* He surely indicates that what is given first and foremost is different from what is added over and above.

The reason is that eternity should be present in our intention, but time in application, so that the former is given, and the latter is certainly added over and above in abundance. Nevertheless, people often ask for the good things of time and do not want the reward of eternity, so they ask for what is added, and they do not desire

*Job 21:15

*Matt 6:33;
Luke 12:31

that to which it would be added. They do not count their petition profitable if they live poorly here in time and there in eternity live rich in happiness; rather, as we have said, they are wholly intent on the visible, and they refuse to trade the labor of petition for the gift of the invisible. If they did seek what is above, they would already display the labor together with the fruit.

When the mind, you see, eagerly desires the form of its maker in its prayers, it is excited by its desire for God, it is united with heaven, and it is set apart from whatever is below; its fervent love opens it up, so that it may take hold of what is above and by taking hold of it be set on fire. To love that which is above already means to go up there, and while it pants after heaven with a profound desire, it tastes in a wonderful way that very reality that it longs to receive. The next verse:

XLVIII. 54. *Since, however, their good things are not in their hands, let their counsel be far from me.**   *Job 21:16
He who despises earthly goods and subjects them to the mastery of his mind has good things in his hand. Whoever, you see, loves them too much subjects himself to them rather than them to himself. Many righteous people were rich in worldly goods; they were upheld by possessions and dignity and seemed to have a great deal, but since in their minds they did not have excessive delight in those things that were in their possession, their good things were in their hands, because they kept them subject to the mastery of their souls.

On the other hand, the unjust people pour themselves out with all their desires in longing for external possessions to such an extent that it is not so much that they hold those possessions as that they themselves are held mentally captive by those things that they have. Since therefore their good things are not in their hands, he is right to add, *Let their counsel be far from me.*

What is the counsel of unrighteous people, if not to seek worldly honors, to disregard eternal glory, to long for transitory security with loss of interior life, and to exchange present sorrows for eternal groans? Let the holy man contemplate these thoughts of the unrighteous people and reject them, saying, *Let their counsel be far from me.* He certainly sees that it is incomparably better and chooses rather to suffer trials here for a short time than to support the punishment of eternal retribution. But not even in this life do those who desire prosperity continue to prosper, because sudden griefs often cut off their enjoyment. So he adds,

XLIX. 55. *As often as the lamp of the wicked goes out.** The wicked person often esteems the life of his children as a light, but when a child who is excessively loved dies, what seemed a lamp for the wicked goes out. Wicked people often consider the glory of present honors a lamp, but when dignity is lost, they are cast down, and the lamp that lit their way as they desired is put out. The wicked often assume that the means of obtaining earthly wealth is at their fingertips, like an immense lantern full of light, but when losses rush in upon them, they will have lost the riches that they loved more than themselves; in that case, what else have these people done but lost the lantern by whose light they walked?

*Job 21:17

Accordingly, they who do not wish to find their joy in eternity cannot even here, where they will to be set up, find joy continuously. After *As often as the lamp of the wicked goes out*, you see, Job adds, *A flood comes upon them, and it will allot the pain of his wrath.** A flood comes upon the wicked when they suffer waves of anguish from some adversity or other. When almighty God, you see, sees himself despised, and when he sees that people find joy in earthly concupiscence, seeing something in the thought of the wicked that they prefer

*Job 21:17

to him, he strikes out at them with sufferings. Job is right
to say, *It will allot the pain of his wrath.*

He who reserves eternal sufferings for the wicked
through retribution also transfixes their mind from time
to time with some transitory pain, because he strikes
blows at them both here and there, and he allots the
pains of his wrath to the wicked. Nor does present pain
that does nothing to change the base desires in the unrighteous soul free that soul from eternal retribution.
That is why the psalmist says, *He will send rain down
upon the sinners; snares, fire, sulphur, and storm winds
make up part of their chalice.** By speaking of snares,   *Ps 10:7
fire, sulphur, and storm winds, he certainly introduces
many pains. Since, however, the sinners are not corrected by these sufferings, they are summoned to eternal
retribution. The sufferings mentioned are not the whole
chalice, but only part of it. Obviously the book of their
sufferings begins here indeed with those various pains,
but it is completed by eternal retribution. So he adds
some words about their final end:

L. 56. *They will be like chaff before the wind, like
ashes scattered by the whirlwind.** When the unrighteous   *Job 21:18
are conspicuously in power, and when they violently
unleash oppression and fury, they are too harsh for the
thoughts of the weak, and they are esteemed as those
well set up in this world. When however the sentence
of the intransigent Judge is passed, all the unrighteous
people will be like chaff before the wind, because, if I
may speak thus, they are lifted up by a sudden gust of
anger and carried away to the fire. They could not be
moved in this world by the tears of the wretched but
were then in their hasty judgments like an overhanging
mountain, hard and heavy. They are lightweight for the
hands of the Judgment that seizes them, they who were
once heavy with injustice against their neighbors.

They will be like ashes scattered by the whirlwind. To the eyes of almighty God the life of the unjust is like so many ashes, because even if for the moment they look vigorous, the eyes of God's Judgment already see them burnt up, because they are reserved for eternal burning. The whirlwind scatters these ashes, because *God will visibly come; our God will not be silent. Fires will burn in his sight. There will be a raging storm all around him.** The unrighteous people are torn away by the whirlwind of this storm from the sight of the eternal Judge. They who hardened their minds here with evil desires will seem there like chaff and ashes, because the whirlwind will tear them away and carry them to eternal retribution. The next verse:

*Ps 49:3

LI. 57. *God will preserve the father's pain for his sons, and when he repays it, then will the father know.** We know that it is written, *You requite the fathers' sins in the sons and grandsons until the third and fourth generation.** It is written elsewhere, *How is it that you have turned this parable into a proverb among you in the land of Israel: "The fathers have eaten sour grapes, and the sons have gritted their teeth"? As I live, says the Lord God, no longer shall this parable be recited as a proverb in Israel. Know that all souls are mine: Just as is the father's soul, the son's soul is mine. The soul that will have sinned will be punished.** In both passages, although we find a different sense, the soul of the hearers is instructed by the sentence passed, in order that they might carefully find the path of discretion.

*Job 21:19

*Exod 34:7

*Ezek 18:2-4

Of course we carry original sin from our parents, and unless the grace of baptism frees us of it, we also carry our parents' sins with us, because we are obviously still united with them. Accordingly he requites the sins of the parents in the children, since the child's soul is stained with original sin on account of the parents' guilt. On the other hand, he does not requite the parents' sins in the children, because once we are free of original sin through baptism, we no longer carry the guilt of our parents, but only the sins we commit ourselves.

It may, however, be understood in another way, because whoever imitates the evildoing of wicked parents is also bound by their sin. On the other hand, those who do not imitate the wickedness of their parents are by no means burdened by their sin. So it happens that evil children of evil parents not only have to atone for their own additional sins but also for their parents' sins, since they know that the Lord is angry concerning the evil ways of their parents, but they are not afraid of adding their own malice to them as well. It is right that those who do not fear to imitate the ways of their evil parents should under the intransigent Judge be forced to atone even for their evil parents' guilt in the present life. That is why it is written in Ezekiel, *The father's soul is mine, and the son's soul is mine. The soul that sins will die.*

Children also, then, sometimes die for their parents' sins in the flesh. As for original sin, however, once it is blotted out, the wickedness of the parents does not stay in the soul. How is it that young children are sometimes seized by demons, unless it is because the flesh of the child is punished for the parents' penalty? The evil parents themselves, you see, are beaten, and they disdain the pain caused by the force of the beating. They are often beaten in their children in order that they might suffer more, and the parents' pain is transferred to the children's flesh insofar as the parents' evil mind is punished by the children's pain.

When, however, not young but sons who are already adult are struck for the parents' guilt, what else are we clearly given to understand but that they also pay the penalties of those whose deeds they imitate? So it is truly said *until the third and fourth generation*. Since, therefore, the children are able to witness the lives of the parents they imitate until the third and fourth generation, the vengeance thereof even reaches them who saw the things they were mischievously to copy.

58. Since guilt blinds the eyes of the wicked but the penalty finally opens them, Job is right to add, *When he repays it, then will the father know*. The impious do not know the evil they do until the punishment for that evil has already begun. That is why the prophet says, *Nothing but harsh treatment will make them hear and*
*Isa 28:19   *understand*.* Then surely they understand what they hear, when they are finally treated harshly for neglecting it. That is why Balaam says of himself, *Thus says the man whose eye has been closed; thus says he who hears God's words, who has seen a vision of the Almighty, who*
*Num 24:3-4   *falls down, and whose eyes are thus opened*.* He indeed offered counsel against the Israelites, but after that in his penalty he sees the crime he already committed. As for the chosen ones, they see beforehand in order that they should not sin, so their eyes are obviously opened before they fall, but the evildoers open their eyes only after their fall, because after sinning they see already in their penalty that they should have avoided the evil that they have done. Concerning this futile knowledge even then Job adds,

LII. 59. *His eyes will see his own death, and he will*
*Job 21:20   *drink the wrath of the Almighty*.* If only he had wanted to see his guilt while he was still placed in this life, he would not afterward drink the wrath of the Almighty. Those who turned their eyes away from the sight of their crimes here cannot there avoid the sentence of condemnation. On the other hand, those who do not dread eternal retribution are often afraid of doing evil here only out of fear of a temporary beating. Some, however, have

so hardened their hearts in wickedness that they are not
even afraid of blows while engaged in doing the things
they take pleasure in, as long as they can fulfill the evil
they planned. So Job adds more words right here about
the hardening of this wicked man's heart:

LIII. 60. *What concern is it of his what happens to*
his house after him? What if the number of his months
should be halved? * We should certainly not take it in
such a way that this wicked man, after he had been condemned to eternal punishment, had no thoughts at all for
his house, in other words, for the relatives he left behind.
Truth himself says that the rich man who was buried
in hell was concerned about the five brothers he left
behind, even when he was in the place of punishment.*

All sinners, you see, will show prudence in penalty,
those who were fools in sin. There, finally, when they
are doubled up in pain, they open their eyes to reason,
which they closed here when they were engrossed in
pleasures. Pain wrenches them and exacts the use of
wisdom of those who acted foolishly here when pride
blinded them. Their wisdom then profits them nothing,
because here where they should have acted wisely, they
wasted their time. They considered it the highest good
to have children here, to fill their house with family and
possessions, and to live long in this corruptible flesh.

But if by chance they should conceive a desire for
something that they cannot obtain without offending
their Creator, their soul is upset for a little while, and
they take thought: if they grasp that thing and incur
offense against their Creator, then their house, their
children, and their very life are forfeited. Their pride,
however, is immediately ruffled and hardens, and whatever reverses they may feel, whether it be the loss of life
or of property, they do not care, as long as they get all
that they wanted, and however long they live they do

*Job 21:21

*see
Luke 16:28

not cease fulfilling their desires. Behold, their house is struck because of their guilt, but *What concern is it of his what happens to his house after him?* Behold, for the sake of vengeance for their evildoing their life, which could have been long, is shortened.

But what concern is it of his *if the number of his months should be halved*? Therefore sinners lift themselves up against God precisely there where almighty God cuts off their self-lifting. Not even the blows they suffer humble their mind, because that mind is hardened by obstinacy in their resistance to God. It is noteworthy how grave the guilt of such a sin is, when people propose to their minds the penalty for a crime and yet not even for fear of torture bow down the neck of their heart under the yoke of their Creator.

Look now, however: when we listen to these things, a question arises in our hearts: why does the almighty and merciful God allow the reasoning power of the human mind to fall into such total blindness? Lest anyone should presume to discourse upon the hidden judgments of God beyond the proper limits, however, Job is right to add,

LIV. 61. *Will anyone teach God knowledge, who* *judges the highest things?* * When we are in doubt concerning those things that happen among us, we ought to turn our attention to the happenings that seem clear to us and put to rest the disquieting thought that has arisen out of our uncertainty. Look now: if trials call the chosen ones back to life, and if not even trials restrain reprobate sinners from evil actions, the judgments of almighty God concerning us are completely hidden, but they are not unjust. But let us lift up the eyes of our minds to the things that are above us, and in them we perceive that we have of ourselves no legitimate complaint. Almighty God, you see, knew the worth of the angels, some of

*Job 21:22

whom he placed in eternal light to remain there without lapse; others, who fell away of their own volition, he threw down out of their position of supereminence into the punishment of eternal damnation. In his dealings with us therefore he is not unjust, he who judged justly concerning a nature that was more refined than ours. Accordingly let Job say, *Will anyone teach God knowledge, who judges the highest things?* It is clear, then, that he who does wonderful things above us beyond any doubt disposes all things wisely concerning us.

After this introduction, Job goes on to say how the human soul is pressed to the limit in questioning. The next verse:

LV. 62. *This man dies vigorous, healthy, rich, and happy; his internal organs are full of fatness; his bones are well supplied with marrow. Another man, however dies in bitterness of soul, without any resources at all.* *Job 21:23-25 When matters stand thus, who could discourse on the hidden judgments of almighty God, or on why he would allow such things to happen? But while the life of the chosen ones and of reprobate sinners is not equal, the decay of the flesh after death is equal. So he adds, *Nevertheless both together will sleep in the dust, and worms will cover them.* *Job 21:26 Why should we wonder, then, if for a while their lives pass differently in the prosperity or adversity of the present world, when they return to the earth in a similar fashion through the decay of the flesh? That life alone, therefore, is the one we must consider, which the resurrection of the body extends to different terminations of retribution. What then is safety or assurance to the wicked, and what are fatness and riches, when everything is swiftly left behind here, and there that retribution that can never be left behind is found? Just as this wicked man's happiness is turned into penalty, so the pain of the afflicted righteous is turned into

happiness. Riches therefore should not extol the mind;
nor should poverty trouble it. So blessed Job among the
losses of his possessions includes no loss of thoughts in
his mind, but in his dispute with those who disdain his
downfall he retorts with the following words:

LVI. 63. *I know your thoughts very well, and your
unjust opinions about me. You say, "Where is the
prince's house, and where the tents of the wicked?"* *

*Job 21:27-28

They believed he was a wicked man, him whom they
saw temporarily fallen from a happy life. But the holy
man considers them with a regard as high as his righteousness was unbent after all his losses. What harm
had those losses done him externally when he had not
lost him whom he loved internally?

64. He already said, *Both together will sleep in
the dust, and worms will cover them.* If anyone should
wish perhaps to take these words as an allegory, we can
briefly fill it out by repeating what we have already said
about the unjust rich man. Job said above, *His internal
organs are full of fatness.* Just as fatness grows from
abundant food, so pride grows from abundant possessions, and it fattens rich people's minds, while their
souls are inflated with self-importance. Pride in the heart
is unquestionably like a certain kind of dense fatness. So
since many people commit sins out of their abundance,

*Ps 72:7

the prophet says, *Their wickedness increases like fat.* *

He continues, *His bones are well supplied with
marrow.* The lovers of this world have something like
bones when they possess power and dignity in this
world. When, however, their external dignity lacks
worldly property and riches, as far as their judgment is
concerned they admittedly have bones, but their bones
have no marrow. Therefore, since this lover of the present world is supported by power in such a way that he
also grows fat on the internal abundance of his earthly

house, Job says, *His bones are well supplied with marrow.* At least the bones of this rich man are his vicious and shameless habits, whereas the marrow in them is his very desire of living licentiously, which is never satisfied, not even when he does all the evil he can. The marrow moistens the bones, as it were, because his evil desires maintain his perverse habits and let him enjoy his pleasures.

65. There are others who have no earthly riches, but they desire them; they long to be proud, but in this world they are unable to obtain what they desire; they are unsupported by any property or dignity. Their consciences, however, turn them over to the interior judge as guilty in his sight of evil desires. All people, you see, are often afflicted in this way, precisely because they do not manage to get rich or exalt themselves. It is concerning such individuals that Job adds, *Another man, however, dies in bitterness of soul, without any resources at all.* This is how rich people unavailingly exult with proud hearts, and others who are poor are still more unavailingly afflicted in their proud hearts. Job wisely adds concerning both of these men, *Nevertheless both together will sleep in the dust, and worms will cover them.* Sleeping in the dust means closing the mind's eye on worldly desires. That is why all sinners who sleep in their guilt are told, *Awake, you sleeper; arise from the dead, and Christ will enlighten you.** ^*Eph 5:14

Worms are born from the flesh, and they cover both kinds of people, because the concerns of the flesh press upon the souls of both, whether rich or poor, because they are proud. In worldly affairs, you see, the base poor and the base rich are alike, because even if they are not supported by equal prosperity, they are troubled by a similar uneasiness, since the first already possess with apprehension what the second anxiously long for, and they grieve because they cannot have it. Let him say it then: *Both together will sleep in the dust, and worms will cover them.* Even if they are not simultaneously supported by worldly goods, they are simultaneously lulled to sleep in their care for worldly goods by the dullness of their minds. Worms cover them both, because thoughts of the flesh urge the one group, that they might have their desire, and the other group, that they might not lose what they have.

66. As for blessed Job, neither had he been arrogant over his possessions nor did he anxiously seek to recoup his losses, so no worms had covered his heart. Because he had not been dejected in mind concerning earthly cares, he by no means slept in the dust. It follows, *I know your thoughts very well, and your unjust opinions about me.* It is written, *What man knows what is in man? It is the spirit of a man which is in him.** That is why it is said here, *I know your thoughts very well.* But when is the spirit of a man unknown by another man? It is when that spirit is not revealed either by words or deeds. It is indeed written, *By their fruits you will know them.** In other words, through what happens externally, whatever lies hidden within is exposed. That is why Solomon also says correctly, *Just as the water reflects the face of him who looks into it, so are the hearts of men revealed to those who are wise.** Accordingly blessed Job, after he said that he knew the thoughts of his friends who spoke, added, *and your unjust opinions about me,* so that he might prove from a clear case that he had discovered what lay hidden in them. So he again added those unjust opinions of theirs: *You say, "Where is the prince's house, and where the tents of the wicked?"*

67. Any of the weak minds, you see, who desire prosperity in this world become very much afraid of great evils as well as severe trials; they see those who

*1 Cor 2:11

*Matt 7:16

*Prov 27:19

have suffered trials, and from their penalty they imagine their crime. They suspect that the ones they see struck down have displeased God. Accordingly blessed Job's friends saw him struck down, and they believed he had done evil. They obviously judged that, if he had not been impious, his tent would still be standing. But only those think in this way who wearily plod through weakness, who plant the feet of their thoughts in the pleasure of the present world, and who cannot cross over to the eternal fatherland with perfect desire. So Job rightly continues,

LVII. 68. *Question any one of the travelers, and you will find that they know these very same things, namely, that the evil man is kept for the day of destruction and led on to the day of wrath.** God's patience often puts up   *Job 21:29-30
for a long time with those whom he already condemns to foreknown punishment, and he allows them to flourish who, as he already sees, will commit still worse crimes. He sees the pit of condemnation that they are headed for, and he figures that it means nothing to them, that they perversely pile up things here that will be left behind. Anyone who loves honor in the present world, however, counts it great happiness to prosper here according to his own wishes, even if he is forced to undergo eternal punishment hereafter. Accordingly, he alone who has already turned the steps of his heart away from the love of the present world knows that the prosperity of the wicked amounts to nothing. So when Job speaks of the following condemnation of the wicked, he rightly begins by saying, *Question any one of the travelers, and you will find that they know these very same things.*

Those are surely called travelers who know very well that the present life is for them a road, not a fatherland, those who disdain setting their hearts on the love of the passing world, who have no desire of holding on to what is passing away but long to reach eternal life. Those on the other hand who do not wish to be travelers in this life by no means disdain prosperity in this life, and they wonder why other people enjoy an abundance of the things they desire for themselves. That is why the prophet David, when his heart had already passed beyond the love of the present world, described the glory of the impious man in these words: *I saw a wicked man overbearing and towering above the cedars of Lebanon.* But because his heart was not enslaved to this world, he rightly despised that man and said, *I passed by again, and he was gone.*

*Ps 36:35

*Ps 36:36

The impious man would surely count for something in David's esteem if his attention had not already passed on from worldly matters. This person would have seemed important to anyone not passing by, but, in fact, he appeared unimportant to the soul passing by, because when we are intent on eternal retribution, we know that present honors mean nothing.

That is why, when Moses sought the glory of heavenly contemplation, he said, *I will pass by and see the vision.* Unless, you see, he had turned away the steps of his heart from the love of the world, he could never have understood heavenly things. That is why Jeremiah demanded consideration for his mourning heart, saying, *All you who pass by on the road, look and consider if there is any sorrow like my sorrow.* Naturally, when people go through the present life, not as though traveling on a road, but as living in their homeland, they cannot understand why the hearts of the chosen ones mourn. Accordingly, Jeremiah wants them whose concern is not to have their soul bound to this world to consider his sorrow. That is why Solomon says, *Open your mouth to speak for the voiceless and for the causes of all the children who have passed by.*

*Exod 3:3

*Lam 1:12

*Prov 31:8

Those are called voiceless who never contradict or resist the preachers' words. They are also the ones who pass on and who disdain the binding of the mind's attention in the love of the present life. Consequently, since the evil person is kept for the day of destruction and led on to the day of wrath, only those who are travelers understand this, namely, that those who set their hearts on the present do not find out what punishments await the wicked, concerning which Job again adds,

LVIII. 69. *Who will blame him for the road he is on, and who shall repay him for what he has done?* * The   *Job 21:31
evil ones who are going to suffer the indignation of their Creator in eternity often experience that indignation while they are living this life as well, when they lose the prosperity they love and find the adversity they fear. Although they can be scolded for their depravity by the tongues of the righteous people even while enjoying prosperity, we know very well that it is when the deeds of depraved people cast them down that the scolding of the righteous people waxes strong.

For what reason, then, is it now said, *Who will blame him for the road he is on?* Even when the righteous are silent, is it not also a fact that as often as the prosperity of the impious is upset by the intervention of adversity, just as often their way is blamed here on earth? But blessed Job, in the same breath as he is speaking of the body of all evildoers, suddenly turns his speech against the head of all wickedness. He sees Satan entering a person at the end of the world, one whom Holy Scripture calls the Antichrist; he is lifted up so high, so absolute is his power, so great are the signs and portents by which he rears himself up with ostentation of holiness, that his actions cannot be blamed by any one, because the signs of his pretended holiness are joined to dreadful power.

Seeing all this Job says, *Who will blame him for the road he is on?* What people, in other words, would dare scold him, when fear of the very sight of him grips them?

Yet not only Elijah and Enoch, who are led back to the fray to reproach him for his ways, but also all the elect blame and condemn him, and they resist his malice with all the power of their soul. They do this, however, not with their own strength but by the grace of God, so Job is right to say, *Who will blame him for the road he is on?* Who indeed is it except God, by whose assistance the chosen ones are supported in order that they might be able to withstand evil? Sometimes Holy Scripture, to be sure, in answer to the question *who,* supplies the Almighty. That is why when it is written, *Who will raise him?** Paul answers, *God raised him from the dead.*† So when the saints contradict the person of wickedness, it is not they who blame his ways, but he by whose grace they are strengthened.

His presence,* by which he will come in a man, will make his persecution much fiercer than it is now, when he is never perceived, since he is not yet shown forth in a special way in that vessel of his, so he is right to say *him.* As for the present time, there are many who denounce and blame the ways of the Antichrist, but they do so, as it were, in his absence, since they denounce him whom they do not yet see in a special way. When, however, the Antichrist comes in that condemned man, whoever withstands his presence blames his ways to his face, him whose power he sees and disdains. Or at least blaming him for the road he is on means to upset the prosperity of his journey by the intervention of eternal punishment. This act is to be accomplished by the Lord alone and by the power that belongs to him, about which Holy Scripture tells us, *The Lord Jesus will slay him with the breath of his mouth and destroy him by the*

brightness of his coming. So it is rightly said, *Who will*   *2 Thess 2:8
blame him for the road he is on?* Job rightly follows
up as well with *Who shall repay him for what he has
done?* Who else is it but the Lord? He alone will repay
that wretched man for what he has done, since he will
break his great power through his coming and condemn
him to eternal punishment. But about this proud prince
of all evildoers, let us hear what he does as long as he
holds his place in this life:

LIX. 70. *He will be led to the tombs, and he will watch
over the heaped-up bodies of the dead.* Tombs cover the   *Job 21:32
dead, so what else do we understand by the tombs but reprobate sinners, whose souls have lost the blessed life and
lie, as it were, in tombs? This wicked man will therefore
be led to the tombs, since he will be received in the hearts
of depraved people, because they are the only ones who
receive him, those whose souls are found dead to God.
The prophet also tells us the truth about him in describing
his punishment: *All around him will be tombs of all those
who were killed and who fell by the sword.* They are   *Ezek 32:22
unquestionably near him in hell, and that same evil spirit
lies dead inside them. They were stabbed with the sword
of his wickedness, and so they fell. So it is written, *You
freed your servant David from the evil sword.*   *Ps 143:10

Job rightly adds, *He will watch over the heaped-up
bodies of the dead,* because he now sets his cunning
traps in the assembly of sinners. Because there is in the
world a scarcity of good people and a large number of
evildoers, he is right to mention the heaped-up bodies of
the dead, in order that the very large number of wicked
people might be signified: *Broad is the road that leads
to ruin, and there are many who travel it.* For Satan   *Matt 7:13
therefore to watch over the heaped-up bodies of the dead
means for him to act with cunning and malice in the
hearts of reprobate sinners, about which Job again adds,

*Job 21:33

LX. 71. *It was sweet for the gravel of Cocytus.* In
the Greek language *Cocytus* means lamentation, and
lamentation usually refers to women or to those who are
weakened in some way. Those who are worldly wise are
excluded from the light of truth, and they have tried to
hold on to certain shadows cast by the search for truth.
So they invented Cocytus, a river that flows through hell,
obviously signifying that those who perform grievous
acts quickly go to hell and reach the place of lamentation. But let us disdain the shadow of carnal wisdom;
we already hold the light of truth, and we know by the
words of the blessed man that *Cocytus* means lamentation of the weak. It is written, of course, *Act like a man
and strengthen your heart.* Those who refuse to find
their strength in God, you see, are headed for lamentation through the weakness of their soul.

*Ps 30:25

As for gravel, we are accustomed to give that name
to the little stones found in rivers, dragged along by the
running water. What else, then, does the gravel of Cocytus
mean but reprobate sinners who have surrendered to their
own pleasures, as though they are always being dragged
down to the bottom of the river? Those, you see, who
refuse courageously to withstand the pleasures of this
world become the gravel of Cocytus, because they are
headed for lamentation by their own daily sins, that they
may later wail for eternity, they who now rest delightfully
in the enjoyment of their pleasures. So when the ancient
enemy enters into that condemned man and makes him
his vessel, when he bestows his gifts on the depraved,
when he exalts them in this world with honors, when he
displays portents before their eyes, when loose minds
admire him in these portents and follow him, then it is
well said of him, *It was sweet for the gravel of Cocytus.*

While the chosen ones disdain him, and while
they condemn him and stamp on him in their minds,

his loving followers are being dragged down to perpetual lamentation as if by the waters of pleasure, those who fall down to the bottom by daily sins through worldly concupiscence like gravel. To some he offers the taste of his sweetness through pride, to others through avarice, to others through envy, to others through deceit, and to others through lust. As many kinds of vices as he entices them to, so many different sweet drinks does he offer them. When he persuades the mind to any kind of pride, his words become sweet, because the perverse person likes to seem important to other people. When he is ready to suggest avarice to the mind, what he secretly says becomes sweet because need is averted through abundance; when he suggests any kind of envy, what he says becomes sweet because when the perverse mind sees somebody else lose ground, he exults at seeing himself by no means insignificant in consequence. When he suggests any kind of deceit, what he says is sweetened because when he deceives others, he seems so much more prudent to himself. When he speaks of lust to the deceived mind, what he suggests seems sweet because he weakens the soul by pleasure.

So for as many vices as he inserts in the hearts of carnal people, he offers as many sweet drinks to them, as it were. This sweetness of his, as I have already said, only those perceive who have given themselves over to the pleasures of the present life and are being dragged down to eternal lamentation. So it is well said, *It was sweet for the gravel of Cocytus*, because what is bitter to the chosen ones is sweet to reprobate sinners. He therefore only feeds with his delights those whom he is shoving by daily sins to lamentation. The next verse:

LXI. 72. *He drags all men behind him, and in front of him are too many to be counted.** In this verse *men* *Job 21:33
means those who have a taste for what is human. But

since all men outnumber those who are too many to be counted, we must find out why he says that those in front are too many to be counted and those he drags behind him are all. Is it because the ancient enemy enters the man of perdition and then drags all the carnal people along beneath the yoke of his sovereignty? But now before he appears he also draws along those who are too many to be counted, but not all the carnal people. Every day many of them are called back from carnal works to life, and some through a brief period of repentance, others through a long one, return to the state of justice. In the present time, although he does not display the stunning signs of his deception, he does seize souls too many to be counted. But when he has done wonderful prodigies before the eyes of the carnal people, then he drags behind him not those who are too many to be counted, but all of them, because those who enjoy present good things subject themselves to his power without drawing back.

But as we have already said, it means more to drag all people than to drag those who are too many to be counted. Why then does Job first say that he drags all of them, and then in addition say that his subjects are too many to be counted? Reason demands that he should first give what counts less and afterward give the greater number in addition. We should realize, however, that it meant more to say *too many to be counted* in this verse than *all*. He drags all people behind him, you see, because in three and a half years he binds under the yoke of his dominion all those whom he found eager for the life of the flesh. In front of him, however, he holds those who are too many to count, because for five thousand years or more, although he could not drag along all the carnal people, in such a long period of time there were many more whom he seized—they were too many to count—than all of those whom he found to be seized in such a short time of three and a half years.*[4]

*Dan 12:7; Rev 12:6-7, 14; 13:5

So Job is right to say, *He drags all men behind him, and in front of him are too many to be counted*. Then he takes fewer, although he will have taken all, but now he seizes more, although he does not invade the hearts of all. Blessed Job discoursed against the prince of all the wicked people in a wonderful way, against him who is allowed to extol himself in this life but is destroyed at the coming of the Lord. Concerning himself, Job clearly shows that it was not for displeasing the Lord that he received his blows. If any wicked person is allowed to prosper in this world, it is necessary that God's chosen one should be kept in check by blows. On this account he argues with his friends, saying,

LII. 73. *Why then do you comfort me in vain, when your replies have been shown to be at variance with the truth?** Blessed Job's friends could not comfort him, because their discourses flew in the face of truth. Because they called him a hypocrite or an impious man, they themselves lied and committed a crime, and in so doing they unquestionably aggravated the pain of the just one who was covered with wounds. The minds of the saints, you see, love truth, and for that reason they are tortured by the sin of someone else's deceit. The more they see how grave a crime it is to lie, the more they hate lies, not only their own but also those of others.

*Job 21:34

---

[4] Gregory's "three and a half years" is equivalent to the calculation of the end time in the biblical passages (Dan 12:7: "a time, two times, and half a time"; Rev 12:14: "a time, and times, and half a time"; Rev 12:6-7: "one thousand two hundred sixty days"; Rev 13:5: "forty-two months").

BOOK 16

Those whose charges against the words of Truth fall short often go so far as to repeat matters that are already well known, lest they should seem losers by their silence. So now Eliphaz, being pressed hard by blessed Job's speech, speaks out concerning truths that no one is ignorant of. Here is what he says:

I. 1. *Can man compare himself to God, even if he had perfect knowledge?* * Compared with God's our knowledge is obviously ignorance. Our wisdom comes from participation in God, not from comparison. What, then, is surprising about that which he utters as dogma, when it could be known even if unspoken? As if he were defending God's power, he further adds,

II. 2. *What advantage is it to God, if you are just? What do you bestow on him, if your life should be spotless?* * Indeed, all the good that we do helps us, but does not help God. That is why the psalmist says, *I told the Lord, "You are my God. You have no need of anything good from me."* * He is truly Lord to us, because he is certainly God, and he does not need the goodness of his servant; rather he bestows the goodness that he receives, so that the goodness offered might profit not himself, but those who first receive and then give back. Even when the Lord comes with Judgment, he says, *As often as you benefited one of these, the least of my brothers, you benefited me.* * With admirable loyalty he speaks here of the compassion of his own members. For the very reason that he is our Head, he helps us himself, and through our good works for his own members he too is helped. Eliphaz again adds something that everybody knows and says,

*Job 22:2

*Job 22:3

*Ps 15:2

*Matt 25:40

264

III. 3. *Is it because of fear of you that he accuses you and enters into judgment with you?* * Who, even if out of his mind, would think that God would accuse us out of fear or out of dread pronounce judgment against us? But those who do not know how to weigh their own words beyond doubt allow useless speech to proliferate, and if they never correct themselves for such behavior, they are quick to move on to hurtful and insulting words. So Eliphaz, who began with useless words, now bursts out with an insulting speech and says,

IV. 4. *Is it not because of your many vices and innumerable wicked deeds?* * Take heed of the sluggish heart that turns to useless words and from useless words has burst out first in the sin of deceit and then in insults. These are unquestionably instances of growing guilt, when the tongue is not restrained but never lies still where it has fallen; instead it continues to fall into worse sins. The words that follow, however, are clear enough from the story, so they do not need literal interpretation.

5. Since we have said that blessed Job's friends play the role of the heretics and that Job himself signifies Holy Church, we will now at this point show how the words of Eliphaz correspond with the false teaching of heretics. The next verse:

V. 6. *You have taken away a pledge from your brothers without a cause, and you have deprived the naked poor of their clothes. You provided no water for the weary, and you have withheld bread from the hungry. By the force of your arm you have taken possession of the land, and being the most powerful lord, you held it.* * In Holy Scripture the word *pledge* sometimes means the gifts of the Holy Spirit and sometimes the confession of a sin. *Pledge* means the gifts of the Holy Spirit, for example, when Paul says, *He gave us the pledge of the Spirit.* * We receive a pledge for this reason, you

*Job 22:4

*Job 22:5

*Job 22:6-8

*2 Cor 1:22

see, that we may have certitude concerning a promise made to us. The gift of the Holy Spirit is accordingly called a *pledge*, because it fortifies our soul and gives us certitude of interior hope. On the other hand the word *pledge* tends to be understood as the confession of sin, since it is written in the law, *When your brother owes you anything, and you take away a pledge from him, you* *Exod 22:26* *must return the pledge before sundown.**

Our brother becomes our debtor when any one of our neighbors shows that he has failed us in some way. We indeed call sins *debts*. Thus the sinful slave is told, *Matt 18:32* *I forgave you the whole debt.** We pray every day in the Lord's Prayer, *Forgive us our debts, as we also forgive* *Matt 6:12* *our debtors.** From our debtor we receive a pledge when we already hold a confession of his sin from the one who is known to have sinned against us, and through that pledge we are asked to forgive the sin that has been committed against us. The one who admits the sin he has committed and receives forgiveness has already given a pledge, as if it were for a debt. That pledge assuredly we are commanded to return before sundown, because before the sun of justice goes down in our hearts through sorrow, we must acknowledge our forgiveness to the one from whom we receive confession of guilt, in order that the one who mentions failure in duty against us might duly feel forgiven by us for his failure.

Because, consequently, Holy Church receives any of the heretics who turn back to the true faith, she first persuades them that they should confess the guilt of their error. So it is in the guise of the heretics that Eliphaz says, *You have demanded a pledge from your brothers without a cause.* In other words, "You have uselessly required of those who come to you from us confession of error." If, on the other hand, as we have already said, we take *pledge* to mean the gifts of the Holy Spirit, the heretics say that Holy Church has demanded a pledge from their brothers in the sense that they suspect that those who come to her lose spiritual gifts. So he goes on, *You have deprived the naked poor of their clothes.*

7. Those whom the heretics attract by their false preaching, they expect to wear the tenets of their doctrine as though they were wearing clothes, and they think they are wearing those clothes just as long as they imagine they keep the tenets they preach to them. So when some of them return to Holy Church, the heretics forthwith suspect that they have lost the clothes of their doctrine. Since, however, a naked person cannot be despoiled, we must ask how it is that one who is first described as naked can later be despoiled. On the other hand we must know that everyone who enjoys purity of heart is without the covering of duplicity and is therefore naked.

There are some of the heretics too who have purity of heart, even though they receive the perverse dogmas that they teach. These people are unquestionably both naked because of their own purity and dressed, as it were, with the preaching of their mentors. Every one like them easily returns to Holy Church, because they are strangers to malicious duplicity; the heretics admit that those who they say have been despoiled of their clothes by the church are naked, because they consider each one of them simple, slow, and dull-hearted, considering them lost as far as their depraved teachings are concerned.

8. Eliphaz goes on, *You provided no water for the weary, and you have taken away bread from the hungry.* Since the heretics have no solid foothold in truth, they sometimes endeavor to excel in fluency, and they boast against the catholic faith as though they knew doctrine. They go after all those they catch sight of in order to

interest them in their perverse conversation, and when they associate other people with themselves to their ruin, they suppose they are acting vigorously. We call those people weary who are tired of the heavy load of this world. That is why Truth himself says, *Come to me, all you who labor and are burdened, and I will give you rest.** *Matt 11:28

Consequently the heretics, since they do not stop preaching their dogmas, deride Holy Church for her inexperience, as it were, and say, *You provided no water for the weary, and you have taken away bread from the hungry.* They suppose they are giving water to the weary when they offer their error as a drink to certain ones who are struggling under an earthly responsibility. They opine that they have not taken away bread from the hungry, because even when they are asked about invisible and incomprehensible matters, they answer with colossal boldness. They think themselves more learned than anybody else when they presume so far as to speak of things unknown, which is still sadder.

Holy Church, however, when she sees anyone hunger for something that for his own good he should not receive, either she modestly holds it back if it concerns knowledge that she has, or if it concerns a truth that is still unknown, she humbly admits that she does not know. She calls back the heretics to an attitude of due humility, and she tells them through her chosen preacher, *Do not be wiser than befits wisdom, but be wise for the sake of right conduct.** He says elsewhere, *Do not think too highly, but rather be afraid.** It is written further, *Do not seek anything higher than yourself, nor should you examine anything beyond your power.** In another book we find, *If you have found honey, eat only what satisfies you, lest if you should exceed your capacity, you might vomit it out.** Surely the finding

*Rom 12:3
*Rom 11:20

*Sir 3:22

*Prov 25:16

of honey is equivalent to the tasting of the sweetness of holy intelligence. That only a sufficiency is eaten implies that our understanding is moderated according to the measure of perception, because too much honey causes vomiting, and those who desire to understand more than they are able also lose what could nourish them. Since, therefore, Holy Church does not allow weak minds to study high truths, blessed Job is told, *You have taken away bread from the hungry.*

9. Since the heretics also envy her greatness, because she holds all the peoples in the true faith, when they find themselves in times of material prosperity, they exceed moderation in raising proud voices against her, and they reproach her openly just as much as they previously secretly envied her power. Here is what they say: *By the force of your arm you have taken possession of the land, and being the most powerful lord you held it.* It is as if he said openly, "That your preaching has reached and won the whole earth is due to the force of power, not reason and truth." Because they see the Christian princes loyal to her preaching, they suspect that all that the peoples' credit her with is due not to the worth of righteousness, but to the force of worldly power. The next verse:

*Job 22:8

VI. 10. *You have sent the widows away empty-handed, and you have weakened the arms of orphans.* The peoples who subjected themselves to the preaching of the heretics conceive depraved offspring from carnal understanding of their errors, and they are associated with them in condemnation. But when Holy Church either receives the preachers of error themselves, once they are won over by reason or, when they are still obdurate in their attachment to perversity, confines them with the chain of discipline, the heretics find themselves forsaken when the peoples without preachers stay with

*Job 22:9

them, so what else do the heretics groan about to Holy Church but abandoned empty-handed widows? In the absence of the teachers of heresy, the heretics consider the ministry of their disciples impaired, and the heretics complain that the church has weakened the arms of orphans.

Certainly Holy Church, while she receives some of the heretics who come to her, obviously contradicts their former error. There are those, you see, who so strongly support physical virginity that they condemn marriage, and there are others who praise fasting so highly that they curse those who take necessary food. Paul speaks about such as these when he says, *They forbid marriage and enjoin abstinence from foods which God created for the faithful to partake of with thanks-*
*1 Tim 4:3 *giving.*[*] Accordingly, because Holy Church calls them back from the carnal attraction of their fanaticism, and the heretics see them living differently from the way they taught them, they curse the church for having weakened their arms from the practices that they formerly followed. Accordingly, during this time of discipline, if any adversity comes upon the church, they maintain that it has happened as a just punishment for her sins. So he continues,

VII. 11. *Now you are surrounded by traps, and*
*Job 22:10 *sudden fear troubles you.*[*] Sudden fear troubles those who neglect the consideration of the imminent ruin that threatens them because of the coming of the intransigent Judge. The heretics believe that the faithful people are troubled by the guilt of bad faith, so they charge that they are surrounded by traps. They suppose that these people do not foresee the future, and in the people's tribulation they think the people are troubled by sudden fear. Still hurling taunts at the people, the heretics add, *You thought you would see no darkness, and you did*

not expect to be engulfed by the onset of flood waters.   *Job 22:11 It could be said more clearly thus: "Hopefully you predicted security and peace for yourself, and on that account you boasted of your presumption as of the coming of light, supposing you would never be oppressed by trials. But see now how you are afflicted by misfortunes that have come upon you, and the darkness of trials is showing whether the faith you hold is correct." Eliphaz compares these trials to flood waters, because while some trials follow fast on the heels of others, they are like rising waters with more waters following fast upon them. The next verse:

VIII. 12. *Do you not know that God is higher than heaven, and that he is loftier than the tops of the stars? Do you say, "What does God know?" and "Does he judge through gloomy darkness?" Clouds are his hiding place, and he has no consideration for our concerns. Rather he walks on the vault of heaven.* Many people *Job 22:12-14 are so dense that they cannot be afraid of anything that they do not see with their physical eyes. Thus it happens that they do not fear God whom they cannot see. The heretics, however, think they are wise, and they produce words of scorn against the catholics, who, they suspect, do not fear God whom they cannot see physically, so that through mental dullness they regard their Creator, who exists higher than heaven and beyond the tops of the stars, as being unable to see at such a distance. Thus, because between us and the heavenly throne lie the various levels of the upper air, it is as though God were wrapped in a cloud and pronounced Judgment out of darkness; intent on the higher realms, he would pay no attention to the lower reaches; he who presses against the hinges of heaven by encircling them would not see anything below.

But who would be so foolish as to suppose such a thing of God, who is unquestionably always the

Almighty and attends to everything in such a way that he may be immediately present to each one; conversely he is present to each one in such a way that he may not be absent from all. Even if he should desert some sinners, he is nevertheless present through Judgment to the very same ones whom he seems to assist by his absence. He accordingly surrounds the world externally in such a way that he may fill it internally; he fills it internally that he may surround it externally. He rules the highest in such a way that he may not be absent from the lowest; he is present to the lowest in such a way that he may not leave the highest.

He hides his appearance in order that he may be known in his actions; he is known in his works in such a way that he can nevertheless not be comprehended by the appraising knower; he is not present in such a way that he can be seen; he cannot be seen, and yet his very Judgment testifies to his presence. He allows himself to be understood, and yet the very ray of understanding darkens his being for us. On the other hand, he restrains us by the darkness of ignorance, and yet rays of his glory flicker here and there in our minds, inasmuch as the darkness is lifted for something to be seen and driven back trembling. The mind cannot see him as he is, but it knows by seeing to a certain extent. The heretics, however, do not judge that Holy Church knows all this, because they think in their foolish opinionatedness that they alone are wise, and they typically continue in the same vein:

IX. 13. *Do you wish to follow the world's path, which wicked men have trod?** Just as the path of our Redeemer is humility, so the world's path is pride. Accordingly the wicked tread on the world's path, because through the desires of this life they walk arrogantly. Concerning such wicked people he also adds,

*Job 22:15

X. 14. *They are taken away before their time, and a river overturns their foundation.** Since the length **Job 22:16* of our life is doubtlessly fixed beforehand by God's foreknowledge, we must certainly ask ourselves what is the reason that now prompts him to say that the wicked are taken away from the present world before their own time. Even if almighty God does often change a decision, he never changes his Judgment. Accordingly, that time when anyone is taken out of this life is the time foreknown by God's power before time began. But what we must know is this: almighty God creates and directs us according to the merits of each single person, and he also arranges each one's end, so that such and such an evil person should live only briefly, lest he should prove a bad influence on many people who do what is right, or such and such a good person should last longer in this life, in order that he might assist many people in the doing of good works. On the other hand an evil person might be allowed to live longer so that his depraved actions might grow worse and the just might be purified by the temptation offered by such actions, and his own life might be improved thereby, or the good person might be quickly taken away, lest if he lived longer on this earth, malice might corrupt his innocence.

We must nevertheless realize that God's kindness reaches so far as to grant the sinners time for repentance. But because the time so received is not used for the profit of repentance but is rather turned to the doing of evil, the merit they could have gained from God's mercy is lost. In any case, almighty God foreknows the time of each person's death, the day his life ends, so no one could die at any other time except the very day of his death. If, as we read, fifteen years were added to Hezckiah's life,* his lifetime indeed grew from that mo- **2 Kgs 20:6* ment when he should have died; accordingly God's plan foreknew the time at which he afterward took him away from this life. If such is the case, what do these words mean: *The wicked are taken away before their time*? Is it not that all those who love the present life promise themselves long enjoyment of it? But when death does come upon them and takes them out of the present life, the length of their life, which they were accustomed to make longer in their imagination, is cut off. So he is right to say of them, *A river overturns their foundation*.

15. The wicked, you see, disregard the heart's journey out to eternity as long as they do not see that everything in the present world is passing; they fix their mind on the love of the present life and construct a foundation, as it were, of a long stay in that life, because their desires are firmly planted in the soil of earthly affairs. In this way Cain is the first to be described as the founder *Gen 4:17 of a city on earth,* and he is thereby clearly portrayed as a stranger, because he dug a foundation on the earth, and he was an exile from the solid ground of the eternal homeland. Surely a stranger from the highest position, he who located his heart's resting place in worldly plea-

Gen 5:3, 18 sure sunk his foundation in the lowest place. So Enoch, which is interpreted "dedication," was the first to be born in his family. In the group of the chosen, however, Enoch[1] is said to have been the seventh, because reprobate sinners in this life, which is the first age, dedicate themselves by building; the chosen, however, await the dedication of their building until the end of time, that is, the seventh age.

---

[1] If one counts Adam's descendants in Genesis 5:3-18 and adds Cain, Enoch is the seventh. Apparently Gregory identifies this Enoch with Cain's son mentioned in Gen 4:17. This whole passage appears to be a meditation on Hebrews 11:10.

You could see, in fact, many people focus on worldly aims alone, go after honors, pant after obtaining possessions, and aim at nothing after the end of this life. What, then, are they doing but dedicating themselves in the first generation? As for the chosen ones, you would never see them focusing on anything concerning the glory of the present life; rather you would see them freely accepting poverty and calmly undergoing misfortune in the present life in order that they might be crowned at its end. For the chosen ones, then, Enoch is born in the seventh generation, because they are aiming at the dedication of their joy in the glory of the final retribution. In the meantime the mortality of the present life goes on with daily loss of time, and by taking away the reprobate sinners it destroys their dedication; Zophar rightly says about the wicked men, *A river overturns their foundation.* In other words the very course of changeability that the sinners run overturns the fixed state of their perverse building. The next verse:

XI. 16. *They said to God, "Leave us."** Who would doubt that blessed Job also said this?* Lest we tire the reader, we avoid repeating the exposition we have already given of blessed Job's words. The next verse: *Their evaluation was that there was just about nothing that the Almighty could do.** In this speech he uses different words but expresses the same sentiment. What in fact blessed Job said was namely, *Who is the Almighty that we should serve him?** Eliphaz repeats, *Their evaluation was that there was just about nothing that the Almighty could do.* He continues,

XII. 17. *Yet he had filled their houses with good things.** The Lord fills the houses of evildoers with good things, because he does not deny his gifts even to those who render him no thanks, in order that they might either become embarrassed, considering the kindness of

*Job 22:17

*see book 15.XLIV.50

*Job 22:17

*Job 21:15

*Job 22:18

the Creator, and return to goodness, or that when they show contempt for any idea of a return, their punishment hereafter might be greater for the fact that they repaid the abundant bestowal of God's good gifts here below with evil. Thus heavier punishment would in the next world overtake those whose malice in this one not even gifts won over. The next verse: *Let their purpose be* *far from me.** This too is one of blessed Job's maxims.

*Job 22:18

*Job 21:16

He said in fact, *Let their counsel be far from me,** even if *purpose* is slightly different from *counsel*. Purpose indeed is in the mouth, but counsel in thought. When accordingly Eliphaz prefers to be far from an evil purpose and blessed Job from evil counsel, it is certainly clear that the former wishes to separate himself from evil words and the latter even from evil thoughts. The next verse:

*Job 22:19

XIII. 18. *Righteous men will see it and be glad,* *and the blameless man will deride them.** When the righteous people see the unrighteous ones go wrong in this world, they cannot rejoice at their going astray and being lost, because if they are glad because of their going wrong, they are not righteous. On the other hand, if their gladness is caused by exultation, because they perceive that they are themselves not like other men, they are certainly proud men. That is why the Pharisee lost justification when he boasted of displaying himself above the publican's merits, saying, *I thank you* *that I am not like the rest of men: robbers, criminals,*

*Luke 18:11

and adulterers, or even like this publican.* On the other hand, if we say that righteous men can exult with perfect joy over the death of evildoers, what is our joy worth in this world over the retribution of sinners, when even the life of the righteous people is in question? Let us distinguish accordingly the time for fear from the time for exultation.

The righteous people, therefore, even now see the unrighteous ones, and they repine because of their wickedness. When they see them struck down, however, they become uneasy about their own lives as well. When, therefore, shall the righteous people see the ruin of the ungodly and be glad, if not when they have united themselves finally with the intransigent Judge with perfect security in exultation, and when they see their condemnation in that Final Judgment, having no longer any reason to fear for themselves? So now they see reprobate sinners and they sigh, but then they will see and deride them, because in their exultation they will despise those whom, not without a sigh, they once looked at behaving wickedly, and not without fear saw them die for their evil works. So in the following paragraph we are told about their final condemnation, as Eliphaz forthwith continues,

XIV. 19. *Is not their temerity immediately cut short, and does not the fire consume what is left of them?* *   *Job 22:20
Here below the wicked act with temerity, and they rear themselves up in their depraved behavior, because they both behave perversely and for their depraved behavior are never beaten. They sin and they flourish; they sin some more, and their earthly possessions multiply. Their temerity is cut short, however, when they are plucked from the present life to their ruin or dragged away from the eternal Judge's presence to the eternal fire of hell. Furthermore, although they leave their dead bodies here, they receive them back again at the resurrection, in order that they may burn in that same flesh in which they sinned. Just as their guilt resided in mind and body, so their penalty will be felt both in their souls and in their flesh. Since therefore not even that which they left dead here below will be free of torment for them, it is rightly said here, *Does not the fire consume what is left of them?* The next verse:

XV. 20. *Give in to him and have peace. By that means you will bear abundant fruit. Receive the law*
*Job 22:21-22 *from his mouth, and keep his words in your heart.** The sin of pride amounts to the teaching of better people, and that is what the heretics always do: they take their own depraved thoughts and try to teach them to catholics. Then indeed they think catholics give in to God when they happen to consent to their own perversity. They promise peace to those who give in, because against those who consent to them they finally stop quarreling. They promise excellent fruit to those who give in to them, because they consider only those to be doers of good works whom they boast of having won over to their dogmas. So that is their due that he adds: *Receive the law from his mouth.* It is their own thoughts, you see, that they surmise are proceeding from God's mouth, so it continues, *Keep his words in your heart,* as if he added, "Which you have held in your mouth up to now, but not in your heart." Because Job rejected their perverse dogmas, you see, they charge him with having kept God's word not in his thoughts but by showing off. So they administer the virus of their pestilential persuasion in the form of a kind of meekness, in order that they might counsel the church to keep the word of God in her heart, though if it had ever left her heart, she would not hear such words from them. The next verse:

XVI. 21. *If you return to the Almighty, you will be*
*Job 22:23 *rebuilt, and you will keep evil far away from your tent.** The heretics think the faithful people have receded from God, because the heretics see them resisting the heretics' own preaching. When they also see the people troubled by the misfortunes of the present time, they try to draw the people, as it were, to the Creator's grace by admonishing them. Here is what they say: *If you return to the Almighty, you will be rebuilt.* In other words, "By

resisting our dogmas you have receded from God, so the building of justice has been destroyed in you."

As for the tent, we sometimes take it to mean the dwelling place of the body and sometimes the dwelling place of the heart. Just as the soul dwells in the body, you see, so we dwell in the heart through thoughts. Accordingly, wickedness in the tent of the heart is the perverse intention in the focused thought, but wickedness in the tent of the body is the completed perpetration of a carnal action. So Eliphaz, being a friend of the blessed man, understood some things that were true, yet he deviated from righteousness in other matters, and in these he plays the role of the heretics. He was unaware of the fact that blessed Job had been struck down because of his virtues, and he believed that the one whom he saw prostrate had gone astray, and he promises him that if he returns to the Almighty, *You will keep evil far away from your tent.* It is as if he said openly, "Whoever returns to God after going astray will be purified both in mind and in action." The next verse:

XVII. 22. *Instead of earth he will lay down hard stone, and instead of hard stone he will release torrents of golden water.** What does the earth signify but impotent action, and what does hard stone signify but strength? What do we take the torrents of golden water to mean but the teaching of internal glory? Almighty God lays down hard stone instead of earth for those who turn to him, because instead of impotent action he confers the strength for vigorous work; instead of hard stone he releases torrents of golden water, because instead of vigorous work he gives an abundance of glorious internal teaching. Thus any repentant sinners can come out strong from weakness, and in their strength they can rise even to the level of speaking out words of internal glory, inasmuch as their impotent action,

*Job 22:24

in which they sink like the earth, becomes strong with the vigor of righteous living. And since perception is drawn from life, rivers of golden water can flow out of that vigor, because in the mouth of those who live righteously glorious teaching flows abundantly. The next verse:

XVIII. 23. *The Almighty will be against your enemies, and silver will be heaped up for you.* What other greater enemies do we have than the evil spirits, who besiege us in our very thoughts, in order that they might be able to break into the city of our minds and hold it captive under the yoke of their dominion? As for the word *silver*, the psalmist bears us witness that it means Holy Scripture. He says, *The word of God is pure silver, tested by fire.* When we are intent on Holy Scripture, we often suffer more grievous attacks from the evil spirits, because they throw the dust of worldly thoughts into our mind's eye, so that they might obscure the light of interior vision we were intent on.

That is surely what the psalmist had undergone when he said, *Get away from me with your malice, and I will search the commandments of my God.* He clearly insinuates that he could not search out God's commandments as long as he endured the hidden traps of evil spirits in his mind. We notice that the same thing is symbolized in Isaac's relations with the crooked Philistines, who stopped up the wells that Isaac had dug with heaped-up soil.* We certainly dig wells for ourselves when we search deeply in the hidden places of Scripture with our minds. These wells the Philistines secretly stop up when the unclean spirits put in worldly thoughts while we are intent on the highest realities, and as soon as the water of the knowledge of God is found, they take it away. But since no one overcomes these enemies by his own strength, Eliphaz continues, *The Almighty will*

*Job 22:25

*Ps 11:7

*Ps 118:115

*Gen 26:15

be against your enemies, and silver will be heaped up for you. It is as though he said openly, "While the Lord drives the evil spirits from you by his own strength, the glowing talent of God's word within you continues to grow." The next verse:

XIX. 24. *Then you will have abundant delight on account of the Almighty.** Abundant delight on account of the Almighty means food that satisfies the appetite that is the love of Holy Scripture. In her words we unquestionably find as much delight as we receive different kinds of knowledge for our profit, so that at times naked history nourishes us; at other times the moral sense of allegory, hidden beneath the veil of the literal text, feeds us internally; at other times contemplation leaves us suspended on high, already shining with eternal light even in the darkness of the present life. Remember that anyone who has abundant delight is freed, as it were, and unimpeded, and he rests from his intense labor as though in weariness, obviously because when the soul begins to have abundant interior delight, it no longer consents to dwell on worldly occupations. Rather it is captivated by love of the Creator and by its captivity is henceforth free, so it weakly pants for the contemplation of his presence. As if by growing weary it were growing strong, since it is no longer able to carry base encumbrances, it quietly hurries to him whom it loves internally.

That is why someone also wrote in wonder at the bride, *Who is it who is going up from the desert with abundant delight?** Unless Holy Church had abundant delight in the word of God, you see, it could not go up from the desert of the present life to a higher plain. Accordingly it has abundant delight, and it goes up, because as long as it feeds on mystical knowledge, it is daily lifted up to heavenly contemplation. So the

*Job 22:26

*Song 8:5

psalmist says for his part, *Night is my illumination in my*
*Ps 138:11
delight.* This means that the eager mind is refreshed by
mystical knowledge, so that the darkness of the present
life is already illuminated for her by the brightness of
the day that is coming; the intensity of that future brightness can then burst forth with understanding even in the
darkness of this corruption, and the soul can learn by
foretasting its nourishment what the delight in the word
of God is, and what it means to hunger for the food of
truth. The next verse:

*Job 22:26
XX. 25. *You will lift up your face to God.** Lifting up
one's face to God means raising one's heart to search out
the highest realities. Just as we are known and visible to
humans bodily through our human face, so also through
our interior image God sees and knows us. When, however, we are cast down by the guilt of sin, we are afraid
to lift up the face of our heart to God. As long as we
are not supported by any confidence in good works, the
mind is afraid to look at the highest realities, because our
very conscience accuses us. When however our guilt is
once more washed away by the tears of repentance and
we mourn for what we have done in such a way that we
would never do anything again that would be worthy of
mourning, great confidence is born in the soul, and the
face of our heart is joyfully lifted up to see the eternal
reward that is waiting. All this, however, Eliphaz would
be saying truthfully if he were speaking to a weakling.
When it is a just man whom he despises for the trials he
undergoes, what else does he do but ignorantly dump
out words of knowledge? Surely, if these words should
be applied to the type of heretics, as we have said, they
falsely promise to lift up our faces to God. It is as though
they plainly told the faithful people, "As long as you will
not bow to our preaching, your heart is pressed down to
the lowest depths." Since, however, Eliphaz admonished

blessed Job to return to God, from whom that blessed man had never turned away, he again adds a promise:

XXI. 26. *You will ask him, and he will answer.**   *Job 22:27

Those who scorn the orders of the commanding Lord indeed ask the Lord, but they do not deserve an answer. That is why it is written, *The man who closes his ears to keep from hearing the law: his prayer is accursed.**   *Prov 28:9

As long, accordingly, as Eliphaz did not believe that blessed Job would get an answer, he certainly judged him to have gone astray in his actions. So he again adds, *You will pay your vows.**   *Job 22:27

He who promises prayers but is unable to fulfill them because of weakness is dealt with according to the penalty of sin, in such a way that he is unable to do what is right when he wills to do so. On the other hand, if any outstanding guilt is wiped away in the presence of the interior Judge, the immediate result is the possibility of prayer. The next verse:

XXII. 27. *You will decide a thing, and you will get it.**   *Job 22:28

This opinion is normally found to be characteristic of weak minds, that they suppose any person to be just to the extent that, as far as they can see, he gets whatever he wants, although we know very well that just people are sometimes deprived of worldly goods, which however are granted to the lawless in great abundance; it is the same with physicians who order that their patients who have no hope of a cure should be given whatever they ask for, whereas those who they discern can be cured, they deny whatever they ask. But although Eliphaz enters these arguments concerning spiritual gifts, we must realize that a thing is decided and gotten when the virtue is desired and sought, and when God grants it, it even grows by performance. So he again adds,

XXIII. 28. *The light will shine on your road.**   *Job 22:28

For the light to shine on the road of the just means that they spread abroad the signs of their glory through wonderful works of virtue, so that wherever they go on their straight path, they drive away the night of sin from the hearts of those who meet them. They let the light of justice shine on them by the example of their own works. But however great the justice of their works may be, it amounts to nothing in the eyes of the internal Judge if it is inflated by mental pride. So he again adds,

XXIV. 29. *He who has been cast down will be glori-*
fied, and he who lowers his gaze will save himself.* This statement is not at variance with the one uttered by the mouth of Truth: *All those who exalt themselves will be humbled, and he who humbles himself will be exalted.** So also Solomon says, *Before it is ground down, man's heart is exalted, and before it is glorified, it is humbled.** Eliphaz is right to say, *He who lowers his gaze will save himself.* However much it can be found out by one's physical deportment, the first manifestation of pride is usually in the eyes. So it is written, *You will humble the eyes of the proud.** So we are told about the very head of the proud ones, *He sees all that is lofty.*† So also it is written about the one who clings to him through infidelity, *Her generation includes those who have proud eyes, and whose eyebrows are lifted up on high.** To lower one's gaze means to avoid any look of disdain but at the same time to consider oneself less than and unequal to all those whom one sees. Those who lower their gaze will therefore save themselves, because those who abandon the false pinnacle of pride will ascend to the high place of truth. The next verse:

XXV. 30. *The guiltless man will be saved, saved, however, by the purity of his hands.** If these words express retribution in the Kingdom of heaven, they are confirmed by truth; it is written of God, you see, *He will render to each man according to his works.** At the Last Judgment the justice of the eternal Judge saves

Margin notes:

*Job 22:29

*Luke 14:11

*Prov 18:12

*Ps 17:28 LXX
†Job 41:25 Vulg

*Prov 30:13

*Job 22:30

*Rom 2:6

the one whom here God's own loyalty delivers from debased actions. If, however, each person is believed to be saved by the purity of his own hands here in the sense that he would become a guiltless person by his own merits, beyond doubt Eliphaz is wrong, because if heavenly grace does not prevent a person from guilt, never, unquestionably, will it find a guiltless person to reward. So we find Moses saying these true words: *No man is guiltless before you of himself.*

*Exod 34:7
Vulg

Accordingly it is heavenly grace that first operates in us without our help, in order that our free will may also follow God's lead and that he, along with us, may also bring about that good that we already want, which he, through his superabundant grace, rewards in us at the Last Judgment, just as if it had proceeded from us alone. Since God's goodness goes ahead of us to make us guiltless, Paul says, *By God's grace I am what I am.*

*1 Cor 15:10

Since our free will follows that grace's lead, he adds, *His grace has not been fruitless in me, but I have labored more than any of them.* He is well aware, however, that he is nothing of himself, so he continues, *But it is not I.* Yet he also knows he is something when grace finds him, so he again adds, *It is the grace of God in me.* He would not say *in me* if, along with God's anticipatory grace, he did not have a free will to follow up. Accordingly, in order that he might prove that he is nothing without grace, he says, *It is not I.* In order that he might show that his free will had come into play along with grace, he added, *It is the grace of God in me.*

The guiltless, consequently, will be saved by the purity of their hands, because they who here below are anticipated by the gift of innocence are rewarded for merit when they come to Judgment. All this, as we have already said, Eliphaz correctly spoke out, but he did not really know the man to whom he spoke, because a better man should not be taught but listened to. All his words, however, typically correspond with the heretics' promises. Every one of the faithful whom they find suffering affliction in the present life they suppose to be struck down for the sin of bad faith, and they promise them healing innocence through the purity of good works, if only they will follow their teaching. But the mind of the faithful disdains them all the more intensely the more clearly they see that they do not possess the innocence they promise. So Solomon is right to say, *It is in vain that the net is cast before the eyes of birds.** Surely the birds are the spirits of the faithful, and while they are flying to heaven through the hope of truth, they avoid the little nets of deception cast by depraved people. The next verse:

*Prov 1:17

XXVI. 31. *Job spoke in reply, "Now again is my speech bitter, and the hand that strikes me is heavy over my groans."** As usual, blessed Job begins with words that are very straightforward, but he concludes his speech with attention to deep mystery. The suffering of the afflicted one ought certainly to have been alleviated by the comfort offered by friends, but because that comfort vented itself in flattery and deception, the suffering of the afflicted one became more intense. Eliphaz, you see, had no hesitation in promising improvement for his conversion, so, as if bad medicine had been administered, his wound grew worse. So he is right to say, *Now again is my speech bitter, and the hand that strikes me is heavy over my groans*, since the intention of misdirected comfort aggravated the blow that it should have softened. Actually these words are spoken in his role as a type of Holy Church, in which the sufferings of the faithful are also to be seen, those who cry out all the more because they see how evil men use flattery, as Paul says, *The hearts of the faithful are led astray by sweet words and blessings.**

*Job 23:1-2

*Rom 16:18

32. These words are correctly applied to the more careful consideration of the mind of the faithful people as well, those who cannot be without bitterness in this world even if they seem to enjoy prosperity. But when adversity comes in addition, their suffering is redoubled. So Job is right to say, *Now again is my speech bitter,* in order that he might clearly show that the mind of the chosen people could not be without bitterness, even in the midst of prosperity. He also correctly says, *The hand that strikes me is heavy over my groans.* The hand that strikes certainly means a forceful blow. The chosen ones consider that their first blow, you see, is that they have been separated from the vision of their Creator, that they never enjoy the glory of interior illumination, but that in the exile of the present life they groan as though banished to a dark place. They always have their groan present to them, accordingly, in this striking hand. But when they also suffer adversity in this life, the striking hand is still heavier over their groans. Even when adversity was absent from their lives, they had groans and suffering. But the bitterness of the first blow increased with the trial of adversity. So he says, *The hand that strikes me is heavy over my groans,* because adversity in this life did not strike any just man in happiness, but rather multiplied the pain of his wound. It is because of a wonderful dispensation of almighty God, then, that when the mind of the just man suffers more from adversity in this world, he thirsts all the more for the contemplation of his Creator's face. So he adds the following suitable words:

XXVII. 33. *Who will grant me the gift of knowing him, of finding him, and of coming to his throne?*[*] Not one of the elect would love the Lord, be assured, if he did not know him. But it is one thing to know the Lord through faith and quite another to know his form, one

*Job 23:3

thing to find him by believing, another by contemplation. That is how it happens that all the elect who have known him by faith yearn to see his form as well. They burn with the fire of love, because they already taste the sweetness of his charm in the very certitude of their faith. This is the reality that the man who was delivered from demons in the region of the Gerasenes represents: he wanted to go away with Jesus, but the Lord of salvation told him, *First go back home and proclaim all that God has done for you.* So upon the lover another delay is imposed, in order that the desire of postponed love might earn a greater merit and reward.

*Luke 8:39

Accordingly almighty God becomes a charming miracle worker for us, yet he remains hidden in his high domain, in order that by showing us something of himself by his hidden inspiration he might also ignite his love in us; on the other hand, by hiding the glory of his majesty, he would increase the power of his love through the heat of desire. Unless, you see, the holy man aimed to see him in his majesty, he would certainly not add, *I will come to his throne.* What is the throne of God, anyway, but the holy angels, who, as Holy Scripture bears us witness, are called thrones.* He, consequently, who wants to come even to God's throne, what else does he desire but to be among the angelic spirits, that he might no longer suffer any failing moments of time but rise with permanent glory in the contemplation of eternity?

*Col 1:16

34. These words, however, also fit the just who are still placed in this life. When they see anything done that is against their wish and desire, they have recourse to God's hidden judgments, that they may see there that what seems to happen inordinately in the external forum is not arranged inordinately in the internal forum. When with the eyes of faith they contemplate the Creator of the world presiding over the angelic spirits, of course they

come to his throne. Since they reflect how wonderfully he governs the angels, they surely see that his providence over humans is not unjust, and they discover that rational causes are indeed just, even while these same causes seem unjust externally; while they are humbly considering the matter, they often reproach themselves for their willfulness, and they sometimes pass judgment on their own wishes, because they understand that the Creator's arrangements are better. So he again adds with reason,

XXVIII. 35. *I will set my case before him, and I will fill my mouth with reproaches.** To set one's case before God means to open the eyes of our consideration to the terrible sight of his majesty within the hidden reaches of our mind through the eyes of faith, to consider what humankind, the sinner, deserves to expect, and how terrible the Judge, who is now hidden and silent, appears hereafter. That is how it happens that the soul is called to a more demanding self-knowledge, and because the soul sees that the hidden Judge is still more terrible, she is more dreadfully cornered by her actions. She anxiously troubles herself, keeps lamenting her sins, cries out in repentance, and remembers how bad she has been.

*Job 23:4

So now again, after Job has said, *I will set my case before him*, he correctly adds, *I will fill my mouth with reproaches.* He who pleads his case in God's sight fills his mouth with reproaches, because while he is gazing on the exact scrutiny of the terrible Judge directed at him, he turns a bitter invective of repentance against himself. As long as we neglect the thought of our sins, you see, we are often unaware of what follows their reproach in the Judgment; however, as long as we keep after them with repentance, we find out what the Judge can say about them to us in his interrogation. So he again adds with reason,

XXIX. 36. *Let me understand the words with which he answers me, and let me know what he will say to me.** We bewail our sins at the time that we begin to weigh their gravity, but then we weigh them more exactly when we bewail them more anxiously. From the lamentations of our heart arises plentifully that with which God's intransigence threatens sinners, the disgrace of reprobates, terror, and the turning away of implacable majesty. Then the Lord will tell reprobate sinners in his anger all that his justice allows them to suffer. Those are certainly the words of his sentence that the righteous people carefully feared all the while and so avoided hearing. But who could be found righteous in that scrutiny if God should scrutinize the life of humankind according to his majestic power? So Job wisely adds,

XXX. 37. *I do not want him to deal with me very energetically or to press down upon me with the weight of his greatness.** The mind of any just person, whoever he may be, if he is judged strictly by almighty God, is pressed down by the weight of God's greatness. By these words, however, we must also understand that when the holy person avoids God's energy, he does nothing else but wish him to be weak. Is it not written, *The weakness of God is stronger than men?** So he forthwith adds, *Let him act with fairness against me, and let my judgment win the victory.** Who else but the Mediator between God and men, the man Christ Jesus,* is intended by the word *fairness?* Of him it has been written, *God has made him our Wisdom and our Justice.**

He is certainly that Justice who came into this world against the conduct of sinners, him by whom we are victorious over the ancient enemy who made us his captive. Let him then say, *I do not want him to deal with me very energetically or to press down upon me with the weight of his greatness. Let him act with fairness against me,*

*Job 23:5

*Job 23:6

*1 Cor 1:25

*Job 23:7
*1 Tim 2:5

*1 Cor 1:30

and let my judgment win the victory. In other words, let him send his incarnate Son to make me ashamed of my ways, and then I will victoriously shut out the insidious enemy through my acquittal at the Judgment.

If the only-begotten Son, you see, remained invisibly in the power of his divinity in such a way that he took upon himself nothing of our weakness, when could weak humans have been able to find access to him by grace? The consideration of the weight of his greatness would certainly have oppressed us rather than helping us. Rather, he who is strong above all things appeared as weakness among all things, in order that the weakness assumed might render him like us, and so that he might at the same time elevate us to his permanent strength. In the highest reaches his divinity could not have been understood by us, small as we were, but he prostrated himself before humankind by his humanity; we ascended, as it were, to him who was lying prostrate; then he arose, and we were lifted up. The follow-up is immediate, whereby divinity can be shown both invisible and incomprehensible. So he goes on:

XXXI. 38. *If I go east, he will not be there, if west I will not perceive him; if I turn left, what can I do? I will not reach him; if I turn right, I will not see him.* *   *Job 23:8-9
The Creator of all is of course not in a part, because he is everywhere. He is then less to be found when he who is totally everywhere is sought for in a part. His spirit is not enclosed, but he has all things within himself, those things that, however, he surrounds by filling, fills by surrounding, supports by transcending, and transcends by supporting. Job already said it all: *If I go east, he will not be there, if west I will not perceive him; if I turn left, what can I do? I will not reach him; if I turn right, I will not see him.* But now he adds, *He really knows my path.* * It is as if he said, "I cannot see   *Job 23:10

292 Gregory the Great

him who sees me, and him who sees me thoroughly I
cannot look upon." He wants to demonstrate that he is
just as carefully to be feared as he is inconspicuous. He
who looks upon us in such a way that we cannot look
upon him is for that reason more to be feared, since he
sees all things and is never seen. When we think that
anyone is hiding in ambush against us, we are the more
afraid of him because we see him not. And when we
by no means find out where his ambush is, we also fear
it where it is not. But our Creator, who is everywhere
complete and who sees everything without being seen
himself, is all the more dreadful the more invisible he
remains, and we know nothing about what or when he
discerns concerning our actions.

These words of Job, however, can also be understood in another way. We go east when we lift up our
minds to the consideration of his majesty. But he is not
there, because mortal thought does not succeed in seeing
what he looks like in his own nature. *If [I go] west, I
will not perceive him.* We go west when the eye of our
heart is lifted up to God, but beaten back by the very
intensity of light, we return to ourselves. In this way we
wearily learn that what we sought was too high above
us. Then considering our mortal nature we realize that
we who wished to see the immortal are still unworthy.
If I turn left, what can I do? I will not reach him. To
turn left means to consent to sin's pleasure. It stands to
reason that the one who still grovels in sinful pleasure
at the left hand cannot reach God. *If I turn right, I will
not see him.* He doubtless turns right who is lifted up to
the life of virtue, but he cannot see God, who is happy
with his good works and rejoices privately, because the
eye of his heart is covered by the tumor of pride. That
is why it is said elsewhere, *Do not turn aside to the
right or to the left.*[*] In all these ways the soul is often

dispersed and cannot even find herself integrally. So he rightly adds the following:

XXXII. 39. *Yet he really knows my path.** In other words, "I interrogate myself strictly, but I cannot know myself perfectly. Yet he whom I cannot see sees in detail all that I do." The next verse: *He tries me like gold that passes through fire.** Gold in the furnace reaches the brightness of its nature when it loses its dross. So like gold that passes through fire, the souls of the just are tried; by the burning action of trials their vices are removed and their merits increase. Nor was it out of pride that the holy man compared himself situated in tribulation to gold, because he was called just by God's voice before his affliction, so it was not on account of any vices that had to be purged that he was permitted to be tried, but his gold was purified in the fire in order that his merits might increase. Accordingly he thought less of himself than he was when he was given over to trials, he who thought he was being purged although there was nothing in him to be purged.

40. We must realize that however little the mind of the just might think of itself, the just people look upon their actions as righteous, but they presume nothing on account of their rectitude. So Job now adds, *My foot has followed his tracks; I have kept on his path, and I have not turned aside from it. I have not departed from the commandments of his lips, and I have stored the words of his mouth in my breast.** But let us see whether in all these words he considers himself to be something. These words follow: *He is the only One.** By this additional phrase he shows that in all his good works he thought of himself as nothing. But we will repeat these words of his mentioned above, in order that we might touch on them again.

*Job 23:10

*Job 23:10

*Job 23:11-12

*Job 23:12

*Job 23:11   XXXIII. 41. *My foot has followed his tracks.** Like footsteps or tracks of God are those works of his that we look upon, by which all people, good and bad, are ruled, by which righteous and unrighteous people find their places and their rank, and by which each one of his subjects is led to better things every day and every one of his adversaries becomes daily worse, but tolerated. The prophet surely spoke of these footsteps: *They saw* **Ps 67:25*   *your tracks, O God.** Accordingly, when we contemplate the strength of his forbearing love and from this contemplation make the effort to imitate him, what else do we do but follow in his footsteps in imitating the outermost traces of his works? Truth himself advised us to imitate these traces of his Father when he said, *Pray for those who persecute you and speak falsely against you, that you may be sons of your Father who is in heaven, who* **Matt 5:44-45*   *makes his sun rise upon the bad and upon the good.**

Blessed Job had already said, assured by faith, *I know that my Redeemer lives, and on the last day I will* **Job 19:25*   *rise from the earth.** He can therefore look upon the future acts of Wisdom, who is to become incarnate, just as we today behold by faith the past works of the same Wisdom: namely, that the Mediator of God and men was kind in giving, humble in endurance, and patient in offering an example. While blessed Job was looking on that life with anxious attention, filled with the heavenly spirit as he was, he foresaw his future humility and meekness; he had recourse to it as to an example proposed for his imitation, in order that, whatever he did in this life, he might cling by imitation to his footsteps, inasmuch as he could not see his deep hidden plan. Rather he looked upon the earth and stuck to the following of his footsteps, concerning which Peter wrote, *Christ suffered for you, leaving you an example, that you* **1 Pet 2:21*   *might follow his steps.** He continues in the same vein:

XXXIV. 42. *I have kept on his path, and I have not turned aside from it.** He keeps and does not turn aside who works at this attentively. Keeping attentive is surely the same as not turning aside in operation. This is precisely the anxious concern of righteous people, that they examine their actions daily and compare them to the way of truth, using that way as a yardstick to keep them from turning away from its course of rectitude. They try to move each day above themselves, and where they are carried forward toward the pinnacle of virtue, they heedfully judge and reprove whatever selfish habits remain inside themselves. They are in a hurry to pull every aspect of their personality to that place where they discover that they have partially arrived. The next verse:

*Job 23:11

XXXV. 43. *I have not departed from the commandments of his lips.** Just as good slaves who obey their masters are always attentive to their presence, in order that they may quickly hear and zealously fulfill whatever they command, so also the minds of righteous people are in attendance on almighty God and pay attention to him. They listen to Holy Scripture as though they were in his presence, and because God makes known his whole will through Holy Scripture, the more they understand his will as expressed in his word, the less are they at variance with that will. So it happens that his word does not pass through their ears fruitlessly, but it takes hold in their hearts. So he adds,

*Job 23:12

XXXVI. 44. *I have stored the words of his mouth in my breast.** We store the words of his mouth in our inmost heart when we hear his commandments, not in a passing way, but as something to be fulfilled in action. That is why it is written about his virgin mother herself, *Mary, on the other hand, kept all these words and pondered them in her heart.** These words we are talking about, when they proceed to external acts, also

*Job 23:12

*Luke 2:19

remain hidden in the bosom of the heart if through what is done externally the soul of the doer is not internally lifted up. When the word is conceived and led forth into action, you see, if by that action the praise of humans is looked for, the word of God is obviously not hidden in the bosom of the mind. But I would like to know, O blessed man, why you examine yourself with such close attention and why you repress yourself so anxiously?

XXXVII. 45. *He is the only One, and no man can turn his thought away.** Are there not angels and men, heaven and earth, air and sea, all the birds, four-footed creatures and reptiles? It is surely written, *He created them all and made them be.** Since, therefore, there are so many beings in the world of nature, why does the blessed man now say, *He is the only One*? Being, however, is one thing, but first being is something else; changeable being is one thing, but unchangeable being is something else. All these things have being, but they do not have first being, because they absolutely do not subsist in themselves, and unless they be held in the Pilot's hand, they simply cannot be.

All things subsist in him who created them, nor do they who live give themselves life, nor are those non-living beings that are moved made to move by their own power. Rather, he moves all things, he who gives life to some, but others that have not been given life he appoints as the final beings, and he preserves them admirably. All things have undoubtedly been created out of nothing, and their being would again be reduced to nothing unless the Creator of all things held them fast in his ruling hand. Accordingly, all things that have been created cannot succeed in subsisting or moving by themselves, but they do subsist insofar as they have obtained their being, and they are moved insofar as they are forced to move by a hidden urge.

**Job 23:13

**Wis 1:14

Look at the sinner; he must be requited by human acts. The earth grows dry as he labors. The sea grows stormy and wrecks his ships. The air takes fire, and he sweats. The sky grows dark with rain for his discomfiture. Humans grow angry enough to oppress him, and even the angelic powers are moved against him. Are those beings that we call lifeless or living moved by their own instincts, or are they not rather moved by God's action? Consequently, whatever happens externally, his being is to be understood, he who has brought it about internally. Therefore he who is the first being is alone to be feared in every cause. It is also he who tells Moses, *I am he who is. Tell the Israelites, "He who is sent me to you."* * So when we are buffeted by things that we see, we should anxiously fear him whom we do not see. Let the holy man accordingly despise everything externally dreadful and everything that, unless it be guided by its own essence, would go back to nothing, and let him disregard everything and gaze on him alone with his mind's eye, in comparison with whose essence our being is non-being. Let him say, *He is the only One.*

*Exod 3:14

46. Concerning his unchangeability Job forthwith adds wisely, *No man can turn his thought away.* Like his unchangeable nature, his will too is unchangeable. No one indeed can turn his thought away, because no one succeeds in resisting his hidden Judgment. Even if there have been some who by their prayers seemed to have turned his thought away, his internal thought was such that they could turn aside his decision by prayer, and they received from him what they should do in his presence. Let him then say, *No man can turn his thought away.* His Judgment once fixed can never be changed. That is why it is written, *He made a precept which will not be forgotten,* * and again, *Heaven and earth will pass away, but my words will not pass away,* * and again, *My*

*Ps 148:6

*Mark 13:31

thoughts are not your thoughts, nor are my ways your

*Isa 55:8 *ways.** So although his decision seems to change externally, his internal plan does not change, because concerning any single matter, whatever is done externally
and changeably has been unchangeably fixed internally.
The next verse:

XXXVIII. 47. *Whatever his soul wanted, that he*

*Job 23:13 *did.** Since God is outside of all bodies and inside of
all minds, that force itself by which he penetrates and
rules all things is called his soul. Not even those things,
take notice, that seem to happen contrary to his will
resist his will, because he sometimes allows even that
to happen which he did not command, in order that
through its means what he did command might be done
more surely. The apostate angel's will is unquestionably perverse; nevertheless God arranges events in so
wonderful a way that even the very traps that he sets
serve the advantage of good people, whom they purify
at the same time as they tempt. That is how his soul did
whatever he wanted, in order that he might do his will
even there where his will seemed to meet opposition.
Accordingly, let the just man be terrified and consider
the weight of such awesome majesty, recognizing his
weakness in its presence.

48. But faced with these words we are free to inquire, "O blessed Job, you are situated among such
awful trials, why do you fear even greater ones? You
are already surrounded by troubles, and you are already
cornered by afflictions without number. That evil should
be feared that has not yet come about. What do you fear
when you are situated in such intense pain?" Now see
how the just man answers our questions as he adds,

XXXIX. 49. *When he has realized his will in me, he*

*Job 23:14 *has many more similar trials ready to send.** It is as if he
said openly, "I am now counting my sufferings, but I still

dread what I may have to suffer. He is fulfilling his will
for me, since he is buffeting me with many afflictions.
But he has more like them ready to send, and if he plans
to strike, he already knows where the wound can grow."
From these reflections we may conclude how fearful he
was before the trials came, since even after the blows he
still dreads being struck. He surely estimates that there
is in himself an incomprehensible power of self-control
and consideration, and he refuses to consider himself a
just man or one who is safe from blows. So, still afraid,
he adds the following:

XL. 50. *That is why I am disturbed in his presence,
and watching him I shake with fear.** He is well advised
to be disturbed in his presence who proposes terror of
God's majesty to the contemplation of his heart and who
is shaken by fear of his governing, since he knows that
he is unable to render an account of himself if Judgment is strict. He is right to say, *Watching him I shake
with fear.* Because no one considers the might of divine
Judgment, no one fears it, so a person feels all the safer
in this life the less familiar he is with the consideration
of internal coercion. Consequently righteous people always return their full attention to the secret place of the
heart, gaze at that hidden coercion, and stand before the
judgment seat of innermost majesty in such a way that
they will one day be all the safer, because they refused
security all the while they lived here below.

As for evil people who refuse to consider what they
fear, they will one day merrily reach that which they
fear in their minds but in no way avoid. Yet here is what
we know about blessed Job: he was constantly offering
sacrifices to God, he freely spent his money on hospi-
tality and on the needs of the poor, he was meek even
in his relations with his slaves, and he showed kindness even to his adversaries, yet he suffered so many

*Job 23:15

trials, and not even after the blows was he safe from fear but still trembled under the threat of the force of God's strict Judgment. What do we miserable sinners say about ourselves, then, if he who behaved in this way was still so fearful? But let him tell us now whether he bore such a heavy burden of fear on his own account. The next verse:

XLI. 51. *God softened my heart, and the Almighty* *Job 23:16 *made me anxious.** The heart of the just man is said to be soft by God's favor, because it is transfixed by the fear of heavenly Judgment. That which is soft can be penetrated; that which is hard cannot be penetrated. That is why Solomon says, *Blessed is the man who is always* *Prov 28:14 *fearful, but the hard-hearted man sinks down into evil.** Job therefore attributes his virtue of fear not to himself but to the Creator when he says, *God softened my heart, and the Almighty made me anxious.* The hearts of good people are not secure but anxious when they weigh the burden of the future Judgment, and they do not want to have a peaceful existence here; rather, they trouble their own security with the consideration of internal severity. They do, however, even in the midst of fearful entreaties, often remind their soul of its gifts, and in order that they might refresh themselves with consolation while yet thinking about the object of their fear, they refocus their eye upon the gifts they have received; thus hope raises up the one whom fear cast down. So he continues:

XLII. 52. *I did not perish because of the threatening* *Job 23:17 *darkness, nor did blackness cover my face.** He who is cornered by trials loses bodily health because of the trials that threaten him, and he is buffeted for past actions in order that he might escape future punishment. The trials suffered by good people in fact either purify them from faults they have committed or shield them from future ones they might otherwise commit. As for blessed Job, on the other hand, when he was in the midst of his trial, he was neither purified from former sins nor shielded from those that beckoned; it was only that his virtue was increased by his trial. So he loyally says, *I did not perish because of the threatening darkness, nor did blackness cover my face.* No darkness of sin hid the face of his heart, because he always kept the seriousness of the fear of God in view. Nor did he whom no penalties threatened lose bodily health because of the darkness that hung over him.

53. It is noteworthy that when he denounces his former sufferings, he never says, "It did not *touch* my face," but *The darkness did not* cover *my face.* Thoughts that arise, you see, often do soil the hearts of even righteous people when they touch the delights of earthly things, but when they are quickly driven away by the hand of holy discretion, it soon turns out that no darkness covers the face of the heart, even if it was already touched by illicit pleasure. In the very sacrifice of prayer, you see, troublesome thoughts often press themselves upon us, thoughts that could snatch away or defile what we are tearfully offering God within ourselves. In this way, when Abraham was offering his evening sacrifice, he diligently chased away the birds that were alighting on it, lest they should seize the sacrifice he was offering.* *Gen 15:11 In the same way we also offer a holocaust on the altar of our hearts, and we guard it against the unclean winged creatures, lest the unclean spirits and bad thoughts seize what our minds hope to offer profitably to God.

XLIII. 54. *Time is not hidden from the Almighty, but those who know him do not know his days.** What do *Job 24:1 God's days mean except his eternity? The latter is often mentioned as lasting one day, as, for example, where it is written, *One day in your courts is better than a thousand.** Sometimes, however, eternity is symbolized by *Ps 83:11

*Ps 101:25

speaking of the length of many days, concerning which it is written, *Your years are as ages and generations.* Accordingly we are involved in time, precisely because we are creatures. God the Creator of everything includes our time in his eternity. So Job says, *Time is not hidden from the Almighty, but those who know him do not know his days.* He indeed sees all that is comprehensible in us, but we can in no way comprehend what belongs to him.

Nevertheless, God's nature is simple, so it is a source of great wonder that prompts Job to say, *Those who know him do not know his days.* There is no difference between him and his days. Rather, God is that which he possesses. He certainly has eternity, but he also is eternity. He has light, but his light is what he is. He has glory, but he also is his glory. He is not being at one time and having at another. So what does it mean to say, *Those who know him do not know his days*, except that those who know him at the same time do not know him? Even those who already know him by faith do not yet know him by encounter. Since he is himself his eternity, as we really believe, we do not know the special quality of that eternity of his.

We hear about the power of the divine nature, but in what we hear we are sometimes accustomed to consider the things we know by experience. Everything that begins and ends is enclosed between the beginning and the end. But if any small delay postpones the end, it is said to be long-lasting; still, if anyone turns back the eyes of his mind over that length by memory and stretches ahead through expectation, it is as though he widened the space of time in his mind. So when anyone hears of the eternity of God, he proposes to his soul, which understands in a human fashion, a long lifetime, and in such matters we always measure backwards what remains in memory and what lies ahead, which we wait for with attention.

55. The more we think such thoughts about eternity, however, the less we still know about it. There indeed is where we find a reality that neither begins finitely nor ends finitely, where nothing future is awaited, nor has anything happened that should be remembered, but there is one reality that always remains being. This being, which we and the angels begin to see beginning, we see without its beginning, and it always continues to be without end in such a way that the soul never waits for what is to follow, as if those things that are were multiplying and becoming long-lasting. Even if the Spirit of prophecy said, *O Lord, you reign in eternity and in the world, and you still reign,*[*] after the fashion of Holy Scripture, the Spirit has spoken to humans in a human way and said *still*, leaving out the idea of waiting. Eternity, you see, has no *still*, because it always has being, and no single part of its length is lost in order that another part could take its place, but all is being at the same time, nor can any non-being be discerned; rather, the soul sees all that is, both the recent non-being and the long-lasting being.

*Exod 15:18
LXX

But while we are talking about the days of eternity, we try to see something greater than what we do see. Let him then correctly say, *Those who know him do not know his days.* Even if we know God by faith now, we do not see the special quality of his eternity, having no past before the ages, having no future after the ages, long without delay, continuous without expectation. Since blessed Job typifies Holy Church, he restrains himself with the strong rein of knowledge, lest he should be wise beyond the proper limits of wisdom; he admits that he cannot comprehend the days of God, and he forthwith turns his mind's eye to the pride of the heretics, who want to know what is lofty and who boast of knowing perfectly what they cannot grasp in any way. The next verse:

XLIV. 56. *Some people have moved the boundaries;*
*Job 24:2
they have seized the flock and pastured it. To whom
is he referring by the words *Some people*, if not the
heretics who are estranged from Holy Church's lap? It
is they who move the boundaries when they by double-
dealing overstep the ordinances of the fathers. Of these
ordinances it has been absolutely stated, *You must not
move the ancient landmarks which your fathers have put*
*Prov 22:28
in place. They seize the flocks and pasture them, because they attract anyone who is unwary to their persuasion by means of their perverse teaching, and they feed
them with destructive doctrines in order to ruin them.
That the word *flocks* is intended to mean unwary people
is testified by the Bridegroom's words when he tells his
bride, *If you do not know, O most lovely of women, go*
*Song 1:7
out and follow the tracks of the flocks. In other words,
if you do not know your glory, which is that of being
created in the image of God, by living uprightly, then
leave my presence where I am contemplated and imitate
the life of unwary people. The next verse:

XLV. 57. *They drive away the orphan's ass and*
*Job 24:3
claim it, and they take the widow's ox for a pledge.
Whom do we understand by orphans in this passage but
God's chosen ones, whose mind is impressionable, who
are fed by the great grace of faith, and who do not yet
see the face of their Father who already died for them?
There are many members of the church who see certain
people desire heaven and show contempt for everything
worldly; although they wear themselves out in the toils
of this world, they provide for the needs of those whom
they see sighing for heaven with the worldly goods that
they possess. Although they are unable to live a spiritual
life themselves, they freely provide support for those
who are headed for the heights. The ass, you know,
customarily bears people's burdens, and they are like

an ass, so to speak, for the chosen ones, who zealously perform services for the chosen ones by their worldly actions, bearing burdens for the use of people. When the heretics turn away such a one from the lap of Holy Church, as they often do, it is as if they drove away an orphan's ass, because when they attract him to their own false belief, they tear him away from his ministry to the saints.

58. What should we understand by the widow if not Holy Church, who for a while is deprived of the sight of her husband, who was killed? This widow's ox is the preacher, whoever he may be. It often happens that the heretics attract by their perverse teachings even those who seemed to be preachers. They take the widow's ox when they snatch away from Holy Church even those who are preaching. But he is right to add, *for a pledge.* A pledge, you see, is taken, and it is something that is held, but something else is wanted when it is taken. The heretics often try to draw away the preachers, precisely in order that they may also draw away their followers. Accordingly the widow's ox is stolen for a pledge when the one who preached is grabbed so that others may follow him. After his downfall it often happens that those also leave Holy Church's lap whose behavior there was good, so that they might look like the meek and lowly ones. So he goes on:

XLVI. 59. *They have misguided the path of the poor, and along with that they oppressed the meek of the earth.** It is often customary to use the word *poverty* to express humility, and sometimes those who seem to be meek and humble, if they do not know how to observe discretion, are led by the example of others to their downfall. There are some heretics, on the other hand, who shun association with other people and who seek the seclusion of private life. Those whom they find they

*Job 24:4

often infect with the pestilence of their own persuasion to such an extent that they seem to them more respectable because of the merits of their lives. Concerning them he has more to say:

XLVII. 60. *Some, like wild asses, go out to the des-*
*Job 24:5
*ert to do their work.** The wild ass, you see, is a rough country brute, and heretics are rightly compared in this passage to wild asses, because they are abandoned to their own wills and are strangers to the fetters of faith and reason. That is why it is written, *The wild ass is accustomed to the wilderness; in the desire of his soul*
*Jer 2:24
*he draws in the wind of his love.** The wild ass is absolutely accustomed to the wilderness, because he does not cultivate the earth of his heart with the effort of discipline, and so he makes his home there where there is no harvest. In the desire of his soul he draws in the wind of his love, because the thoughts he conceives in his mind with the desire of knowledge succeed in inflating themselves, but not in edification. Holy Scripture speaks out against them, *Knowledge inflates, but love*
*1 Cor 8:1
*builds.** That is why he also says advisedly, They *go out to do their work.* It is not God's but their own work that they pursue when it is not correct teaching but their own desires that they seek to fulfill. It is again written, *He who walks in the way of innocence is the one who*
*Ps 100:6
*ministered to me.** Accordingly, he who does not walk in the way of innocence ministers to himself, not to the Lord. The next verse:

XLVIII. 61. *Others are on the watch for spoil to*
*Job 24:5
*prepare food for their children.** They are on the watch for spoil, because they are always trying to twist the speeches of righteous people around to their own meaning, in order that they might use them to prepare food of error for their stubborn children. This food is obviously what is spoken about by Solomon when the words of

a woman are applied to the perversity of heretics as a type, where it is written, *Stolen water is sweet, and secret bread is rich.** The next verse: *Prov 9:17

XLIX. 62. *They reap a field that is not their own, and they harvest the vineyard of the man they oppress.**   *Job 24:6
The word *field* may symbolize the extent of the knowledge of Holy Scripture; although the heretics harvest it, it does not belong to them, since they take various thoughts from it that are far from meaning the sense they take. The word *vineyard* also has this signification, because Holy Scripture offers the grapes of virtues through the maxims of truth. The Lord of that vineyard, the Creator of Holy Scripture in other words, is the one they oppress, because they try to twist the meaning of Holy Scripture violently. It is he who said, *You made me a slave by your sins, and you made me labor by your iniquity.** They harvest his vineyard, because they   *Isa 43:24
gather the grapes of maxims from it for the purpose of their own interpretation. The word *field* or *vineyard* can also mean the universal church reaped by deceitful preachers, who also oppress its Maker in his members; they harvest the grapes, because they persecute the grace of our Creator by seizing some of his members who seemed to be behaving correctly. What else are they taking but heads of grain or grapes of souls? Concerning these people he again adds,

L. 63. *They send the men away naked, and they take away the clothes of those who have nothing to cover them against the cold.** Just as clothes cover the body, so   *Job 24:7
good works cover the soul. That is why someone is told, *Happy is he who is on his guard, keeping watch over his garment, lest he go around naked.** When, accordingly,   *Rev 16:15
the heretics ruin good works in people's minds, they undoubtedly take away the garments that cover them. He is right to say, *They have nothing to cover them*

against the cold. Covering, you see, is connected with justice, but cold with guilt. There are those who sin in certain situations but perform good works in others. He consequently who sins in some of his actions but seeks justice in others, what else is it but that he is clothed against the cold? He feels the cold and covers himself. He is warmed for justice by some good work, he who by a different work grew cold with guilt.

So when the heretics take away good works from some people, they so arrange things that they have nothing to cover them against the cold. So he is right to say, *They send the men away naked, and they take away the clothes of those who have nothing to cover them against the cold.* The cold of guilt alone kills them whom the warmth of some other work would at least partly cover. On the other hand, cold could mean desire, and clothing works. There are many whose evil desires still seethe, but they fight themselves spiritually; they resist themselves with righteous actions, and they cover with good works that evil shiver that they perceive in themselves through temptation. So when they desire evil, they become cold; when they perform good works, they clothe themselves. The heretics, however, deny them the works of righteous faith by their twisted pronouncements, and thereby they bring it about that, when they feel the cold of carnal desires, they die without the clothing of good works. The next verse:

LI. 64. *Rain from the mountains wets them; they have no clothes, and they hug the rocks.** *Rain from the mountains*: these are words spoken by teachers. The voice of Holy Church says of these mountains, *I have lifted up my eyes to the mountains.** Rain from the mountains wets these people, because the words of the holy fathers run down and fill them. Clothing, as we have already said, we take to mean the covering of good

*Job 24:8

*Ps 120:1

works, with which all people are clothed, in order that their foul depravity might be hidden from the eyes of almighty God. So it is written, *Blessed are they whose sins are forgiven, whose misdeeds are hidden.*   *Ps 31:1

But whom do we take the word *stones* to refer to, if not the strong people within Holy Church? They are told by the first shepherd, *You are like living stones in a building made into a spiritual house.* Accordingly, they   *1 Pet 2:5 have no confidence in any works of their own, but they have recourse to the protection of the holy martyrs, and they tearfully stand near their bodies, begging God that they might have the grace of forgiveness through their intercession. What, then, are these people doing in their humility when they have no clothes of their own good works but hugging the stones? The next verse:

LII. 65. *They have violently robbed the orphans, and they have despoiled whole crowds of poor people.*   *Job 24:9 When the heretics are not prosperous in the present life, they convince feeble-minded people with flattery that they should act unlawfully. If, however, they should enjoy any kind of prosperity in the present time, they do not even then stop urging those whom they forcefully persuade. They accordingly are distinguished by the word *orphans*, they who have been incorporated into Holy Church and are still fragile, whose life the merciful Father saved by dying himself, who have already been led forth to a good purpose but who have not yet been strengthened in good works by any virtue. Consequently the heretics violently rob the orphans, because they proceed against the weak minds of the faithful with the violence of their words and actions. The crowds of poor people are the untaught people who, if they had the riches of true wisdom, would never lose the clothing of their faith. There are unquestionably some educated people who are like senators within the ranks of Holy Church, who have accumulated knowledge in their minds, and these people certainly abound with true riches in themselves, but the heretics despoil whole crowds of poor people, because although they gain no ground against the educated ones, they strip the uneducated of the garment of faith one by one with their destructive preaching. The next verse:

LIII. 66. *They take the ears of corn away from the naked people who walk around without any clothes in their hunger.** He repeats the idea *naked* in the words *without any clothes*. It is one thing, however, to be naked but something else to walk around naked. Anyone who does neither good nor evil is both naked and indolent. He, on the other hand, who does evil walks around naked because he follows the path of depravity without the covering of any good action. Then again there are those who know how wrong their evil ways are, yet they hurry to be filled with the bread of justice, and they desire to hear the words of Holy Scripture. As often as they turn over the declarations of the holy fathers in their thoughts for the purpose of edification of their minds, they carry ears of corn from a good harvest.

The heretics accordingly take the ears of corn away from the naked people walking around without any clothes in their hunger, because they are either indolent people employing themselves in no good works, or they follow the path of shamelessness without the covering of any good works. Even if they desire finally to return to repentance and wish for the food of the word, the heretics take the ears of corn away from these hungry people, because they undo the effect of the declarations of the holy fathers in their minds by their ruinous persuasion. We do not say unadvisedly that the ears of corn signify the declarations of the holy fathers, because as often as they are offered through figurative speech, we

*Job 24:10

strip them of the sheath of the letter, as if they were the peelings of grain, so that we may nourish ourselves with the spiritual marrow. The next verse:

LIV. 67. *They take their noonday rest among the crowds of those who tread the winepress and are thirsty.*   *Job 24:11
All the persecutors of Holy Church are nothing other than treaders of the winepress. What they do is permitted by God's providence, in order that the grapes of souls might flow as spiritual wine; having divested themselves of corruptible flesh, these grapes run on to the Kingdom of heaven, as though to the wine storage vats. As long as unjust people oppress those who are just, they tread them underfoot like grapes. When these grapes have been pressed, their abundance overflows for the heavenly banquet of those who once hung free in the air of this world.

The prophet David foresaw the affliction of Holy Church and wrote the psalms inscribed *for the winepress.*   *Pss 8; 80; 83 Vulg
All the persecutors of the lives of the faithful tread and thirst; by acting with cruelty they become fiercer still, and they are so blinded by the guilt of their impiety that they keep turning around to commit worse crimes, where they have already committed serious ones. The heretics, although they have no power of themselves to persecute, impel the powers of this world and influence their minds to persecute, and whomever they can they incite by persuasion. Those whom they notice acting with cruelty against the lives of catholics, they rest among, as though under the very heat of the sun. So he is telling the truth here when he says, *They take their noonday rest among the crowds of those who tread the winepress and are thirsty*, because they join the multitude of those whom they see already acting with cruelty and still thirsty for more cruelty. As long as their zeal satisfies their own desire, they rest in their actions as though at midday. The next verse:

*Job 24:12

LV. 68. *They caused the men from the cities to sigh.*
The word *cities* takes its origin from the people who live together within them, so churches of the true faith are not unreasonably called cities; they are situated in all parts of the world, and together they make up the one catholic church, in which all the faithful who have a correct understanding of God live in harmony together. The Lord traced out the plan of this harmony in the gospel, where his servants would live together even when separated by location: as he was about to satisfy the people with five loaves, he ordered them to recline in groups of fifty and one hundred,* obviously in order that the crowd of the faithful might receive its food while being separated locally but united morally.

*see Mark
6:34-44

The repose of the jubilee is contained in the mystery of the number fifty, and fifty multiplied by two comes to one hundred. Since accordingly the soul first ceases from bad action in order that it may afterward be completely at rest in thought, some recline in groups of fifty and others in groups of one hundred, because there are some who are already at rest from bad action externally, and there are others who are already at rest from bad thoughts in their minds. So, since the heretics often attach themselves to depraved people with worldly power and they persecute good people who enjoy social life and concord, we are now correctly told, *They caused the men from the cities to sigh.* Blessed Job rightly singles out such people, because it is especially they whom the heretics keep turning around to ruin; it is they who run with perfect steps on God's road, not in a wavering or weakly manner, but in a manly way. When they see the faithful little ones inflicted by the wound of false faith, they always return to cries and groans. So he is right to say,

LVI. 69. *The souls of the wounded ones have cried out, and God does not let them go away unavenged.*

*Job 24:12

The souls of the just are indeed wounded when the faith of the weak ones is troubled, whose cries already show how they pine away because of another person's fall. God however does not let them go away unavenged, because even if he allows something unjust to happen in due order, he does not let the injustice go on unavenged, as he allowed to happen in his justice, because even in the injustice of depraved people he strikes at certain faults of the chosen people that he observes in them; nevertheless, eternal justice is not slow to strike at the injustice of the strikers. The next verse:

LVII. 70. *They were rebels against the light.** Perverse individuals often know the truth they ought to follow, yet they scorn the following of the truth they know. They are accordingly rebels against the light, because they follow their own desires, and they pour scorn on the good that they know. They sin not through ignorance but through pride, and they hold up the shield of their pride to turn aside the arrows of truth, in order that their heart might not be struck advantageously. Furthermore, their pride obviously brings it about that just as they refuse to do what they know they ought to do, they no longer know the good they should do;* rather their blindness entirely shuts them out from the light of truth. So he again adds,

LVIII. 71. *They did not know his ways, nor did they return by his paths.** Those who are knowingly rebels in the beginning are later blinded so as not to know, as it is written concerning some of them: *Although they knew God, they did not glorify him as God or give him thanks.** Again a little later he says of them, *God gave them up to a base mind, that they should do what is indecent.** Accordingly they refused to glorify him whom they had known, so he gave them up to a base mind, and they were abandoned to the point that they should no

*Job 24:13

*See
Rom 7:19

*Job 24:13

*Rom 1:21

*Rom 1:28

longer be able to think that what they were doing was evil. So he is right to say, *They did not know his ways, nor did they return by his paths.* A path is of course narrower than a way, so those who disdain to do the good works that are more conspicuous never succeed in understanding the more refined ones.

Almighty God expected them to walk on his paths; well, if only they would at least return by them, in order that the journey of life they refused to follow in their innocence they might keep through repentance. We are shown in this matter how deep the bosom of mercy is in almighty God, when he begs them whom he sees leaving him to return. That is why, after having enumerated the sins of the failing synagogue, he calls her back through the voice of the prophet and says, *Therefore, at least now call me "My Father," and say, "You are the Lord*
*Jer 3:4   *of my maidenhood."* * The next verse:

LIX. 72. *First thing in the morning he rises to do murder; he kills the needy and the poor man. At night,*
*Job 24:14   *however, he acts like a robber.** Since the murderer ordinarily walks at night, when it is especially quiet, to kill his neighbors, how is it that in this passage we are told that the murderer rises first thing in the morning to kill the poor man and the needy, whereas at night he is said to act like a robber? But when the very words do not make literal sense, we should recall them in order to search out spiritual mysteries. Holy Scripture customarily uses the word *morning* to signify either the appearance of the Lord's incarnation or the coming of the exacting Judge, who is then terrible, or indeed the prosperity of the present life. As for the coming of the Lord's incarnation in the morning, it has happened as
*Isa 21:12   the prophet says: *Morning comes and night again,** because the beginning of new light has shone out in the

Redeemer's presence, yet the darkness of their unbelief has not been wiped away from the persecutors' hearts.

On the other hand, the coming of the Judge is also signified by morning, as the psalmist says, *Every morning I killed all the sinners in the land.** As though playing the role of all the chosen ones, he said, *In the morning I will stand before you, and I will see.** Again morning signifies the prosperity of the present life, as when Solomon says, *Woe to you, O land, when the king is a child, when the princes feast in the morning.** Morning is the first time in the day, and night the last, so we are never going to feast on the prosperity of this life that has already gone before, but we shall have those things that follow at the end of the day, that is, at the end of the world. They who are thrilled about the prosperity of this world consequently feast in the mornings, and as long as they impetuously care for the present joy, they think nothing about the future.

Everyone who hates his brother is a murderer.* Accordingly the murderer rises first thing in the morning, because all the crooks stand up for honors in the present life, and they threaten the lives of those who thirst for the glory that follows, as it were, and yearn for the fulfillment of the evening. Every depraved person seizes the dignity of fleeting power in this world, and inasmuch as he shows himself ever more ruthless in fulfilling his evil designs, he shows that he has no love for anyone, since he lacks the deep source of charity. As often as his thoughts wax cruel against good people, so often does he destroy the lives of those who are blameless.

73. If by God's providence he should lose the honorable power he has received, he changes his domicile, but he does not change his disposition, because he forthwith slides into the state of mind announced

*Ps 100:8

*Ps 5:5

*Eccl 10:16

*1 John 3:15

by the second half of the verse: *At night, however, he acts like a robber.* Surely in the night of tribulation and dejection, even if he cannot stretch out his hand for cruelty, he offers perverse counsel to those whom he sees as the ones in power. He rushes around here and there, and whenever he can he suggests ways to attack good people. He is rightly called a robber, because even while he is giving perverse counsel, he is afraid of discovery. He who murders the needy and the poor man in the morning hides out like a robber at night, because all perverse individuals threaten the lives of the poor by oppression while they are enjoying the prosperity of the present life themselves, whereas when their position is lost in adversity and dejection, they secretly hurt the poor by their perverse counsel. That which they cannot perpetrate themselves they get done by their attachment to those in power in the world.

LX. 74. *The eye of the adulterer watches for the* *Job 24:15 *darkness, and he says, "No eye will see me."* * There is nothing to prevent this point from being understood literally, namely, that the man who desires to perpetrate adultery requires darkness. Since, however, the thought is expressed against the heretics, the words are fittingly understood mystically. Paul says, *We do not, as some do,* *2 Cor 2:17 *adulterate the word of God.* * The adulterer, to be sure, seeks in the carnal union not offspring, but pleasure. The perverse man and the slave of vainglory is rightly said to adulterate the word of God, because his desire is not to bring forth children for God through Holy Scripture, but to make a show of his own knowledge. He who is urged to speak by an unbridled lust for glory expends his resources for his own enjoyment rather than for the sake of offspring. So he is right to say, *No eye will see me,* because when adultery is committed in the mind, it is extremely difficult for human sight to perceive it. So the perverse mind perpetrates adultery all the more securely the less he is afraid of being seen by anyone, which is what he is ashamed of. We should also remember that just as the one who commits adultery unlawfully joins the flesh of someone else's spouse to himself, so all the heretics who seize the faithful soul and trap it in their errors take away, as it were, another person's spouse. The mind obviously clings to God spiritually and is married to him as if it were in the embrace of love; so when it is led by perverse persuasion to depraved dogmas, like someone else's spouse, it is corrupted and stained. So he is right to add,

LXI. 75. *He will cover his face.** The adulterer obviously covers his face so that he may not be seen. All who live an evil life by thought or act cover their faces, because their intention in holding perverse doctrines or actions is that they may not be recognized by almighty God at the Judgment. That is why he will tell some souls at the end, *I never knew you. Get away from me, you evildoers!** What, then, is the face of the human heart, if not its likeness to God? That is obviously the face that perverse people cover in order that they may not be recognized, when they mess up their lives either by evil actions or by bad faith. But when such people see the righteous being supported by prosperity in the present life, they are far from daring to persuade them to act perversely. If, however, the storms of adversity should overtake them, then the perverse will surely spout words of pestilential persuasion. So he adds,

LXII. 76. *They dig through houses at night, just as they had plotted during the day, and they have not known the light.** What does the word *houses* signify in this passage if not the consciousness in which we live

*Job 24:15

*Matt 7:23

*Job 24:16

while planning our actions? That is why a certain man was told after he was cured, *First go back home and proclaim all that God has done for you.* In other words, he was told to return to his own consciousness, safe now from the disease of sin, and to awaken his conscience to the voice of proclamation. As for the just, accordingly, when their newfound prosperity is noised abroad, the masters of error are afraid to try persuading them of perverse doctrines.

*Luke 8:39

Those perverse people take counsel, however, and they anxiously await the failure of the prosperity of the good, in order that they might dig through their minds in the darkness of adversity by persuasion and speak of perverse doctrines, as they never dared to do while the good were living in prosperity. But as soon as the perverse see the good people in adversity, they are ready to declare that the good suffer such things for no other reason than the wages of sin, because they love only the honors of the present life and count trials as condemnation. Accordingly they dig through houses at night, because they undertake the corruption of the minds of good people from the very adversity of those people.

He is also right to say, *Just as they had plotted during the day,* because when they saw that the fame had spread about the prosperity of the righteous people and they could then say nothing, they merely called an evil council against them. So whether it be the heretics or any other perverse people, they rejoice when they see the righteous dejected. When, on the other hand, they see them burst forth in the very pinnacle of ruling authority, they are troubled, they worry, they pine away, and they are afflicted. So he again adds,

LXIII. 77. *If the dawn should suddenly break, they consider it the shadow of death.* The wicked are always waiting for the affliction of the faithful, and they desire

*Job 24:17

to see their tribulation. They dig through their houses at night while they corrupt the hearts of those who are innocent but also feeble, with their radically evil talk in the time of their downfall. It often happens, however, that while they are watching some downtrodden good people, a hidden arrangement of God suddenly brings it about that the just person who seemed crushed gets support from a worldly source of power, and prosperity in the present life smiles upon the one whom the darkness of adversity formerly crushed. When the crooks see this prosperity of his, of course, as we said before, they are panic-stricken. They forthwith return to their hearts and recall to their mind's eye all the evil that they remember having done, and they are afraid that they will have to pay for every crime; so where the fortunate one who receives power is radiant, there all the crooks anxiously cower in darkness, fearing retribution.

So Job is right to say, *If the dawn should suddenly break, they consider it the shadow of death.* The dawn is certainly the mind of the righteous person, which abandons the darkness of his sin and already breaks forth into eternal light, as it is written somewhere about Holy Church: *Who is she who is coming forth like the dawn rising?** Accordingly, when any righteous person, *Song 6:9 shining with the light of justice, is raised and dignified in the present life, the darkness of death falls before the eyes of crooked people, because they remember the crimes they have committed, and they are very much afraid of going straight. Their desire is always to relax in their depraved conduct, to live unreformed, and to find pleasure in their guilt. This fatal gladness of theirs is itself conveniently expressed when Job forthwith adds,

LXIV. 78. *So they walk in darkness, as though it were light.** Their depraved mind exults in their crimes, their *Job 24:17 guilt draws them closer every day to their punishment, and yet they are unconcerned. That is why Solomon says, *There are evil men who feel as secure as if they had done deeds of justice.** About these impious people it is again written, *They rejoice when they do evil, and they exult in wayward behavior.** That is how they walk in darkness, as though it were light, because they are as glad in the night of sin as if the light of justice surrounded them.

*Eccl 8:14

*Prov 2:14

At least in another sense darkness not unsuitably expresses the present life, where the consciousness of one person is unseen by another; our light is the eternal homeland where, just as we see one another's faces, so we also see our own hearts mutually. The wicked, however, love the present life so much, and they embrace the time of this exile just as if they already reigned in the homeland; so he says it correctly: *So they walk in darkness, as though it were light.* They are just as glad in their present blindness as if they were already basking in the light of the eternal homeland. The next verse:

*Job 24:18

LXV. 79. *The face of the water is smooth.** He returns from plural number to singular, because one person often begins doing evil, and many follow by imitating him. The guilt however falls principally on the one who showed the example of wickedness to his perverse followers. The accumulated sentence therefore comes back to him who was the source of the guilt. The surface of the water is churned up back and forth by the wind; stabilized by nothing, it is moved here and there. The mind of the wicked person is accordingly smoother than the surface of the water, because whatever wind of temptation touches it, no hesitation or resistance keeps the temptation from drawing the mind to itself. So if we think of the heart of any perverse person as lax, what else do we see but the surface of water open to the wind? Now the wind of anger moves him, now the wind of pride, now the wind of lust, now the wind of envy, now the wind of deception, and he is pulled along. He is then smoother than the face of water, moved by whatever wind of error reaches him.

So the psalmist too is right to say, *O God, make them like a wheel, like stubble before the wind.** The wicked are made like a wheel, because they have been set to work in an endless circle; to what is in front of them they pay no heed, but to what should be left behind they return; they are lifted up from behind, and they fall headlong. They are rightly compared to stubble before the wind as well, because when the wind of temptation arises, they are supported by no weight of gravity, so they are lifted up and dashed to the ground, and often enough they consider themselves to be worth something when the wind bears them off to the high reaches of error. The next verse:

*Ps 82:14

LXVI. 80. *Cursed be his lot on earth, and let him not walk on the vineyard road.** Whoever acts uprightly in the present life and puts up with adversity seems indeed to struggle against adversity, but he ends up with the blessing of eternal inheritance. On the other hand, anyone who acts perversely and yet receives prosperity, who still does not abstain from evil actions even after the abundance of gifts, seems indeed to enjoy prosperity, but he is bound by the penalty of eternal malediction. So Job is right to say here, *Cursed be his lot on earth.* Even if he enjoys temporary blessings, he is held fast by the penalty of malediction.

*Job 24:18

The following half-verse applies to him: *Let him not walk on the vineyard road.* The vineyard road is the righteousness of the churches. Consistent with this interpretation, nothing prevents us from understanding the one talked about as any heretic or carnal person, since the vineyard road, that is, the righteousness of the churches, is lost when either correct faith or the righteousness of justice is not maintained. He therefore walks the vineyard road who ponders the teaching of Holy Church universal and turns aside from the rectitude neither of faith nor of good works. Surely to walk on the vineyard road means to look upon the fathers of Holy Church as if they were clusters of grapes hanging from her and to pay attention to their words in the fatigue of the journey, that they might be inebriated with the love of eternal life. The next verse:

LXVII. 81. *Let him pass over from the snow waters*

*Job 24:19   *to the region of torrid heat.*** Wickedness is compared to extreme cold, because it presses upon the sinner's mind like numbness. So it is written, *Just as a cistern has made its waters icy cold, so he has made his mal-*

*Jer 6:7   *ice frigid.*** On the other hand, love is heat, because it obviously inflames the mind that it fills. It is written about this heat, *Wickedness will spread far and wide,*

*Matt 24:12   *and the love of many will grow cold.*** Yet there are those who, while the extreme frostiness of their wickedness is turning aside, come to the true faith or to the condition of holiness. Still, because they depend on their senses more than is expedient, they often want to examine in the faith that they receive something that they do not receive, in order that they might cleave to God rather by reason than by faith. The human mind, however, cannot examine God's mysteries, so whatever they cannot examine by reason they disdain to believe, and through excessive investigation they fall into error.

These people, accordingly, when they did not yet believe, or when they were still dallying with wickedness, were like snow water. When, however, they abandoned the works of the flesh and were led to faith, they desired to explore in that faith more than they received, so they obviously warmed up to it more than they should have. It is rightly said consequently about this perverse person (the judgment of a prophet rather than a wish), *Let him pass over from the snow waters to the region of torrid heat.* In other words, "He whose disloyalty or coldness in perverse actions is not humbly controlled by the bridle of discipline falls into error through excessive wisdom."

That is why the illustrious preacher also rightly avoids this excessive heat of the wisdom so carefully sought out by his disciples in their hearts and says, *Do not be wiser than befitting wisdom, but be wise for the sake of right conduct.*[*] He does not want to risk the chance of too much heat ruining those whom the snow water, or rather disloyalty, formerly held in its grip, or perhaps the frigidity of half-hearted acts, of which they would have died. It is extremely difficult, you see, for the one who considers himself wise to return to humility and to believe the preachers of correct doctrine; it is difficult for him to abandon his twisted notions, so Job is right to add,

LXVIII. 82. *Let his sin go down to hell.*[*] His sin is undoubtedly taken all the way down to hell unless it is removed before the end of the present life by correction and repentance. John tells us concerning this sin, *There is such a thing as mortal sin, and I do not say that you should pray about that.*[*] Mortal sin is the sin that leads all the way to death, apparently because for the sin that is not done away with here we ask forgiveness in vain. He adds more about that sin: *Let his mercy be forgotten.*[*] The mercy of almighty God is said to be forgotten for the one who has forgotten the justice of almighty God, because whoever does not fear his justice now cannot find his mercy later. This judgment is certainly not aimed at the one alone who abandons the preaching of the true faith, but also at the one who belongs to the true faith but lives in a carnal fashion, because no one

*Rom 12:3

*Job 24:19

*1 John 5:16

*Job 24:20

can evade the vengeance of eternal Judgment, whether his sin be against faith or against right action. Even if condemnation be different in kind, when guilt is never removed by repentance, no faculty of absolution can take it away. The next verse:

*Job 24:20   LXIX. 83. *His worm is sweetness.** Anyone who desires prosperity in this world, preferment above others, and abundance of wealth and honors, for that person certainly worldly cares are desirable, and he rests in labor. His weariness is extreme, if fatiguing worldly cares are absent. Since it is natural for worms to be constantly on the move at every moment, it is not incongruous for restless thoughts to be designated by the word *worms*. The sweetness of a twisted mind is therefore wormy, because it feeds with pleasure on that by which it is constantly agitated through restlessness.

Flesh too can be even more significantly represented by the word *worms*. That is why it is said below, *Man*
*Job 25:6   *is rottenness, and the son of man is a worm.** We are shown therefore how blind is any lustful person or anyone dedicated to carnal pleasure when we are told, *His worm is sweetness*. What is flesh indeed if not rottenness and worms? Anyone who pants after the desires of the flesh loves nothing else but a worm. The tomb bears us witness to what the substance of flesh is. What parents, what faithful friends, what dearly beloved can touch the flesh that is teeming with worms? Accordingly, when flesh is desired, we should think what it is without the soul, and we will understand what it is we love. Absolutely nothing is better for the taming of the appetite for the desires of the flesh than that each one should consider the living one whom he loves and then what that one is like when dead. Having understood the corruption of the flesh, we will recognize the sooner, when

we desire the flesh improperly, that what we desire is decay. So it is rightly said of the lustful mind, *His worm is sweetness*, because the one who is on fire with desire for the corruption of the flesh pants for fetid rottenness.

I recall now that at the beginning of this third part of the work I made the promise of brevity, and I have indeed dealt with it briefly, in order that I might with God's help be more prolix in the remainder of the work, since the subject matter is involved with much obscurity.

Scriptural Index

BOOKS 11–16, JOB 12:6–24:20

Scriptural references are cited by book and Maurist (Arabic) paragraph. For example, 11.4 refers to book 11, paragraph 4.

Gen		**Deut**		12:14	11.12
2:23	14.72	17:11	16.38	12:15	11.14
3:19	11.5, 11.15,	32:34-35	12.21	12:16	11.17
	11.61, 12.6, 13.26,			12:16-17	11.18
	15.37	**Judg**		12:17	11.19, 11.20
3:24	12.13	15:16	13.15	12:18	11.21
4:6-7	11.12	**2 Sam**		12:19	11.22
4:10	13.26	11:1-26	12.23	12:20	11.23
4:17	16.15, 16.15n1	20:9	15.13	12:21	11.25
5:3	16.15			12:22	11.26
5:3-18	16.15n1	**1 Kgs**		12:23	11.29
5:18	16.15	11:4-8	12.23	12:24-25	11.30
6:3	14.72	17:1	11.49	13:1	11.31
15:11	16.53			13:2	11.32
26:15	16.23	**2 Kgs**		13:3	11.33
41:1-8	11.31	20:1	12.2	13:4	11.34
49:9	15.69	20:6	12.2, 16.14	13:5	11.35
				13:6	11.36
Exod		**Job**		13:7	11.37
3:3	15.68	1:8	11.51	13:8	11.38
3:14	16.45	2:3	14.36	13:9	11.39
4:21	11.13	2:5	14.36	13:10-11	11.40
15:18 LXX	16.55	10:13	12.15	13:12	11.42, 11.43
22:26	16.6	12:6	11.1, 11.2	13:13	11.44
34:7	15.57	12:7-8	11.5	13:14	11.45
34:7 Vulg	16.30	12:9	11.6	13:15	11.47, 11.51
		12:10	11.7	13:15-16	11.48
Num		12:11	11.8	13:16	11.49
17:1-8	14.68	12:12	11.10	13:17	11.50
24:3-4	15.58	12:13	11.11, 11.17		

13:19	11.52, 11.53	15:10	12.33	16:19	13.26
13:20	11.54	15:11	12.34	16:16 LXX	13.22
13:21	11.55	15:12	12.35	16:17 LXX	13.23, 13.24
13:22	11.56	15:13	12.36		
13:23	11.57	15:14	12.37	16:18 LXX	13.25
13:24	11.59	15:15	12.38	16:20 LXX	13.27
13:25	11.60	15:16	12.39	16:21 LXX	13.29
13:26	11.51, 11.61, 11.62	15:17	12.40	16:22 LXX	13.30
		15:18	11.51, 12.41	16:23 LXX	13.31
13:27	11.63	15:19	12.41	17:1	13.32, 13.33
13:28	11.64	15:20	12.42, 12.43	17:2	13.34
14:1	11.65	15:21	12.44	17:3	13.35
14:1-2	12.0	15:22	12.45	17:4	13.36, 13.37
14:2	11.67	15:23	12.46	17:5	13.38
14:3	11.69	15:24	12.47	17:6	13.40
14:4	11.70	15:25	12.48	17:7	13.41
14:5	12.1, 12.2	15:26	12.48	17:8	13.42
14:6	12.4	15:27	12.50, 12.51	17:9	13.43
14:7-10	12.5	15:28	12.52	17:10	13.44, 13.45
14:10	12.9	15:29	12.53	17:11	13.46
14:11-12	12.10	15:30	12.54, 12.55, 12.56	17:12	13.47, 13.48
14:12	12.12			17:13	13.49
14:13	12.13, 12.14, 12.15	15:31	12.57	17:14	13.50
		15:32	12.58	17:15	13.51, 13.52
14:14	12.16, 12.17	15:33-34	12.60	17:16	13.53, 13.55
14:15	12.18, 12.19	15:34	12.62	18:1-2	14.2
14:16	12.20	15:35	12.64	18:3	14.3
14:17	11.51, 12.21	16:2	13.2	18:4	14.4, 14.5, 14.6
14:18-19	12.22	16:3	13.3, 13.4	18:5	14.8
14:20	12.24, 12.25, 14.17	16:4	13.4	18:6	14.10
		16:4-6	13.5	18:7	14.11, 14.12
14:21	12.26	16:7	13.8, 14.30	18:8	14.13
14:22	12.27	16:8	13.9	18:9	14.13, 14.14
15:1-2	12.28	16:9	13.10, 13.11	18:10	14.15
15:3	12.29	16:10	13.12	18:11	14.16
15:4	12.29	16:11	13.14, 13.15	18:12	14.17
15:5	12.30	16:12	13.16	18:13	14.19
15:6	12.31	16:13	13.17, 13.18	18:14	14.20
15:7-8	12.32	16:14	13.19	18:15	14.22, 14.23
15:9	12.32	16:15	13.20, 13.21	18:16	14.24